MY BROTHER'S KEEPER

MY BROTHER'S KEEPER

The Untold Stories Behind the Business
of Mental Health—and How to Stop
the Abandonment of the Mentally Ill

NICHOLAS ROSENLICHT, M.D.

PEGASUS BOOKS
NEW YORK LONDON

MY BROTHER'S KEEPER

Pegasus Books, Ltd.
148 West 37th Street, 13th Floor
New York, NY 10018

First Pegasus Books cloth edition October 2024

Interior design by Maria Fernandez

Library of Congress Cataloging-in-Publication Data is available.

ISBN: 978-1-63936-730-6

10 9 8 7 6 5 4 3 2 1

Printed in the United States of America
Distributed by Simon & Schuster
www.pegasusbooks.com

In gratitude to the thoughtful and strong individuals
who gave me the privilege of sharing their lives and experiences.

Contents

INTRODUCTION

Bedlam by the Bay

I n the fall of 2021, I was returning from the airport on BART, San Francisco Bay Area's rail transit system. It was near midnight, and half my co-passengers seemed to be homeless and using the system for shelter. I missed the connection in the East Bay, and with a handful of others had a half-hour wait at a dark underground station. Joining us was a visibly deranged man, screaming obscenities and threats at unseen persons. As a diminutive and very frightened woman sidled up to me the man circled us, ranting, wildly gesticulating, and attacking a bench, a sign, an intercom phone—fortunately, not us. Appallingly, this is not an uncommon occurrence.

Growing up in the San Francisco Bay Area in the 1960s and '70s, I learned to question established institutions and authority. High school classes were disrupted when tear gas from nearby anti-war protests wafted our way, a commonly seen bumper sticker exhorted us to "Question Authority," and we were told to "let your freak flag fly." Foremost among institutions to be questioned was the mental health system, especially the reviled and rapidly imploding state mental institutions. We cheered at the protagonist McMurphy's exploits in Ken Kesey's *One Flew Over the Cuckoo's Nest*, a devastatingly critical book and later movie about a psychiatric hospital, and *King of Hearts*, a 1966 film depicting an insane asylum's endearingly lovable inmates who appear more sane than those waging war in the outside world. Just how much these films resonated with Americans' feelings about mental healthcare and the asylums is indicated by the praise heaped upon *Cuckoo's Nest*. It swept the Academy Awards, winning Best Picture, Best Director, Best Actor, Best Actress, and Best Adapted Screenplay.[1] Even Kesey's odd disclaimer about the story, "It's the truth, even if it didn't happen," gave a window into the public's views on mental illness and its treatment.

Today, those idealistic ideas about mental illness and its treatment have imploded. As I negotiate bodies and human feces on our downtown sidewalks, endure petty crime, and see people who cycle in and out of jail, I can only shake my head in disgust at our failed mental health system. Once the envy of the world, our healthcare system is consistently rated dead last among developed nations in measures of quality, outcomes, and accessibility. In terms of cost, it's in a league of its own, double that of other developed countries. But the most shameful aspect of our last-place healthcare system is its treatment of mental illness. In 2022 we lost roughly 300,000 people to suicide, excessive alcohol use, and overdose,[2,3,4] more than to AIDS, guns, and motor vehicle accidents *combined*. This is more than we lost to COVID (244,000),[5] which dominated the news and public discussion and overturned our lifestyle. Suicide is now the second most common cause of death in ten- to twenty-four-year-olds in this country, behind only accidents.[6,7] During the pandemic, suicides in the elderly rose to a level not seen since the Great Depression, probably fueled by a great sense of isolation.[8] For all our worry about violent crime, we are more than twice as likely to die at our own hands as at the hands of another,[9] and five times as likely to die by overdose. Yet it's estimated that health insurers allocate little more than 4 percent of healthcare dollars to the treatment of mental illness and addiction.

On graduating from medical school, I seriously considered many specialties, but ultimately chose psychiatry. I believed psychiatry was entering a new era, with advances in medication and neuroimaging, and would be the area of medicine that would evolve and grow the most in the following decades. From my experiences in medical school I saw the great need for mental healthcare, and wanted to be part of our growing capability to fill that need. As a third-year medical student I cared for a woman who had been transferred from the obstetrics ward to the psychiatry unit. She had presented to the emergency room (ER) in labor, and the ER physicians reported hearing "fetal heart sounds." It turned out she was psychotic, delusional, and not pregnant. She suffered from a syndrome called pseudocyesis, a condition in which the patient has all the signs and symptoms of pregnancy except for the presence of a fetus. This had happened to her before, when, as with this time, she had discontinued her antipsychotic medication. Faced with the choice of putting food on the table for her family or paying for medication, she chose the former. Two weeks later she was discharged, much improved, and returned home to her much-relieved husband and joyous children. This, and a number of similar experiences, convinced me psychiatry was the area of medicine in which I could make the most meaningful difference in people's lives.

By the 1960s we had a medicine chest full of relatively effective drugs for a number of formerly hopeless psychiatric disorders, like depression, bipolar disorder, and even schizophrenia, with the promise of newer and better treatments on the way. I had witnessed what one of my professors called "the Lazarus effect," where profoundly psychotic patients returned to coherence after beginning medication. I saw patients so depressed they could not rise from their bed or eat—who were literally starving to death—get up, begin talking again, eat, and go home to productive lives. Advances in neuroscience were blending with psychotherapy to promise new and more effective forms of treatment. We could now treat both peoples' brains and minds. The dark days of Kesey's mental institutions seemed behind us, with the closing of state asylums and the blossoming of effective and humane community care for the mentally ill, particularly the establishment of Community Mental Health Centers in 1963 under President

Kennedy. It seemed society could begin to welcome back into the community those it formerly shunned and locked away in packed dungeons. But it was not to be.

Over my forty-year career in psychiatry I've worked in many settings. I've been a teacher and researcher at several major medical schools, an administrator directing inpatient units and outpatient clinics, and through it all a clinician, in settings as varied as VA medical centers, university clinics, community mental health clinics, homeless centers, and private practice. Everywhere I worked, despite the promise we'd sensed in the 1960s and '70s, it felt like we were falling behind in our battle against mental illness. During the latter part of the twentieth century and early part of the twenty-first, there have been no major breakthroughs in our understanding of these brain diseases, nor major advancements in their pharmacological or psychotherapeutic treatments as had been anticipated. In fact, the most effective drugs we have for major psychiatric disorders like schizophrenia and bipolar disorder are now all more than fifty years old. We still do not know the root causes of any of the major psychiatric illnesses, which are diagnosed by sign (observable behaviors) and symptom (subjective reports by the patient) clusters. We refer to these disorders as "functional," because they affect functioning but have no measurable physical causes; we still have no true "tests" for them. We do not even know if diseases like bipolar disorder or schizophrenia are discrete entities. We separate or lump these disorders by their signs and symptoms despite many that overlap, like delusions and hallucinations.

Neither discarding psychoanalysis, or "talk therapy," for the "biological" revolution in psychiatry—which based treatment on drugs, and research on brain imaging—nor "the decade of the brain," in the 1990s have unlocked the mind's secrets or significantly improved our treatment effectiveness. In fact, in many ways we are now providing worse care for our patients by treating with medications alone instead of offering more comprehensive treatment interventions that combine drugs with psychotherapy and social supports like housing or drug treatment. New drugs studied in clinical trials (and subsequently approved by the Food and Drug Administration) ameliorate symptoms only moderately over placebos, and no better than older, cheaper, and better tested drugs. Part of this phenomenon may be due to the fact that more complicated and thus difficult-to-treat subjects enter into drug studies. People who respond to available drugs don't generally sign up for drug trials where they may receive a placebo. Nonetheless, we are left with rafts of patients referred to as "treatment resistant"—a euphemism meaning they show little or no response to medications we can offer, as if it is their fault rather than our system's dismal failure to advance our understanding and treatment of mental illness.

Psychotherapy has expanded beyond the rigid orthodoxies of psychoanalysis, with its expectation of meeting four to five times a week, to include contributions from self-psychology (the understanding of how one views their "self" in relation to the rest of the world), object relation theory (in which our internal representations of our relationships with others guides our behavior and emotions), and cognitive behavioral techniques (how our thoughts and behaviors are interrelated, and affect our sense of well-being), based on the 2,000-year-old teachings of the Stoic philosophers. This growth and augmentation has expanded the applicability and palatability of various psychotherapies such as cognitive behavioral therapy (CBT) and psychodynamic therapy, without the need for daily sessions. But these advances have produced only limited improvement in outcomes, with the possible exceptions of insomnia and some anxiety disorders. Meanwhile, the number of diagnosable psychiatric disorders and people filling these categories has exploded. Despite touted advances, it seems we are less able to relieve the suffering of those with mental illness than half a century ago.

Most tragically, the Community Mental Health Centers were underfunded and failed to live up to expectations. America's most vulnerable, the seriously mentally ill, have moved from relatively safe state asylums to our streets, jails, and prisons. (Here is where *One Flew Over the Cuckoo's Nest* and *King of Hearts*, which reviled state asylums, missed the mark.) Currently it is estimated that two-thirds of our homeless population have mental illness and/or substance use issues, and nearly 400,000 people behind bars have serious mental illness. [10] In fact, in "the land of the free," more people with mental illness are in jails and prisons than in hospitals. Americans with mental illness are up to ten times more likely to be incarcerated than hospitalized, and once imprisoned, are unlikely to get treatment. It is estimated that mental illness is responsible for 14 percent of deaths worldwide, and nine of the top twenty-five most disabling illnesses are mental illnesses. [11] Yet in this country we squeeze the mentally ill out of healthcare, despite the fact that treatments for psychiatric illness (when properly implemented, combining medication with other modalities such as psychotherapy and social supports) are, on average, just as effective as those for other chronic illnesses. [12] We don't throw up our hands and call someone with difficult to control diabetes or hypertension, or for that matter cancer, "treatment resistant." We redouble our efforts to help.

A number of books and innumerable news and journal reports have documented the inefficiency, inequity, and outrageous costs of our healthcare system. Blame abounds, directed mainly at the venality of health insurers, the pharmaceutical industry, and organized medicine. What this uproar fails to acknowledge is that our healthcare system was not foisted on us. Instead, we, perhaps unknowingly, chose and embraced it. It is a sad story of good intentions gone bad, and as things deteriorated, clinging to a failing system all the tighter.

In the second half of the last century it seemed we could overcome anything with American ingenuity and capitalist zeal (and financial motivation). To combat rising healthcare costs, we turned to our financial wizards: economists, business leaders, and entrepreneurs. If we could put a man on the moon, conquer polio, become the richest nation on Earth, and make the dollar the standard of the world, certainly we could vanquish illness and the high cost of healthcare.

But while capitalism could bring down the Berlin Wall, disease and death turned out to be more formidable foes. Encouraging economic priorities in healthcare, such as with the Health Maintenance Organization (HMO) Act passed by Congress in 1973, had unintended consequences: in making medical care a business, patients were turned into consumers, or "clients," and healers became "providers." In short, patients were turned into articles of trade, where the priority was profit rather than improving health. Healthcare workers in turn have become cogs in corporate machines rather than dedicated healers. As the physician Victor Montori laments, "Money has shifted from a resource for patient care to the product of healthcare."[13] For 2,000 years, medicine had been a social and ethical contract, yet in a few short decades it became beholden to financial imperatives.

Immediately, beginning in the 1970s, consumer and patient rights advocates raised concerns that converting medical care into a business rather than a calling, a paradigm that set profits in opposition to care, would trample patient rights and quality of care. Being a patient arms one with certain ethical and legal rights, ones not afforded to a customer of a business. Doctors have a fiduciary responsibility to their patients; that is, they must put their patients' needs above their own. Businesses have fiduciary responsibility to their investors, not their clients. Indeed, advocates' concerns seem to have been well justified. Since abandoning our formerly largely nonprofit stance, US healthcare expenditure has ballooned to nearly 20 percent of our GDP, almost three *times* more than it was in 1973 when Congress passed the HMO Act, a law specifically implemented to lower costs.

Many claim that our healthcare system is broken. This is wrong, and misses the point. Our for-profit healthcare model is working exactly as it is designed to. In fact, it is working quite well for some: healthcare corporations and investors. It's just not working that well for most people, especially the chronically ill, and most of all those with mental illness. Fiddling with it as we have through piecemeal legislation aimed at the most outrageous profiteering, and even the implementation of the Affordable Care Act to increase access to care, does not fix its fundamental problems. As it turns out, the promotion and maintenance of good health do not respect the usual rules of commerce; health is not a fungible article of trade. One can buy and sell services and products, but not health. Our need for care, which increases with age and infirmity, tends to vary inversely with earning power. This is a lousy business model. Those who need care the most can least afford it, and those who can afford it least want it. The sick get poorer and the poor get sicker. The current industry behemoth thrives by charging outrageous prices and the effective marketing of costly and unneeded care to those who can afford it—such as overpriced drugs that are no more effective than older and better tested ones, or expensive but unneeded testing—and conversely, by not caring for those who can't, such as the indigent and especially the mentally ill. This book specifically examines these skewed priorities, why we embraced them, and why we won't let go of them.

For example, framing healthcare as a business or consumer issue helps us avoid painful decisions about who gets care by reducing our sense of obligation to help those without means. It makes it more palatable to decline to care for someone who has no insurance or can't pay for care at the going rate. After all, that's how a business operates. Our business model of healthcare thus helps manage our feelings of helplessness in the face of so much suffering. In most societies, medical care is viewed more as a public service, needed by all in the community at one time or another, not an elective commodity. Like highways, clean water, fire departments, and working sewage systems, good healthcare benefits us all. When even a few suffer, the rest of society suffers. One person's cancer diminishes our community; one homeless person begging in front of the supermarket touches us all. The current US healthcare system serves the economic desires of a vast for-profit industry, but too often, not the health needs of its citizens. But nowhere are our priorities more distorted than in our handling of the mentally ill.

With discriminatory coverage by insurers for mental health treatment, its availability has shrunk. Fewer people enter the field, and many leave, while the need has exploded. Insurers pay fines for failing to provide equal coverage for mental health treatment, but just view this as a cost of doing business: the relatively small fines they pay cost less than it would to provide adequate treatment. Psychotherapy is now largely reserved for the wealthy who can afford the out-of-pocket expenses—*if* they can find an available therapist. Most are just plain out of luck. Every night, across our country, *thousands* of adolescents languish in emergency rooms, sometimes for weeks, while staff and families search for somewhere they can get appropriate treatment, often in vain. Worst off perhaps are the seriously mentally ill (SMI), those who are least able to hold down a job, pay for health insurance, or figure out how to navigate our byzantine systems in order to access care.

More than any other field of medicine, beginning in the 1970s, mental health and addiction treatment embraced this new economic model as healthcare corporations charged high fees to the rich and excluded the SMI from treatment. Embracing economic incentives has permitted us to look the other way, portraying the suffering of those with mental illness as a choice, or a crime requiring avoidance or incarceration, rather than the consequence of illness and needing care.

Downtown, I continue to circumvent tent cities and walk the gauntlet of ragged beggars. I see people stop to give the homeless a dollar, or twenty dollars, yet we all know that this is not the way to actually help the underlying problem. The SMI are struggling human beings, deserving of care and respect like the rest of us, not a small handout. What we don't do is put adequate resources into the care of the SMI. Mostly, we try to avoid them.

Our aversion toward mental illness, and the barriers to its treatment—such as lower insurance payments for mental as opposed to physical healthcare, lack of accessibility, and a shortage of competent mental health clinicians—have effectively banished the mentally ill from our society. We all pay the societal costs for the exclusion and incarceration of the treatable mentally ill. We rail against our system, yet paradoxically we avoid considering alternatives. We now blame the healthcare corporations we constructed and enabled for doing exactly what corporations are designed to do: maximize profits by restricting expenses. What has become clear is that this model is not compatible with improving the cost, availability, appropriateness, advancement, or quality of our healthcare.

Examining our history of the treatment of mental illness, and the personal and societal influences that guided our choices, reveals powerful lessons. Although we separate mental and physical healthcare in this country, it is a false dichotomy, based in fear and prejudice. They are not so different. But what is different is our emotional response to mental illness. While illness striking the various organs of the body, such as the heart or kidneys, evokes care and empathy, a diseased brain often evokes fear and revulsion. Using mental health as the worst-case example of the healthcare industry and a cautionary tale, I examine these issues, how they lead us to behave the way we do, and why we built and continue to tolerate our appalling healthcare system.

We did not end up in this mess by random chance. We made and continue to make, mostly through inaction, choices about our healthcare, yet fail to adequately examine our motivations. Why would doctors, who devote their lives to serving others, take pharmaceutical company kickbacks? Why would well-intentioned healthcare executives charge outrageous prices for lifesaving care, effectively sentencing their customers to disability and death? Why would we pay insurance premiums that exceed the cost of a home mortgage for low-quality care? Clearly, our system serves deep-seated emotional needs—if not explicitly, then in the security it promises. In understanding these motivations we can look clearly at what needs to be done to improve our healthcare.

I had high hopes for the field of mental health when I began my career as a psychiatrist. I still do, and I think the hard lessons learned over the past few decades can serve as a guide for our management of healthcare as a whole. A 2023 Gallup poll found that rates of depression in this country are skyrocketing, with more than one in six

Americans saying they are currently depressed or receiving treatment for depression and 29 percent reporting that they have been diagnosed with depression at some point in their life.[14] A 2022 survey by the U.S. Department of Health and Human Services found that nearly forty-nine million adults in this country, more than one in six, had a substance abuse disorder.[15, 16] That same year a CNN/Kaiser Family Foundation survey found that *nine out of ten* adults said they believe there's a mental health crisis in the US today,[17] and a 2022 survey by IPSOS, a global market research and public opinion firm, found that mental health is now the single greatest health concern for Americans, surpassing even COVID.[18] Who among us has not been touched by mental illness or addiction? Who does not personally know someone, maybe a family member or friend, whose life was upended by mental illness? Yet our healthcare consistently marginalizes and ignores mental illness and drug misuse.

Many of us recall the May 2023 incident involving Jordan Neely. Mr. Neely, a desperate mentally ill young man screaming for help, a man arrested more than forty times, in and out of a dysfunctional "revolving door" mental health system for years—including many involuntarily hospitalizations—who had recently broken an elderly woman's nose, was strangled to death on a New York subway by Daniel Penny as a crowd looked on. Where does sympathy or blame lie in this tragedy? In the lost, crazy, and violent Mr. Neely, who was on his own at fourteen after his mother was strangled to death? Or with Mr. Penny, who was just trying to get somewhere on the subway and no doubt felt under attack? How would he have responded if Mr. Neely were having an asthma attack instead? How about those in the crowd that watched, and helped restrain Mr. Neely, even filming the incident as life drained from his body?[19] Is this who we have become, and how did we get here?

In this book I will examine this decline and the history of the disastrous economic revolution in healthcare with a focus on mental health. Step by step I will examine the impact of this revolution on patients and their families, the practice of psychiatry, the practice of psychotherapy, and the insidious ethical and practical consequences of reframing patients and clinicians in business language. Finally, I will look at the reasons why we maintain this healthcare system that we loathe so much and ways we can turn it around. Let's back up and look at why we built this system and what needs it serves. Only then can we implement real solutions. Every other developed nation has managed to modify their healthcare systems in ways that have resulted in higher quality and more cost-effective care. We can, too.

CHAPTER ONE

A Little History: How and Why We Made This Mess

HEALTHCARE 101: HOW WE GOT HERE

The Price is Right

Formerly a model for the world, relative to other developed nations, our healthcare system is now a bloated embarrassment. It consistently ranks at the bottom in measures of quality, access, and good health outcomes. Even more, it has spawned a fundamental mistrust of healthcare companies and public health decisions, as we saw so clearly in the COVID pandemic. What led to this decline? While the reasons are many, there is a key factor that started us on this slide more than fifty years ago. Prior to the middle of the last century, our healthcare was based on nonprofit principles, principles based in beneficence and community. Starting in the 1960s we embraced a for-profit free-market approach to virtually everything, including healthcare.

It was part of the ascendancy of a new American model. Following the ideas of Milton Friedman, the influential Nobel Prize-winning University of Chicago economist, we put blind faith in free-market business interests as the way to prosper, avoiding government (as well as legal and moral) interference. We put a man on the moon, had remarkable prosperity (at least for many), but it was the collapse of the Soviet Union in 1989 that finally solidified this consensus. The division of the world between communist and capitalist societies was one of history's great natural experiments, and the results were clear. "The Cold War is over, and the University of Chicago won it," crowed the conservative columnist George Will in 1991.[1] Embracing our free-market identity, we went so far as to introduce a popular TV game show in 1956 called *The Price is Right*. The show tested contestants' ability to guess market price for merchandise, and it still airs today, the longest running game show in history. If free-market economic principles helped us win the Cold War, put a man on the moon, and made for good entertainment, certainly it could help rein in healthcare costs.

Rising healthcare costs were becoming a national concern, reaching 7.3 percent of our gross domestic product (GDP) in 1973. To speed the shift to economic, rather than medical or ethical priorities, Congress and then-President Nixon enacted the Health Maintenance Organization (HMO) Act of 1973. It provided federal grants and loans to private companies to encourage the development of "managed care" HMOs. These companies were to foster free-market competition and implement business strategies intended to promote economic efficiency. Unfortunately, this reorientation had an unintended consequence: it legitimized the view that healthcare was an area of *business*, and one in which vast fortunes could be made. The result was that American healthcare shifted from its long-standing not-for-profit principles to a for-profit model.

Some raised concerns about this shift in paradigm. In 1970 Barbara and John Ehrenreich coined the term "medical-industrial complex,"[2] and in 1980 Arnold Relman, editor of the *New England Journal of Medicine*, expanded on the consequences of this industrialization of healthcare. He described how, just as the military-industrial complex lifted us out of the Depression and helped win World War II, our country embraced this new complex, trusting it could vanquish illness and rising medical costs.[3] Presciently, Relman warned that these companies, by virtue of holding the purse strings, effectively had control over who receives care and who does not. He predicted, correctly, consequences such as cream-skimming, the elimination of low-profit but necessary services, exclusion of unprofitable patients, and how these businesses would acquire unwarranted influence.

Your Money and Your Life: Healthcare as a Commodity

How has this shift worked out? That depends on who you ask. US healthcare expenditures, which had reached $3 trillion in 2019, topped $4 *trillion* in the pandemic. It now consumes 20 percent of our GDP,[4] almost triple that of 1973, the year the HMO Act was put into law. One of every five dollars spent in our country is spent on healthcare. As a result, many Americans simply cannot afford it anymore. Meanwhile, revenues of healthcare corporations have soared such that, for example, annual profits for the five biggest health insurance companies went from $15 billion in 2009 to $25 billion in 2015 and their share prices tripled.[5]

The healthcare giant UnitedHealth's earnings jumped almost 14 percent in 2023, to $32.4 billion.[6] Even the "nonprofit" Kaiser Permanente raked in $4.1 billion in profits in 2023.[7] Healthcare, primarily mental healthcare, is now the largest and most profitable sector for private equity and venture capital investment.[8]

The American Experiment

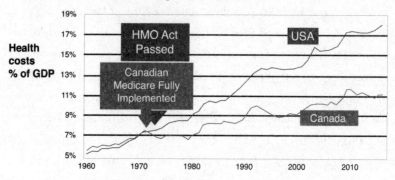

Relative cost of healthcare in the United States and Canada, as a percentage of GDP.

For others, like my patient Sandy, things have not gone so well. Much of my work and interest as a psychiatrist has been in the inter-action between physical and emotional health. One aspect of this is performing psychiatric evaluations on people hospitalized for medical and surgical reasons. When asked to see Sandy, a forty-year-old single mother in the hospital with ovarian cancer, I cringed. I am usually able to help people see a way through their challenges, to help them figure out how to put their situation in a different context, to find ways to lessen or at least help them endure their suffering. This was hard in Sandy's situation. She had not seen a doctor in years; what little money she could scrape together for healthcare was spent on her kids. So she ignored her abdominal pain and put off the care she knew she needed but could not afford. By the time she saw a doctor her cancer had metastasized. Her length of survival was estimated in weeks to months, not the decades she had hoped for. But her greatest sorrow was that she knew she would not live to see her kids reach adulthood; in fact, she would not see them through middle school and had no idea what would happen to them after she was gone. Tragically, Sandy is not an anomaly. A 2022 Gallup poll found that more than a third of Americans report that they or a family member have put off medical treatment over the cost, including more than one in four who have a serious condition.[9] That number jumps to 83 percent among the uninsured.[10]

Basing our healthcare on private for-profit insurance, which most often requires employment, just doesn't make sense and has been instrumental in converting our health into a business venture rather than a social contract. If you think about it, health insurance is not really insurance in the usual sense. Insurance is intended to spread the impact of infrequent or unlikely disasters across a community, blunting the impact on individuals. Everyone pays a small amount so that if they are involved in an accident, die, or their house burns down, they and/or their family are not ruined.

But illness and the benefits of good healthcare are not unlikely or unexpected. Health insurance does not protect us against the consequences of illness—disability insurance and life insurance do this. It is supposed to assist in the payment for care that protects us from illness in the first place. Preventive healthcare helps one to stay healthy and to live longer. But US health insurers exist to make a profit, and they have an incentive to keep us from using healthcare, which would cut into their bottom line. Insurance companies have developed strategies to make it difficult for patients to access care, then try to avoid paying claims when care is rendered. They also try to offload responsibility onto another payer, such as the Veterans Administration or other governmental plans like Medicare and Medicaid, or another insurance company, whenever possible.

Free-market economic models are based on the assumption that people are savvy consumers who act in a focused and self-interested manner, competing for limited resources. But healthcare is very different than most business markets. The customer is most often not the primary payer, and good health and its promotion do not behave like typical commodities. The need for healthcare is not voluntary nor can the time of need be chosen. Free-market incentives don't apply well to things we need as opposed to things we merely want. Healthcare is, as economists call it, inelastic. As care costs go up, people don't stop needing it. They pay. That is, if they can.

We undervalue healthcare when we are well. But when we need it, we don't quibble—who bargains with their doctor over price while they are being wheeled into the operating room for an emergency coronary bypass graft, or with the pediatrician when their child is dying from meningitis? In neither situation are we the "savvy consumer" at the core of economic theory. In fact, a 2023 Gallup poll found that a mere 17 percent of Americans, around one in six, report that they knew what their healthcare products or services would cost before they received them.[11] Although I did have a veteran patient who, realizing he was having a heart attack, drove to the airport and hopped on a flight to LA all the while popping nitroglycerine tabs to control his pain so he could get to the VA medical center for bypass surgery because he had no insurance.

As a 2021 *New York Times* article revealed, some hospitals understand this lack of choice all too well and use predatory billing practices on car-crash victims sent to their emergency rooms to boost their income. They charge up to five times their usual rates and refuse to bill insurers, then use lien laws to claim any accident settlement victims may receive.[12]

Further, free-market assumptions don't apply to a community's health. One individual's good health benefits everyone in the community, while another's illness can adversely affect all. Using local officials' emails, a *Wall Street Journal* investigation found that hospitals with available ICU beds turned away critically ill COVID patients from overflowing nearby hospitals because of their insurance status, endangering *everybody* in the community regardless of their wealth or insurance status.[13] Focusing on short-term profits and keeping the economy alive has encouraged this sort of dangerous action, excluding some from healthcare and increasing the spread of diseases and subsequent deaths.

A number of books, including Maggie Mahar's *Money-Driven Medicine*[14] and Elisabeth Rosenthal's *An American Sickness: How Healthcare Became Big Business and How You Can Take It Back,* as well as a position paper by the American College of Physicians,[15] describe the consequences of this shift to economic priorities. As Rosenthal succinctly summarizes, "In the past quarter century, the American medical system has stopped focusing on health or even science. Instead it attends more or less single-mindedly to its own profits."[16] She cites concrete examples of how the usual market forces do not work in healthcare: In 2014 the "usual and customary" fee for gallbladder surgery in Queens, New York, was around $2,000, but twenty miles east in Nassau County, Long Island, where more doctors are in private practice, it was $25,000.

Similarly, drug prices do not follow market forces, but are protected vigorously by market manipulation and patents. A 2021 Rand study found that prescription drug prices in the United States average two and one-half times those in other nations.[17] Even generic drugs are not free from pricing scams. The generic drug company Teva Pharmaceutical agreed in 2022 to pay $420 million to settle shareholder litigation alleging the company hid an anti-competitive price-fixing scheme.[18] Mind you, this was to pay off shareholders. No compensation was offered to the patients who overpaid for the drugs or those who were harmed by being unable to afford them. Even when competition is present, studies show that companies just pass on the increased cost of marketing to patients by increasing drug prices.[19] The top-selling drug in the world is the patent-protected Humira, used primarily in autoimmune diseases, with sales of over $20 billion per year. Until some equivalent drugs were finally allowed in the US in 2023, the average cost for a years' treatment (after rebates) was $38,000. In 2023, even after some equivalent medications were allowed, market manipulation kept Humira's price at nearly $30,000. Meanwhile, in European countries, equivalent drugs cost less than one-fifth of this amount.[20, 21, 22]

The Greek physician Hippocrates stated that doctors should forgo fees whenever possible. Until the latter half of the twentieth century, patients mostly paid for doctor's visits out of their own pocket, and most paid on an informal sliding scale in proportion to their ability to pay, or bartered with reciprocal services or goods. As Rosenthal points out, "Paying a doctor's bill was not really a commercial transaction."[23] Today, insurance plans forbid physicians from discounting care to their patients, and to do so would be considered fraud. Prices for treatment are mandated by insurers, often negotiated in secret between healthcare systems and insurers without the input or knowledge of patients, doctors, or government or community representatives. Under a government ruling enacted in 2021, which the healthcare industry sued to block[24] and some companies are refusing to comply with, hospitals must now make these prices public. Using this new ruling, the *Wall Street Journal* uncovered wildly divergent prices charged at Sutter California Hospitals. For example, one complex cardiac procedure was billed at less than $90,000 to some insurers, whereas the charge was over $325,000 to those who paid out of pocket.[25] In fact, private individuals are most often charged more for treatment than are insurance companies. Medical care has changed from something most people could afford, or barter for, to something that, without insurance, most cannot.[26]

Similarly, mining this newly available data, a *New York Times* investigation found that having insurance is no guarantee of a good price. The secret prices negotiated between insurance companies and healthcare delivery systems vary widely even within the same insurer depending on the plan: ". . . a single insurer can have a half-dozen different prices within the same facility, based on which plan [they are enrolled in]." Hospitals and insurers hide behind the contracts they've signed, contracts which prohibit them from revealing their rates. "We had gag orders in all our contracts," reports Richard Stephenson, who worked for the Blue Cross Blue Shield Association from 2006 until 2017.[27] Six months after passage of the transparency ruling, the majority of US hospitals have not complied and their pricing is still not available.[28]

By holding the purse strings these companies effectively control who receives care, and what kind of care, and who does not, functioning as corporate death panels that enforce policies that amount to economically driven eugenics.[29] In a particularly flagrant example of this, in 2023 the hospital giant HCA Healthcare was accused of policies that encouraged staff to transfer more patients to palliative and end-of-life care in an effort to increase turnover and boost hospital quality scores.[30] The intention may not be for people to die, but that becomes a cost of running a successful business in healthcare.

Falling Behind

A concern in 1973, the cost of US healthcare is now called a "crisis." As previously mentioned, healthcare costs in the US had reached 7.3 percent of GDP in 1973, roughly the same as countries like Canada, Denmark, and France (5.3–7.9 percent). By 2007, the United States was spending two and a half times the average of other rich countries.[31] The costs of our model are more than economic; as profits have soared, the quality of our care has worsened. In 2000 the World Health Organization (WHO) rated the overall system performance for healthcare of 191 nations. The US was ranked thirty-seventh, the lowest of any developed nation and just behind Dominica (a tiny Caribbean country, not the same as the Dominican Republic) and Costa Rica, an outcome mocked in Michael Moore's 2007 documentary *Sicko*.[32] For the past seven years in a row the Commonwealth Fund has rated US healthcare dead last among eleven developed nations on measures of quality of care, access, equity, efficiency, and healthy lives. Yet it ranked first in per capita cost, more than twice that of the top-rated UK.[33] In 2018 the business news organization Bloomberg ranked fifty-six nations on their health efficiency index. The US tied for fifty-fourth with Azerbaijan, ahead of only Bulgaria, widely viewed as the most corrupt nation in the European Union.[34]

US healthcare spending continues to Outpace Other Wealthy Nations

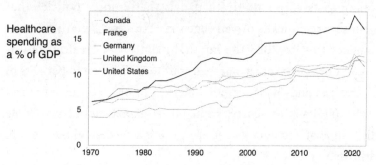

US healthcare spending as compared to other wealthy nations.

Americans born in recent years are the first generation ever to face greater infant and maternal mortality rates and a shorter life expectancy than their parents, and this was before the COVID pandemic. In the midst of rising maternal and infant deaths, rural hospitals are now closing maternity wards to save money.[35] Less widely appreciated is the fact that *four out of five* pregnancy related deaths in the US are entirely preventable, and the most common cause of these deaths are mental health conditions—such as suicide or overdose—not ones we commonly think of like preeclampsia, gestational diabetes, or placenta previa.[36,37]

US life expectancy continues to Fall Behind Other Wealthy Nations

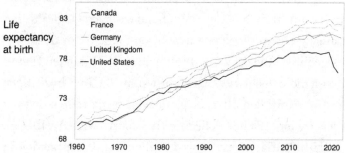

US life expectancy as compared to other wealthy nations.

There are other costs to society when healthcare corporations act single-mindedly in their own economic interest. Economic incentives have crowded out other priorities, such as ethics and humanitarianism, as we shall examine in more depth in following chapters. For example, the pharmaceutical industry's aggressive marketing of expensive pain-killers is cited as a major contributor to our nation's opiate crisis, which kills at least 50,000 Americans a year.[38] And there are many other examples of pharmaceutical companies hiding clear evidence of dangers associated with their products that used to be forbidden in medicine, but not in the business world.

NOTHING TO SEE HERE: MENTAL HEALTH IS FORCED OUT

The Rise and Fall of "Moral Therapy" and the Asylums

As serious as the consequences of the for-profit revolution have been to healthcare, nowhere have they been as devastating as for those with mental illness. This history warrants examination and has lessons applicable to healthcare as a whole. Let's begin with a definition. The seriously mentally ill (SMI) are generally defined as adults who have a diagnosable mental, behavioral, or emotional disorder causing serious functional impairment that substantially interferes with major life activities. Schizophrenia, for example, is a common cause of serious impairment in which hallucinations (false sensory perceptions, frequently voices) and delusions (firmly held beliefs not based in reality such as being followed, persecuted, or having special powers) can render sufferers unable to make rational, healthy, or safe life decisions.

While Hippocrates felt that mental illness, like all other illnesses, could be studied and treated scientifically,[39] most societies have had trouble reconciling themselves to the reality of diseases of the brain. In Greek and Roman times, insanity was a domestic responsibility.

As Roy Porter, the author of *Madness: A Brief History*, describes, "The seriously disturbed were kept at home, whilst the harmless might be allowed to wander, though as evil spirits were thought to fly out of them to possess others, the deranged were feared and shunned."[40] Later, he continues, "In Christian Europe too, the family was held responsible for the deeds of its mad members. As with children, lunatics and 'village idiots' typically remained in domestic care . . . hidden away in a cellar or caged in a pigpen. . . ."

Organized separate housing for the SMI, inspired by the Christian ideal of charity, began toward the end of the Middle Ages, but the accommodations were often dungeons or similar horrific facilities. In London, the religious house St. Mary of Bethlehem, founded in 1247, famously became known as "Bedlam," a now-derogatory term we use for mental health facilities today. Though they are now frequently a subject of derision, our state mental institutions were actually founded in the mid-1800s as a remedy for the inhumane treatment of the mentally ill. They were based on the asylum movement, grounded in the integration of medical care and what was called "moral therapy," which followed principles of kindness, mildness, reason, and humanity. Hence they were given the name "asylum," as in refuge, or place of safety. This refuge was to serve both the ill and their burdened families and communities.

The American asylum system, which lasted in this country from the mid-nineteenth century until the mid-twentieth century, was launched by dedicated mental-health advocates, the most famous being Dorothea Dix. Outraged at how the mentally ill had been confined to poorhouses and jails, these activists lobbied for new, custom-designed institutions that would provide "asylum" and "moral treatment" at public expense. Generally set in bucolic surroundings to calm the troubled by removing them from the stress and strife of city life, they were intended to be a lot like vacation resorts. Initially they worked well, claiming discharge rates of 80 to 100 percent. But while the asylums started with high hopes and good intentions—and some success—they were soon overwhelmed with the sheer number of severely ill patients and conditions deteriorated. Despite this, Dorothea Dix herself chose to spend her last years as a guest of the New Jersey State Lunatic Asylum, which she had founded.

An unfortunate but probably not unintentional aspect of this system was that the asylums sequestered the mentally ill away from society; out of sight, out of mind. Like the tuberculosis sanatoriums and leper colonies of yesteryear, the asylums hid the mentally ill away from the "mentally well." But unlike those with tuberculosis, the mentally ill were not contagious, though they were discomfiting. (The unfortunate lepers, who, like the mentally ill, were upsetting but not highly contagious, were also banished from society. Leprosy, now called Hansen's Disease, is transmissible to only a small percentage of the population, and then only after months of close contact.)[41] And honestly, we had little to offer of help other than compassion, support, and shelter from the deprivation and abuse they suffered in open society. But this was true of virtually all illnesses until a hundred years ago. Medicine could offer compassion and care, but we had very few effective treatments. Initially there were no psychiatrists to staff these institutions. As Porter points out, "The asylum was not instituted for the practice of psychiatry; psychiatry rather was the practice developed to manage its inmates."[42] The Association of Medical Superintendents of American Institutions for the Insane was established in 1844, the first national medical society in the US. In 1892, it changed its name to the American Medico-Psychological Association, and in 1921 it became the American Psychiatric Association (APA).

DAWN OF A NEW AGE:
THE DEVELOPMENT OF EFFECTIVE TREATMENTS

The twentieth century finally began to offer some hope for the wretched housed in mental institutions. Julius Wagner-Jauregg won a Nobel Prize in 1927 for "pyrotherapy," the intentional counter-infection with malaria that proved to be effective against general paresis of the insane, caused by advanced syphilis, then a common reason for institutionalization. In 1935 Egas Moniz (a neurologist) invented the frontal lobotomy, for which he was awarded the Nobel Prize in Medicine and Physiology in 1949. At the time, the lobotomy was celebrated widely. One has to remember just how devastating and hopeless these illnesses were to both patients and their families. Now regarded as a symbol of evil and medical overreach, the lobotomy was, in fact, of help to some of the most desperately ill, hence the Nobel award. It is still in use today, to good effect in specific situations, though extremely rarely. But the lobotomy was grossly overused. Most notorious perhaps was Walter Freeman, also a neurologist, who traveled around the country performing lobotomies. He ultimately performed 3,600 of the procedures, often many in one day. All told, 50,000 lobotomies were performed in this country.

One must remember that in the 1950s *half* of all hospital beds in this country were occupied by patients with mental illness. People were desperate for relief, and surgery had established itself as the vanguard of progress in many diseases. There were very few truly useful drugs in any area of medicine at the time. The Department of Veterans Affairs (VA) hospitals especially, bowing to intense pressure from patients' despairing relatives, embraced the lobotomy and taught the procedure in its training programs.[43] Perhaps the most famous, or infamous, lobotomy recipient was Rosemary Kennedy, sister of John F. Kennedy. Rosemary suffered from developmental disabilities and was emotionally erratic. Her politically ambitious father worried her behavior could jeopardize the political futures of his sons John, Robert, and Ted. Her lobotomy was botched and she was rendered an invalid, hidden away for the rest of her life.

Early in my career I had the opportunity to care for two people who had undergone lobotomies many years before. Both were, as expected, quite placid and lived in supervised "board and care" homes. Both described being relatively content with their lives, far happier than prior to their surgeries, when life had been a living hell. One still needed a supervised living situation, primarily because he was blind, having prior to his lobotomy "enucleated" (gouged out) his eyes in response to hallucinated commands. As restricted as the lives of these two gentlemen were, they were clearly better off and much happier than prior to their lobotomies. One has to wonder how they would fare in today's world now that we have medication that would render their lobotomies unnecessary. The odds are they would not be receiving any treatment and would be homeless, in prison, or, more likely, dead.

Many other somatic (physical) treatments were tried, some quite bizarre.[44,45,46] Early interventions included the use of Metrazol in the 1940s to induce convulsions. It was found to be helpful to some, but the drug was highly toxic. Insulin coma therapy was popular for a time, helpful in some cases but also extremely risky. The Italians Ugo Cerletti and Lucio Bini ultimately found electricity could induce convulsions more safely than Metrazol and "electroconvulsive therapy" (ECT, or electroshock therapy) was born. Cerletti and Bini were nominated for a Nobel Prize for their discovery. ECT was, and is, extremely effective, but like the lobotomy was overused. But what were the options? Today ECT is underused, largely due to false information spread by anti-psychiatry groups. It now carries great stigma. Thomas Eagleton, the democratic candidate for vice president under George McGovern, was dropped mid-campaign when news got out that he had undergone ECT (with great results) for debilitating depression years before. It remains our most effective treatment for severe depression but is only rarely employed and, paradoxically, is often only available to very wealthy patients who can afford to pay out-of-pocket for premium care.

The 1950s and '60s ushered in the era of the tranquilizer. Meprobamate, sold under the name "Miltown," and barbiturates, like phenobarbital, were extremely popular, used mainly to treat anxiety and as sleep aids. These were soon replaced by the benzodiazepines, which are far less toxic but also potentially addictive. The most well-known of these was Valium (diazepam), which gained widespread popularity, eventually becoming the most widely prescribed drug of any kind in the US for fourteen years running (1968 to 1982). Chlorpromazine, the first effective antipsychotic—that is, a drug that can reduce delusions and hallucinations—was licensed in the US in 1953, selling under the catchy names Thorazine (the power of Thor!) and Largactil (its activity was large!). For some, it was indeed a miracle drug. The anthropologist and author Roy Richard Grinker quotes this staggering statistic: "In just one year, from 1955 to 1956, the state of New York reported, the frequency of restraint and seclusion as mechanisms of discipline and care dropped by 50 percent."[47] The term "chemical lobotomy" was applied to the antipsychotics, not as criticism but as praise: medications that could offer benefits of the lobotomy without the need for surgery and the attendant risks and irreversibility. Its maker Smith, Kline & French advocated for its widespread use in "cost-cutting" and "health economics" to offset the expenses incurred by the state institutions and their burgeoning population, setting the stage for changes to come.

Meanwhile, there were other breakthroughs in psychiatric medications. In 1952, Iproniazid, an anti-tuberculosis drug, was serendipitously found to be an effective antidepressant, spawning several other drugs in its class, the monoamine oxidase inhibitors (MAO-Is). In 1958, Roland Kuhn made brilliant observations on the positive effects of imipramine on depressed individuals,[48] launching a raft of tricyclic antidepressants like amitriptyline (Elavil). Soon after, reports of the positive effects of lithium on bipolar disorder, or manic-depression, were making their way over from Australia and Europe. There was growing hope that we would be able to manage mental illness without the need for expensive and restrictive hospitalization. Concurrently, psychoanalysis was fostering hope that these diseases could be treated and even prevented, without medication.

A COMBINATION OF ADVANCES IN TREATMENT, ECONOMIC FACTORS, AND SOCIAL FORCES DRIVES DEINSTITUTIONALIZATION

Joshua, a young man I treat, has schizophrenia. He is only modestly helped by medication, which does keep him from spinning wildly out of control. At his core he is a sweet, shy young man with no history of violence or criminal behavior, who craves the things most guys his age would want: friends, a job, independence, respect, a romantic partner. Tragically, these are beyond his reach and instead he lives in a fantasy world. His speech is vague and rambling, and its content bears little relation to reality. In his mind he lives not in a modest home with his aging parents, but in a mansion in LA, with his famous movie-star girlfriend and their dozen children. In his world he is a famous rap music star and TV and movie producer.

Over the years Joshua has been placed in multiple supervised living situations and group homes. He invariably walks away, not because he is oppositional, but because he can't understand basic rules or his need to be there. He has been found wandering the streets several times, starving, beaten, and near death. The only current option for him, other than living with his parents, would be to commit a serious crime (which he would never do). Then he might be placed in prison or in a cramped "locked" psychiatric facility where he would be incarcerated with other severely mentally ill individuals, most with a recent history of violence. This would only be temporary; he would certainly be discharged after a short while, only to end up on the streets again.

In the 1950s, more than half a million people with mental illness were living in state mental institutions in this country. This did not include those housed in other hospitals and alternate facilities, including jails and prisons. Today, we have a total of roughly 37,000 psychiatric beds in the entire United States, *one-fifteenth* the number we had back then, despite a doubling of our population. Where did all these people go? It's a sad and interesting story, well documented in a number of excellent books. [49,50,51] This process of clearing out the asylums became known as deinstitutionalization, and while well-intended, the consequences for the severely mentally ill like Joshua and their families, not to mention society at large, have been grave.

The discovery of Thorazine and other effective medications to treat mental illness is generally given as the driving force behind deinstitutionalization, but this is a gross oversimplification. While the promise of effective treatments provided a justification for discharging residents, in reality an unholy alliance of social, political, and economic forces, not patient benefit, drove the movement. In deinstitutionalization conservatives saw a way to save money, civil libertarians a way to expand civil rights. A seemingly improbable combination of conservative groups like the John Birch Society, who were suspicious of government intrusion into personal lives in any form, and civil libertarians, most prominently the ACLU, along with the free-spirit and anti-"big-brother" sentiment of the '60s all pushed to close the asylums. These groups caught the receptive ears of legislators, always eager to save money, particularly fiscal conservatives like Ronald Reagan and Nelson Rockefeller. As the governors of California and New York, respectively, they rallied their states to the forefront of deinstitutionalization.

Public sentiment against the asylums had been growing, fueled by horrific tales in popular media of the institutions' abuses. As early as 1946, a *Life* magazine exposé characterized the asylums as a "shame and disgrace." A powerful influence on many was *The Shame of the States*, a 1948 book written by journalist and social activist Albert Deutsch. In it he describes how "I was reminded of the pictures of the Nazi concentration camps in Belsen and Buchenwald . . . swarming with naked humans herded like cattle." But Deutsch was a thoughtful man, and he dug deeper. He quotes a sympathetic and overworked hospital superintendent who said, "we are short of doctors, nurses, maintenance men, social workers, attendants, and everything else—except patients." What these attacks on the state institutions failed to note was that the institutes did not want all these patients, they were completely overwhelmed and would gladly have sent many elsewhere if there was anywhere else they could go. It was society's decision to offload the mentally ill to the asylums. He also noted that the average daily expenditure per patient in state mental hospitals was less than *one dollar and twenty-five cents*, the equivalent of $16 today.[52] Contrast this with the $125 per day we pay today[53,54] to house each of the almost 400,000 mentally ill who have moved to prisons and jails since deinstitutionalization, or the thousands of dollars per day for hospitalization. Another oft-cited anti-asylum trope is *The Snake Pit*, a popular 1948 movie that chronicles the experience of a woman (portrayed by the stunning Olivia de Havilland) who is incarcerated in a mental institution for reasons she cannot remember. The heroine endures degradingly crowded accommodations, seemingly uncaring and highly regimented treatment, and frightening co-patients, but is ultimately cured by a wise and kindly psychoanalyst. The take-home message was that psychoanalysis would render mental institutions unnecessary.

Another nail in the coffin of the asylums, and a devastating blow to psychiatry in general, was the 1973 publication of David Rosenhan's *On Being Sane in Insane Places*. It appeared in the prestigious scientific journal *Science*[55] and became one of the most widely quoted studies in psychiatry of all time, referenced in more than 4,000 books and papers. As described in the "study," Rosenhan and seven others gained admission to psychiatric hospitals simply by claiming they heard voices saying random words like "thud" or "hollow." Once admitted they were supposedly given psychotropic medications and even held against their will, sometimes long after fellow patients had figured out they were not ill.

The public and many in the scientific community ate it up. Psychiatry was ridiculed for not being able to distinguish between the sane and insane. The reality turned out to be somewhat different. The author Susannah Cahalan recently published *The Great Pretender*,[56] an exhaustively researched examination of the Rosenhan study. She concluded Rosenhan likely fabricated patients and data, and grossly distorted

what data that may have been real. Some colleagues characterized
Rosenhan as a "bullshitter." Of his own hospital experience, she
obtained notes showing he claimed to be suicidal and the voices were so
distressing to him that he had resorted to holding copper pots over his
ears to block them. *The Spectator*, the prestigious 200-year-old British
current affairs magazine, called Rosenhan's paper "one of the greatest
scientific frauds of the past seventy-five years, and it was a fraud whose
real-world consequences still resonate today."[57] But most telling was the
eagerness with which society and the scientific community accepted
Rosenhan's deception, how his message resonated with society's ages-
old need to deny the reality of mental illness.

By this point in time, Rosenhan's paper hardly mattered. Deinstitutionalization was largely complete, and psychiatrists had abandoned the
asylums for practices as psychoanalysts in sophisticated urban centers,
treating healthier (and wealthier) patients. The shift was profound:
In 1917 just 8 percent of psychiatrists were in private practice; by the
1960s the proportion was 66 percent. By then the asylums were largely
run by foreign doctors, many of whom spoke little English and were
poorly able to advocate for their institutions or their residents, and
anti-foreigner sentiment may have contributed to public prejudice
against the institutions. Psychiatrists did not vigorously counter
the anti-psychiatry movement, nor did they fight deinstitutionalization
or the dismantling of treatment for the seriously mentally ill. They
had embraced psychoanalysis and its myth of the preventability and
curability of mental illness which would render asylums unneeded.
Psychiatry, the medical specialty formed to manage the asylums, now
fled for the city lights.

An important influence on the treatment of mental illness at the
time was the National Organization for Mental Health (NAMH),
founded in 1946—not the same as the current mental health advocacy organization the National Alliance on Mental Illness (NAMI),
which will be discussed in later chapters. Driven by the advocacy of
Clifford Beers, who himself had been in and out of mental asylums, it

championed the concept of "mental hygiene," whereby community based early intervention could prevent or lessen the severity of mental illness. Its influence helped drive the transition to community care in what were called "mental hygiene clinics," similar in concept to the prevention of dental cavities by dental hygiene.[58] In the end, there were few advocates for the asylums. The inmates were too disturbed and their families too ashamed to effectively organize any real resistance. Meanwhile, European countries that had access to the same medications and psychotherapies as the US reformed rather than closed their asylums, and fostered close alliances between them and outpatient services.

The anti-psychiatry movement, which thrived in the 1960s and is still quite alive today, merits a closer look too. The movement had three prominent figureheads: Thomas Szasz, Ronald D. Laing, and Erving Goffman. Their core argument was that mental illness was not a medical condition, but a social problem—ignoring the fact that physical illnesses throughout history had been solely defined by their symptomology, as well as the clear genetic contribution to mental illness. Szasz, a Hungarian-born American psychiatrist-psychoanalyst, published *The Myth of Mental Illness* in 1961.[59] In it he argued that mental illness was not real, but merely a metaphor for human suffering. Laing was a British psychiatrist who described schizophrenia as ". . . a special strategy that a person invents in order to live in an unlivable situation,"[60] and that insanity was a perfectly rational adjustment to an insane world.

Also in 1961, sociologist and social psychologist Erving Goffman published *Asylums: Essays on the Social Situation of Mental Patients and Other Inmates,* which examined the asylum as a social construct, benefiting society rather than mental patients. Goffman's ideas were in sync with the antiestablishment 1960s and not entirely off-base considering society's historical—and ongoing—wish to marginalize the mentally ill. However, catchy as their ideas were, these critics ignored or dismissed the clear benefits that the new antipsychotic drugs offered to many. As Jeffrey Lieberman, former president of the APA, wrote in his book *Shrinks:* "State governments, which were always eyeing ways to cut funding for the mentally ill especially state mental institutions . . . were only too happy to give credence to antipsychiatry arguments . . . While purporting to adopt humane postures, they cited Szasz, Laing, and Goffman as scientific and moral justification for emptying out the state asylums and dumping patients back into the community."[61]

These moral crusaders were responding to a very real problem: the mistreatment and exclusion of the mentally ill from society. But they failed to understand that the asylums were actually a solution, albeit a flawed one, to the ages-old problem facing societies throughout history: what to do with the mentally ill among us? Desperate families placed their loved ones in an asylum only after exhausting all other resources they had available; they could see very well where their loved one was being sent and did not make the choice lightly. The critics did not appreciate that the asylums served many quite well, or at least as well as any currently known option. They confused removal of care with individual rights. As academics, Szasz and Goffman were divorced from the ugly realities of treating mental illness and naively offered utopian and unrealistic answers. Goffman was not a clinician, and as adherents of psychoanalysis, Laing and Szasz bought into its myth of the preventability and curability of severe mental illness. They thought, and preached, that mental illness would be a thing of the past and asylums would not be needed once societal pressures were reduced. The residual problems, the expectable difficulties of life—teenage angst, divorce, job loss—could be managed using psychoanalytic techniques in a local community setting. As asylums closed, the new Community Mental Health Centers (CMHCs) were to manage these residual troubles.

Concomitantly, the widespread faith placed in psychoanalysis's potential did damage too. Its influence in society and popular culture was tremendous. Some reasoned that if optimal parenting could prevent mental illness, the occurrence of mental illness meant that the individual must have experienced poor parenting. Schizophrenia was allegedly caused by "schizophrenogenic" mothers, who subjected their children to conflicting statements and expectations, called "double binds," or by "refrigerator" moms, who lacked warmth and caused not only schizophrenia but also autism. These popular and cruel theories blamed those already suffering through the tragedy of an ill child, leaving them shamed and further marginalized.

In retrospect, it seems surprising that the anti-psychiatry and anti-asylum critics held such sway, or that Rosenhan's deception was uncritically accepted. But these were different, idealistic times, and our discomfort with the concept of mental illness so strong that their message took hold. In 1986, *Science* magazine, which had published Rosenhan's paper thirteen years earlier, reported on a poll that found 55 percent of the public did not believe mental illness was real.[62] These prejudices persist today; many in our society still are unable to accept that people can suffer from real and heartbreaking illnesses that affect the brain. We still find it more comfortable to blame societal issues, drugs, anything and anybody but recognize that the brain, like every other organ, can malfunction.

On Halloween day, 1963, with what turned out to be the last bill he signed before his assassination three weeks later, President Kennedy enacted an ambitious National Plan for Mental Health. It called for the formation of a "comprehensive" network of Community Mental Health Centers (CMHCs) to replace the old asylums.[63] These were to be outpatient facilities in urban communities modeled on the mental hygiene movement. The shift in care for the mentally ill was seismic: From the over one-half million patients hospitalized in the asylums in the 1950s, by 1989, that number had dropped to around 150,000.

While deinstitutionalization was well-intentioned, justified by the hope placed in psychoanalysis and the new and more effective medication treatments, its real attraction to legislators was economic. The humanitarian promise of deinstitutionalization quickly became the nightmare of financial and societal abandonment. A colleague of mine served as chief of a clinical unit at St. Elizabeth's Hospital in Washington, D.C., in the 1960s. The hospital was quite pleasant; it had its own farm where patients grew vegetables and a large meeting hall where they attended dances. He recalls people like Benny, a sweet man who had lived there stably for years. Benny was devastated when told he would have to leave, and had to be tearfully escorted out. He returned a couple of months later disheveled, starving, and confused, in the throes of a psychotic relapse.

Benny was not unusual. A 1985 study that tracked patients after discharge from Central Ohio Psychiatric Hospital found that over a third had become homeless within six months.[64] Equally troubling, from 1955 to 1970, "although the resident population of state hospitals declined sharply, the number of admissions to hospitals *doubled*."[65] The result was what is known now as "revolving door" treatment, where people have repetitive brief hospital admissions followed by a swift discharge to the outside world where they fail miserably and are rapidly readmitted, with a step down in their functioning and morale with each cycle. That is, unless they are imprisoned or die. From 1978 to 1988 deaths among the homeless by freezing doubled in New York City,[66] and a 2023 study found that San Francisco's homeless were sixteen times more likely to die a sudden death than others in the population.[67] "If your leg is broken, the city will take you away: If your mind is broken, you just lie there forever. . . . Why is rapid suicide illegal and gradual suicide a right?" ask Rael Isaac and Virginia Armat in their book *Madness in the Streets*.[68]

The beloved neurologist and author Oliver Sacks actually began his work as a neurologist at an asylum, Bronx State Hospital (now Bronx Psychiatric Center), in 1966. Writing of his experience there in *The Lost Virtues of the Asylum*,[69] he affectionately describes the great benefit asylums, when properly run, could provide:

> the protected and special atmosphere they offered . . . they were places where one could be both mad and safe, places where one's madness could be assured of finding, if not a cure, at least recognition and respect, and a vital sense of

companionship and community . . . Sadly and ironically, soon after I arrived in the 1960s, work opportunities for patients virtually disappeared, under the guise of protecting their rights . . . This outlawing of work—based on legalistic notions of patients' rights and not on their real needs—deprived many patients of an important form of therapy, something that could give them incentives and identities of an economic and social sort . . . the effects of stopping it were demoralizing in the extreme. For many patients who had previously enjoyed work and activity, there was now little left but sitting, zombie-like, in front of the now-never-turned-off TV.

I've heard countless stories from patients and their families relating how they miss the old asylums, and how much better life was for both then. Joshua, described earlier, now lives in his small room in his parents' house, and rarely goes outside. His elderly parents are spending their "golden years" caring for him, twenty-four hours a day, while wondering what will happen to him when they are no longer able to be there for their sweet, confused boy. The prospects are dismal.

THE FAILURE OF COMMUNITY MENTAL HEALTH CENTERS

While President Kennedy's vision was far reaching, his bill did not provide long-term funding to sustain the new CMHCs, the hope being that states would step in with their own resources. But rather than invest the money saved through asylum closures on mental health clinics, most states spent it on other priorities, such as cutting taxes or shoring up pensions.[70] The CMHCs ultimately failed the severely mentally ill because they were not equipped to serve them. They were grossly underfunded and focused their limited resources on people with less severe mental problems, bolstered by the popular view that insanity

was avoidable and unhappiness was merely a reaction to life's difficulties. They were often administered and staffed by more economical
non-MD clinicians with less training, particularly in the treatment of
severe mental illness.

The National Institute for Mental Health (NIMH), tasked with
setting up the CMHCs, gutted them of the programmatic components that would deal with the chronically ill, such as intensive
outpatient and day treatment programs, monitored medication
administration, supervised living quarters, and basic skills training
linked to supported vocational options. Instead, they focused on
psychotherapy to help negotiate more expectable and manageable
life stress events such as those mentioned earlier: the difficulties of
parenthood, childhood, juggling work-home commitments, divorce,
financial troubles, and family strife. These were certainly laudable
goals, but of little help to the chronically and severely mentally ill
who had been turned out onto the streets by deinstitutionalization
or their long-suffering families.

By 1977, a Government Accountability Office report concluded:
"CMHCs attracted a new type of patient who was not very ill and (was)
not a candidate for hospitalization in a state institution."[71] President
Jimmy Carter, with help from his wife Rosalynn, tried to revive the
CMHCs in 1980 with a bill that would have more than doubled
the federal government's investment in Kennedy's original CMHC
plan. President Carter signed that bill into law, but it was repealed by
the Omnibus Budget Reconciliation Act of 1981 signed by President
Ronald Reagan the following year.

Adding insult to injury, the mentally ill were further squeezed out
of effective treatment by the IMD (Institution for Mental Diseases)
exclusion rule, enacted in 1965 to avoid recreating the asylums. With
the expectation that care would be available through the CMHCs, it
prohibited Medicaid from paying for care in state or private mental
hospitals with more than sixteen beds. Worse, it forbids the treatment
of physical and mental health in the same location on the same day.

Despite the collapse of the CMHCs, this rule remains in effect today, leaving those on Medicaid in an impossible situation.[72]

Blaming mental illness on societal causes like imperialistic governmental policies and poor parenting allowed many to feel these illnesses could be eliminated through social interventions. Mental illness came to be viewed more as a way of looking at the world, or a choice, or at a minimum due to remediable circumstances. It offered a soothing view: It won't happen to me, it happens to others less fortunate, or less strong. This gave us a comforting sense of control; while mental illness might not be fair, we at least understood it, and could control it. Most reassuring, we could feel confident we were not really like *those* insane people. These comforting distortions are now utilized by multiple elements of our healthcare system to marginalize the mentally ill, as we'll see in subsequent chapters.

SHIFTING INSTITUTIONS

Dennis was a "frequent-flier," a slang term for a patient who regularly uses ER services. Mild-mannered and harmless, he was also hopelessly confused, illogical, and always filthy and hungry. He most often showed up after being beaten and robbed on the streets. If we had no hospital beds available, which was almost always the case, he would simply leave and create a disturbance or break something downtown to get himself jailed.

Deinstitutionalization resulted in somewhere over 500,000 people ending up on the streets. According to a 2011 Substance Abuse and Mental Health Services Administration (SAMHSA) report, more than one in four sheltered persons who were homeless had a severe mental illness and more than one in three adults housed in assistance shelters had chronic substance use issues.[73] These numbers reflect only those who are well enough to be sheltered. They ignore those sleeping in doorways, in parks, and under freeways. A 2024 study found that two-thirds of people experiencing homelessness currently had a mental health disorder, and more than three-fourths had a lifetime history of mental illness.[74] This agrees with my experience. I worked for years in an urban homeless clinic where the vast majority of those we saw had mental health or substance abuse problems, most often both. And those that didn't have psychiatric issues before homelessness certainly needed mental health help after spending some time living on the streets. In fact, the 2024 California Homelessness study found that among the homeless who reported regularly using substances, 64 percent started regular use of drugs after becoming homeless. Some cited the need to stay awake and vigilant to ward off an assault or robbery on the streets.[75]

Deinstitutionalization often meant that there was nowhere to send the severely ill except jail. Patients like Dennis learned this and committed petty crimes just to get into a place where they would at least be sheltered and fed. For Dennis, the lack of more supportive and ongoing treatment effectively locked him out of society, while costing that society far more in police, court, medical care, property damage, and incarceration costs. Being transient, and sometimes paranoid, the mentally ill are particularly poorly equipped to negotiate social services or navigate the complex process of obtaining Medicaid, meaning they can obtain neither employer-based healthcare insurance nor access publicly funded alternatives. Sure, Medicare kicks in at age sixty-five, but the average life expectancy of someone with schizophrenia is 64.7 years.[76]

Hospitalization chart

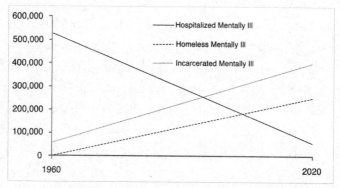

Estimated number of Americans with mental illness hospitalized, incarcerated, and homeless.

Consequently, deinstitutionalization not only caused homelessness to skyrocket, it also spawned a new phenomenon known as trans-institutionalization (not related to the current trans movements relating to gender.) Moving the mentally ill out of the asylums caused many of them to merely transfer to a different sort of institution: jails and prisons. A 2006 study by the Justice Department's Bureau of Justice Statistics found that more than half of all prison and jail inmates had a mental health problem.[77] Currently, Rikers Island Jail in New York, the Twin Towers Los Angeles County Jail, and the Cook County Jail in Chicago serve as our country's three largest psychiatric inpatient facilities. This, according to Kenneth Paul Rosenberg "translates to approximately 383,000 individuals with severe psychiatric disease living behind bars . . . Today, if you are an American with mental illness, you are up to ten times more likely to be incarcerated than hospitalized."[78]

An important step in this process was the 1976 Tarasoff ruling handed down by California courts. It found that the psychiatrist, not the police, could be held liable for the actions of a patient. In the Tarasoff case a young man murdered his ex-girlfriend but the treaters were held responsible despite having alerted the police. This in effect made dangerousness the standard for involuntary hospitalization, not need for treatment, turning doctors into jailers, exactly what deinstitutionalization was trying to avoid.

Compounding this, several pieces of legislation further limited the availability of care. The Lanterman–Petris–Short Act (LPS), signed into law by then California Governor Ronald Reagan in 1967 and used as a model by other states, imposed strict standards on civil commitment. Treatment could be imposed on the mentally ill only if they were deemed to be in *imminent* danger of killing someone or attempting suicide or so disturbed that they couldn't care for themselves. These rulings intimately intertwined treatment with criminal behavior. As Ron Powers succinctly summarizes in his book *No One Cares About Crazy People* about their family's struggles to get care rather than punishment for their sons' mental illness: "Nevertheless, LPS became the national gold standard for clueless, destructive government interference in the interests of mentally ill people. Intended to accelerate deinstitutionalization, it instead served to barricade state hospital doors against the admittance of stubbornly resisting patients—at least until a hearing was held. Not a medical hearing, with psychiatrists, but a judicial hearing, with a judge and lawyers." In the interest of preserving their civil liberties the mentally ill are instead channeled into prisons which "entitle(s) them to beatings and rape by their fellow inmates, beatings and taunting by the guards, solitary confinement that drives them madder still, deprivation of prescription drugs for those few who had prescriptions."[79] In the interest of liberating the mentally ill, they were turned into criminals. Worse, over time, the LPS standard for commitment evolved to become the standard for *voluntary* hospitalization utilized by insurers.

This catch-22 for psychiatric care of the seriously mentally ill was made worse by the Supreme Court's 1975 decision in *O'Connor v. Donaldson*. This ruling determined that a state could not confine a non-dangerous individual who is capable of surviving safely in freedom by themselves, or with the help of willing and responsible family members or friends, as this would violate their civil rights. Thus, if an individual is rendered irrational by mental illness, they may be imprisoned, but not treated. In practice, what "surviving safely" or what constitutes help of a responsible individual has become ludicrous, as evidenced by the legions of mentally ill homeless on our streets.

Our unwillingness to discriminate the need for hospitalization for treatment of mental illness as opposed to incarceration for criminality further restricts those with a serious mental illness's access to appropriate care. As Isaac and Armat point out: "The court did not recognize that, unlike criminal incarceration, involuntary treatment for mental illness offered benefits to the patient, and that unlike criminal and jailer, doctor and patient had a common interest in securing the patient's improved health . . . There was no recognition that a disease process had already curtailed the individual's liberty and that treatment might be necessary to restore the person's autonomy in any meaningful sense of the term."[80]

In 1987, Frank Lanterman, an author of the LPS Act lamented, "I wanted the LPS Act to help the mentally ill. I never meant for it to prevent those who need care from receiving it. The law has to be changed."[81] In the following thirty-five years, it has not been substantially modified.

Once imprisoned, less than one-half of those who were medicated for mental health conditions at admission continue to receive medication.[82,83] In California alone, as an *Los Angeles Times* investigation found, thousands of the mentally ill languish in jail, where they're denied trial or proper treatment.[84] In an even more perverse twisting of priorities, prisoners can be forced to take medication to make them sane enough to be tried for the "crime" caused by their illness, medication that was not available to them on the outside and might have prevented them from committing the "crime."[85] It's estimated that it costs us about $45,771 per year to incarcerate someone in this country.[86] It would cost a fraction of that to provide quality outpatient mental health treatment for even the most severely ill person, and would be a lot less cruel. In a further perversion of logic, the charges against some SMI who commit violent crimes and are felt unlikely to achieve mental competency quickly are dropped. They are discharged back into the community, without care or oversight, only to re-commit violent acts.[87]

When I call my healthcare giant, the voice message says, "If you are having a medical or psychiatric emergency call 911." Why the distinction you may ask? Because the former means you will be sent an ambulance while the latter brings the police. If you fall or have a heart attack on the sidewalk, medical professionals are sent to help you. If you are acting strangely, law enforcement is sent. As Rosenberg points out, "Mental illness crises are the only health emergency in which law enforcement are the first responders."[88] Even in my city where we have a mobile mental health crisis unit, responders will not engage in a mental health emergency without police presence.

According to estimates made by the Treatment Advocacy Center, a national nonprofit organization dedicated to eliminating barriers to the treatment of severe mental illness: "People with untreated mental illness are 16 times more likely to be killed during a police encounter than other civilians approached or stopped by law enforcement . . . and between one fourth and one half of all fatal law enforcement encounters involves an individual with serious mental illness."[89]

Ultimately, our unwillingness to accept the reality of, and confront our aversion to, mental illness causes us to ignore the needs of its victims. Ironically, we have merely recreated the conditions that spawned the asylum movement in this country two hundred years ago. However, the situation today is all the more troubling because we actually have effective treatments. Even when we cannot offer cure, we could at least offer care, which eases suffering. Care is what the asylums offered, and is the core of what medicine has offered for millennia. It seems paradoxical that now that we have the capability to offer at least a partial cure, we have abandoned both care and cure.

CHAPTER TWO

The Impact on
Patients and Families

A DESPERATE SHORTAGE

Justin, a forty-four-year-old Black man, was a patient of mine. A devoted father with a loving family, soft-spoken, a veteran, and with a passion for karaoke, he also suffered from bipolar disorder. Stable for long periods of time when in treatment, he still occasionally lapsed into manic or depressive episodes. One afternoon while in a manic episode he went to visit an elderly friend at her apartment complex. There, he got into a verbal altercation with a known drug dealer he wished to keep away from his friend. The police were called and in assessing the situation questioned Justin. Lacking his usual judgment and restraint he was incensed that he was being questioned along with the dealer. He made an insulting sexual comment to a female officer who replied, "Would you like to go to jail?" His answer: "Yes." In jail he was put in isolation, allowed no visitors, and deprived of his medications. His condition rapidly deteriorated. He became frightened and paranoid. To attract attention he shouted threats against President Obama, someone he respected and supported. He was hauled out of his cell by guards and when he tried to defend himself with a two-inch long mini-golf pencil he was severely beaten. Later he was charged with making "terroristic threats" (while locked in an isolation cell!) and assault with a deadly weapon (the pencil). Ultimately, despite his family and treatment team spending many hours in court explaining his diagnosis and history, he ended up spending months in jail without treatment. The judge, citing his "history of violence," determined he should remain in jail, isolated and untreated, rather than be transferred to a psychiatric hospital. His only "violence" had occurred in jail, off of his medications, at the hands of guards. After release, his nightmare of legal fights, court-ordered monitoring, and restrictions continued. His life in shambles, he ultimately jumped to his death. Rather than a tragic anomaly, Justin's experience is more the norm for people with mental illness in our society, especially for people of color.

This chapter focuses on examples like this—how our healthcare-as-business has impacted the care of patients, people like you and me. As you read the examples I use to illustrate aspects of mental health-care, or more often the lack of it, please stop to think of individuals you undoubtedly know of personally whose stories bear similarities to what I describe. As mentioned previously, in 2023 a Gallup poll found more than one in six Americans, and more than one in four eighteen- to twenty-nine-year-olds, reported they were currently depressed or being treated for depression,[1] and the prior year the Department of Health and Human Services found the same number, one in six, who suffered from a substance abuse disorder.[2] Almost one in two Americans know someone who died by drug overdose. One in eight have had their lives disrupted by a drug overdose death.[3]

Who among us has not experienced, or does not know of someone—a family member or loved one—who has been unable to access adequate mental healthcare, with serious consequences? Who does not personally know someone who has died by suicide or whose life has been upended by mental illness or addiction? As you read these examples, it is crucial to understand that they do not illustrate breakdowns in the system, but rather fully expected consequences of the system working exactly as designed and intended. In subsequent chapters we'll examine how and why our system embraces these seeming paradoxes, as well as why the companies and professionals who are tasked with preserving our health often do just the opposite.

The single biggest problem faced by those needing mental health treatment is that care is simply not available. I hear this story daily. Try as they might, people can't find care. The bottom line is that mental healthcare has been squeezed out of our healthcare system by prejudice toward those with a serious mental illness and financial strangulation by healthcare corporations. In 1955, we had 340 public psychiatric beds for every 100,000 people (and this number was grossly inadequate, psychiatric hospitals were horribly overcrowded then). By 2005 this number had plummeted to seventeen, a 95 percent decrease.[4] There is also a critical shortage of psychiatrists in the US. A 2017 report found that 60 percent of US counties did not have a single psychiatrist, and signs indicate that the shortage is only worsening. The report went on to note that the number of psychiatrist job postings jumped by more than 97 percent between 2010 and 2014.[5]

Children and their families are particularly hard-hit by the clinician shortage. Over the last ten years, the proportion of pediatric ER visits for mental health reasons has approximately doubled, including a five-fold increase in suicide-related visits,[6] with the suicide rate in youth five to nineteen years of age higher in counties with mental health professional shortages.[7] From 2009 to 2019 pediatric acute care hospitalizations for mental health diagnoses increased 25 percent, hospitalizations for self-injury or attempted suicide increased 2.6 fold, and mental health accounted for more than one-quarter of all acute care hospitalization days for three- to seventeen-year-olds.[8] By 2019, prior to the pandemic, 17 percent of outpatient doctor visits for patients ages thirteen to twenty-four in the United States involved a mental health condition. And at 22.4 percent of outpatient visits at least one psychiatric drug was prescribed, suggesting that far more psychiatric problems were present and addressed than were documented.[9] By 2021 American families spent an average of $4,361 per year on child mental health services, which is nearly half (about 47 percent) of all child medical spending.[10]

A 2022 exposé in the *New York Times* described how adolescents spend days, even *weeks*, languishing in ERs while staff hunt for an appropriate psychiatric treatment setting to send them. Every night there are thousands of teens in emergency rooms across the country too sick to go home, waiting for some place they can get treatment. The cost to society in tied-up emergency rooms is staggering,[11] not to mention the other emergencies that don't get timely care due to the backup or the harm done to these teens and their family and friends while they wait desperately for help which may never come.[12]

Signaling their alarm, in 2019 the American Academy of Pediatrics issued a report saying, "Mental health disorders have surpassed physical conditions as the most common reasons children have impairments and limitations . . . Mental health disorders affect 1 in 5 children; however, a shortage of mental health specialists, stigma, cost, and other barriers prevent the majority of affected children from receiving appropriate services."[13] Suicide in teens has been climbing steadily since 2007 and is now the second most common cause of death in this age group, behind only accidents, many of which are undoubtedly misclassified.[14]

For severely ill adults and their families the situation is also especially grim. Even when care is available, the mentally ill and those with substance abuse are often poorly equipped to access that care. Because of instability in their lives, an inability to advocate for themselves, and sometimes an unwillingness to cooperate with or even recognize a need for care, these individuals are left out of America's healthcare system. One such family is Blake and Rita and their two kids, now in their twenties. The kids had trouble launching, they were unable to complete high school or maintain employment which would have allowed them to live on their own. For comfort, or at least some escape, they turned to drugs, and became erratic and paranoid. Attempts by Blake and Rita to convince them to get treatment were met with anger, threats, and even violence. The parents had to tip-toe around their own home, careful not to set off their now-adult kids. They feel trapped. Their only option is to call 911. Yes, the police would then come and assess the situation, and perhaps take the kids to the county hospital for evaluation. But since their kids don't feel they have a problem or need treatment, the only option would be an involuntarily hospitalization—but only if they met the rigid criteria for hospitalization (active threats of suicide or violence) and then only if hospital beds were available. Hospitalization would mean a maximum of seventy-two hours respite (unless they continued to make threats in the hospital), then they would be released to return home. If they refused medication, which is likely, none would be given. What would this charade serve except to inflame an already volatile situation, ask Blake and Rita? So they continue to house their erratic and sometimes violent adult children, feeling like hostages in their own home.

I provide buprenorphine treatment for my opioid-addicted patients, which allows them to keep withdrawal at bay with a relatively safe prescribed oral opioid, much like an office-based methadone maintenance program. While still chained to their medication, they avoid the danger that goes with obtaining street opioids, like hepatitis, HIV, endocarditis, or inadvertent overdose, not to mention having to interact with a crime-driven business run by cartels. But there are nowhere near enough doctors who are trained or comfortable enough to prescribe buprenorphine, especially with the lack of available ancillary support. Plus it takes money (the medication alone runs at least $200 a month for most) or insurance and a relatively stable life to be able to cooperate with the doctor and treatment protocol. Still, my patients are motivated. They know what the alternative is: obtaining heroin on the streets. All of them know someone who has died following that route.

Data from SAMHSA shows the critical shortfall of mental health-care: in 2018 *less than half* of adults with mental health diagnoses received any treatment for their illness (and I'm sure the number is far less for kids), and in the midst of the opioid epidemic, while tens of thousands die annually of overdose, only *one in five* people with an opioid use disorder obtained any treatment at all.[15, 16] As our healthcare system restricted the prescription of opiates in an attempt to slow the epidemic, it did not provide treatment for those it had addicted, so patients had to turn to illegal suppliers for the drugs. This, combined with the spread of the powerful synthetic opioid fentanyl, led to a *tripling* of overdose deaths from 2010 to 2020.[17] A 2023 Kaiser Family Foundation poll found that a staggering two-thirds of American adults ". . . said either they themselves or a family member have experienced addiction to alcohol or drugs, homelessness due to addiction, or an overdose resulting in an emergency room visit, hospitalization or death."[18] More than *one-half* of all people in this country injured or killed in traffic crashes have one or more drugs or alcohol in their bloodstream.[19] Yet our healthcare system acts like substance misuse doesn't warrant treatment.

To give the appearance of offering care, insurers provide online lists of doctors and therapists who are under contract with the company to provide care for people who carry their insurance policy. These clinicians are called "in-network," or on the insurer's "provider panel." But the reality is very different from what these online lists suggest. Many insurers have set up what are known as "ghost networks" of psychiatrists and therapists that include the names and numbers of clinicians who, despite being listed, are not available to patients.[20] I have found my name on lists of "in-network contracted providers" of insurers I have never worked for, along with names of long-deceased colleagues. In a recent study, researchers called 360 psychiatrists on Blue Cross Blue Shield's in-network provider lists in Houston, Chicago, and Boston. Some of the phone numbers on the list were for McDonald's locations, others were for jewelry stores. When the researchers actually reached psychiatrists' offices, many didn't accept the insurance or weren't taking new patients. After calling every number twice, the researchers were able to make appointments with only one out of four of the psychiatrists on the list.[21] In a similar study among child psychiatrists, researchers were able to make appointments with only one out of six of the doctors listed as in-network by Blue Cross Blue Shield.[22] As we'll explore in Chapters Five and Six, the poor reimbursement and other restrictions placed on mental healthcare have caused many mental health professionals to refuse to work with insurance companies. Among psychiatrists, only 55 percent accept *any* insurance plans at all,[23] far fewer than other medical specialties,[24] and then often only the most favorable one or two. Among those that do accept insurance, most are too busy to take on new patients, especially those on insurance who will reimburse less and carry other insurance-mandated restrictions on care. However, they might flex for patients willing to pay much higher out-of-pocket rates.

There is a similar critical shortage of non-MD mental health professionals, such as psychologists and social workers. Lisa, a twenty-eight-year-old 911 operator, came to me in crisis. The stress of her job and its sixty-plus hour work week while juggling family obligations left her at her wit's end. Her HMO offered her a group for depression that started in eight weeks, which met at a nonnegotiable time in the middle of her work shift. She was told the wait for an individual therapist would be many months, at least. A 2021 *New York Times* investigation that polled non-MD mental health professionals found what they termed a "mental health crisis." They reported, "Nearly one in three clinicians said that it could take at least *three months* to get an appointment or that they didn't have room for new patients at all." Six in ten reported an increase in those seeking medication, which because they are not MD's these therapists are not permitted to prescribe.[25]

For reasons we'll explore further in Chapter Six, like psychiatrists, non-medical therapists strive to avoid insurance and build private practices made up of primarily out-of-pocket self-pay patients. Thus many mental health patients, if they are able and if they can find a clinician with time, have to pay out of pocket for care. A recent study found that the percentage of self-paid visits to psychiatrists was more than *fifteen times* those to primary care physicians (26.7 vs. 1.7 percent), and the gap is increasing.[26] Most often, patients who cannot pay out of pocket are simply left out.

THE CRUSHING FINANCIAL AND EMOTIONAL IMPACT ON FAMILIES

Anna was a sweet, smart child who had a troubled adolescence and never seemed to pull herself together afterward. She became rebellious, took chances, wandered from her hoped-for path. It's not clear if she developed schizophrenia or became delusional from her use of drugs, or both. When she uses meth (methamphetamine), she becomes wild and irrational. During periods of abstinence her mind clears and she is remorseful about her behavior. But she's never clean long enough for anyone to know if she will be totally free from her paranoia and idiosyncratic ideas, or just how forthcoming she is. Now thirty-five, her intermittent life on the streets and drug use have taken their toll. Toothless and with many scars, she looks twice her age. Her parents are heartbroken, having seen her cycle in and out of rehab programs, promptly relapsing when returned to the outside world and its challenges. She has spent time in jail, always followed by a firm conviction to stay clean and sober and maintain a stable lifestyle.

Her parents know they must be wary: she has broken into their home and trashed it while in the throes of drug-fueled paranoia. Their financial resources drained, their hopes have been built up then dashed too many times. Their life is dominated by caring for Anna's child, father unknown or unnamed, but long gone. Anna was thrown out of the most recent apartment they paid for after she let it be used as a drug haven by "friends" she met on the street. Her parents have to keep Anna at a distance lest she damage their home again. They can't afford to pay for another hospitalization and watch and wait helplessly as Anna returns to the streets. They live in dread of "that phone call," from the police, the hospital, or the coroner, which is sure to come someday.

Anna is not unusual, nor is the dilemma her parents find themselves in. Most homeless mentally ill have families who love them, or tried very hard to love them. I find that much of my work with the severely mentally ill is through their family, with little help from society at large. The burden to a family of someone who is delusional, or severely addicted, with judgment and insight so impaired that they may not even recognize that they have an illness, is crushing. We joke about the problems in launching children in today's society. What about a child who will never work? What about one who, if not monitored, will wander out to the streets where they will be beaten, or may burn down the family home? This is currently the fate of Rita and Blake, and the families of Joshua and Anna—and so many, many others—who live in fear of the day that they become too old to care for their family member, who will likely die without their assistance.

While the emotional toll on families is immeasurable, the financial toll of our healthcare system is quite clear—and staggering. In 2024 a Kaiser Family Foundation (KFF) survey found that three in four adults reported that they are "very" or "somewhat worried" about being able to afford unexpected medical bills or the cost of healthcare services for themselves and their family.[27] In 2022 KFF found that 100 million people in America, including a whopping 41 percent of adults, are saddled with healthcare debt. Among these, two out of three reported having to cut back on spending for food, clothing, and other basics to pay this debt, and almost half had used up all or most of their savings.[28,29] Another 2022 KFF poll found that in the past year more than half of all adults reported that they had delayed or gone without medical services due to cost.[30]

From 2009 to 2020 medical debt in collections exceeded *all* other forms of debt for Americans.[31] Two out of every three people who file for bankruptcy cite medical issues as a key contributor to their financial downfall. [32] In an indication of peoples' desperation, the crowdfunding site GoFundMe has become a common lifeline for those trying to escape medical billing nightmares. GoFundMe started as a crowd-funding site for underwriting "ideas and dreams," but it is estimated that over one-third of all funds raised on the site now are to pay for medical care. [33]

In 2022 the Consumer Financial Protection Bureau found that even *friends and family* of patients have had to declare bankruptcy, had their wages garnished, and had their homes repossessed after signing "admission agreements" with nursing facilities to help their friend or relative obtain treatment. [34] And of course there is the health toll of medical debt. Medical debt is associated with both physically and mentally unhealthy days, and increased mortality due to both physical illnesses and suicide. [35]

Medical debt and aggressive collection is so accepted now, it is a standard part of billing. In a sad commentary about today's world, I receive copies of insurance company explanation of benefit (EOB) forms for my patients. Anthem Blue Cross EOBs include the standard line items "Interest," "Penalty," and "Levy/Garnishment."

Merely trying to access health benefits can draw patients into a black hole of time. A 2020 study estimates that people in the US spend *half a billion* hours a year on the phone with health insurers, [36] which is certainly more time than they spend with their doctors. One in four patients report that administrative hurdles have caused them to delay or go without care. [37]

As always, in mental health the situation is worse than for other ill-nesses. For the many with mental illness, dealing with insurance claims is an impossible barrier to overcome. But without adequate insurance, hospitalizing a confused, uncooperative and uninsured family member is expensive beyond reason. As ABC news recently reported, a five-day psychiatric hospitalization for an uninsured woman resulted in a bill for $21,000. [38]

Kari, a successful hi-tech worker with many friends, a responsible job, and her own condo, had, under the stress of career expectations, let alcohol take over her life. From a glass of wine to unwind at the end of the day, she progressed to staying drunk virtually any time she was alone. Her family spent dozens of hours researching potential treatment programs. One quoted them $90,000 for one month of inpatient treatment. They eventually did find a program their insurance would help pay for, but only for a maximum of twenty-eight days. Follow-up was equally difficult to arrange due to the extreme shortage of outpatient therapists and programs—only made worse by the pandemic—and inadequate at best; weekly meetings with a counselor and voluntary sobriety meetings, both by Zoom. Within days of discharge Kari had relapsed. Rather than an aberration, Kari's experience is the norm. A 2012 study of the costs of psychiatric treatment in community hospitals found that charges were *2.5 times* higher than the hospitals' reported costs to deliver that care. The study found numerous pricing tricks, including "a large gap between charges and reimbursed amounts, potential cost shifting between payers, and potentially extended lengths of stay to offset reduced per diems (daily rates)."[39] That is, hospitals were using any trick they could such as tacking on other charges—like charging for group meetings, extra medications and tests, and various add-on treatments—all to jack up costs. Some of these tricks will be examined further in Chapter Three. The result of these manipulations has been outrageously expensive, but sketchy and inadequate treatment at best, but most often no treatment at all.

Even turning to nonprofit, "grassroots" patient advocacy organizations for mental health support can hold perils. Many of these organizations have been swept up by the for-profit industry and are now derisively referred to as "astroturf" organizations because the grassroots (community) are fake. They serve as fronts for the pharmaceutical industry, advocating for use of the company's expensive medications. For example, between 1999 and 2001 NAMI, the largest, well-respected advocacy group for the mentally ill, was directed by Gerald

Radke, pharmaceutical giant Eli Lilly's marketing manager, whom Lilly loaned to NAMI complete with salary. Lilly also donated more than $2.5 million to the organization during that period, [40] and paid for projects like a fleet of charter buses to take NAMI members to Sacramento, California's capital, to lobby legislators to approve funding for the use of Lilly's expensive then-new antipsychotic Zyprexa®.

It's one thing to be taken advantage of financially. In a business transaction we almost expect it and are on guard. In most financial transactions, the worst outcome is that you will be harmed financially, but you will still have the possibility of redress or to rebuild. In healthcare the stakes are so much higher. Those fleeced of healthcare often cannot complain, or recover; they are disabled and marginalized, or dead.

LIMITING THE RIGHTS OF PATIENTS

Clara, an elderly woman who suffers from severe anxiety, arrived at my office in a terrified state. Her primary care doctor of twenty years had retired and the HMO-run clinic reassigned her to another. This new doctor told her that to receive care she would have to discontinue her medication (alprazolam, Xanax®) immediately, per "clinic policy." This, despite the fact that the medication had worked quite well for over twenty years and the certainty that an abrupt discontinuation would precipitate a severe exacerbation in her symptoms. She came to me, which meant she was paying entirely out-of-pocket for care. I've worked with Clara for several years now and she has successfully transitioned to a less addictive medication and will in all likelihood be able to discontinue it within the next year. But Clara is an exception, someone with financial resources and the ability to advocate, strongly, for herself. I wonder how Clara's new HMO doctor felt when she had to tell Clara she would have to abruptly discontinue Xanax®? I'm sure she felt in a bind. How does one best serve patients if doing so means your contract with the clinic won't be renewed and you won't be able to offer them your care at all?

Patients themselves are placed in similar binds. To receive treatment they often must sign away their constitutional right to legal representation should they be mistreated by accepting a binding arbitration agreement. In so doing they are agreeing, in advance, to an arbitrator of the company's choosing, with no further recourse beyond arbitration. A 2020 *Forbes* article says it all, ironically titled, "The Doctor Will See You Once You Sign This Binding Arbitration Agreement: As it buys up medical practices, private equity is popularizing a favored Wall Street cost-cutting tactic—and stripping patients of rights."[41]

With our insanely expensive healthcare, when an insurer limits or denies payment they are, in effect, dictating what care we can, or cannot, receive. Despite not being healthcare practitioners, they are making medical care decisions they are not qualified to make on individuals they do not know. Wendy Mariner, professor and an expert on health law at Boston University, cites the example of *Kuhl v. Lincoln National Health Plan of Kansas City, Inc.*, where the insurer refused to pay for Mr. Kuhl's transfer from an in-network hospital to one out-of-network that could perform potentially lifesaving surgery. Mr. Kuhl died and the family sued. However, "The court of appeals found that there was no valid malpractice claim because the plan did not make a medical decision. Instead, it characterized their suit as a business dispute; a claim for denial of benefits or improperly processing a claim for benefits defined by the group health plan."[42]

These sorts of business-driven barriers interfere with patient care on a daily basis. For example, insurers restrict medications they will pay for (called "being on formulary") based on what's most favorable for them financially, not what's best for the patient. A few years ago, the insurer of another of my patients who suffers from panic attacks refused to pay for lorazepam (Ativan®), a relatively inexpensive and generically available benzodiazepine. They would, however, pay for alprazolam (Xanax®), the drug Clara had been taking. Most consider

Xanax® riskier in terms of its potential for abuse and addiction. Yet her insurer insisted she switch to alprazolam, undoubtedly because they negotiated a cheaper price for it. Then, last year, she went off to graduate school on the East Coast, and the clinic that took over her care refused to prescribe her alprazolam. Sure enough, she suffered a major exacerbation in her panic attacks, nearly forcing her to drop out of school. She resumed seeing me regularly for psychotherapy to manage her symptoms, via Zoom, with her parents footing the bill.

MAGNIFYING INEQUALITIES

Sam's crime sounds laughable in retrospect. He walked into a bank, in broad daylight with no disguise or weapon, and demanded money from a teller. When she questioned his request he admitted he really wasn't sure why he was there. He put up no objection or resistance when the police were called, waiting patiently in the lobby until they arrived. He was whisked off to jail, where he was nicknamed "psycho" by his cellblock mates, who tormented him for entertainment. They would assist each other in sexually assaulting him while the guards looked the other way. A favorite activity there was to place him, naked, on the low wall dividing the showers and throw burning matches at him to watch him writhe in fear and pain. Again the guards, fully aware of what was going on, merely stood by. But Sam was a fortunate exception. His prior military service earned him access to free care when he got out. With steady treatment through the Department of Veterans Affairs, Sam's psychosis cleared. His life stabilized and he eventually married, but obtaining employment with the felony bank "robbery" on his record proved impossible. And the shame he carried always kept him on the margins in social situations.

Similar to the racial disparities in the distribution of wealth in this country, since healthcare requires wealth, it too is unevenly distributed. This disparity is even greater in mental healthcare. As we'll see in Chapter Six, Black Americans access mental health services less than *half* as frequently as White Americans, and psychotherapists are overwhelmingly Caucasian, adding another barrier to persons of color in a crisis. Even in primary care settings Black people and Hispanics are given less care for anxiety and depression than White people with equivalent symptoms.[43] While Black Americans constitute 13 percent of the population, they make up over 40 percent of the homeless[44] and over half the prison population. Unable to afford either insurance or legal services, mentally ill people of color are disproportionately excluded from mental healthcare and shuttled into the criminal justice system. Adding insult to injury, our country's bail requirements mean that the mentally ill, who are unable to pay bail, must remain incarcerated while awaiting trial even if they are innocent, further disrupting relationships, housing, and employment, as well as torpedoing any hopes of future employment.

This was driven home to me recently during a BART ride home at 11:00 P.M. on a Monday night. I observed a Black man in his early twenties approach a Hispanic woman in her thirties who was improbably dressed in a thin cotton sweatshirt and sweatpants. Noting the manila envelope she was clutching, he asked her, "Are you just out of jail?" When she registered surprise he showed her his manila envelope. Curious, I joined in their conversation and learned that each had been discharged from jail, different ones, he from "850," she from Santa Rita, each with nothing but a BART ticket and their discharge papers. They had each spent the better part of a week in jail following arrests for driving under the influence, their cars and belongings impounded. Neither had money or a working cell phone. The woman explained that the provision of the BART tickets was a recent addition since the authorities had learned that predators lurked around the jails at night looking for discharged women attempting to walk home. Multiple attacks and rapes prompted the concession. DUIs are a serious offense that can result in death. But what chance do we give to this young man and woman to learn from their experience, make amends, and re-enter society? In my practice, I've found the double whammy of mental ill-ness or substance use and legal problems to be a near-insurmountable barrier to re-entering society as a productive member. In my area, a credit report and background check are routine for someone applying for rental housing. Without our help, these two people will most likely become tragedies and long-term drains on our society.

As we accept that the business model drives our healthcare, money takes precedence and corrodes other values. Incentives are oriented to maximize and consolidate economic gain rather than community welfare. As long as profits are healthcare's goal, a focus on billing, pushing over-hyped expensive (and often ineffective) treatments, and price gouging will be the norm. Our for-profit system effectively obscures long established ethical responsibilities of those who care for the ill. Healthcare companies and their employees have no respon-sibility to protect the health of their clients, which, oddly enough, is supposed to be the goal of their business. Doctors, nurses, and other caregivers may have a sworn duty to put their patient's needs above their own, but this is squeezed out by conflicting employer requirements.

There are other downstream effects when healthcare companies are the drivers of care. Healthcare becomes centralized, its control taken out of the community, away from local elected officials, and into dis-tant boardrooms. Gone are our community and charity hospitals that once served their communities, treating all comers, regardless of their ability to pay. They have been replaced by hospitals owned by large corporations and private equity groups, people and entities who set healthcare standards and pricing, yet live far, far away and may know nothing about a community's needs or resources. Who cares about the suffering of people you can't see and will never meet?

Within us resides an irrational paradox called "tainted altruism." This is a phenomenon where we distrust people who make money by doing good. After all, we figure, one should get adequate pleasure and satisfaction out of the good work itself. Self-promoting pastors of mega-churches and CEOs of nonprofit advocacy organizations are viewed as suspect when they accumulate large sums of money, yet our society idolizes fabulously wealthy entrepreneurs who are acting purely in self-interest. Thoughtful or altruistic exchanges like donating an organ, carrying a baby (surrogacy), or engaging in consensual sex become what are known as "repugnant transactions" when they are tainted by the introduction of money. Money undoes the reciprocal care and goodwill. Similarly, injecting the profit motive into healthcare converts it from an altruistic endeavor into a repugnant transaction, one motivated by profit rather than the kindness and satisfaction that both practitioners and patients hope for. While procedures that are billable are given top value in our current medical industry, other elements that historically have been important to medical treatment like care, kindness, and empathy are not reimbursed.

Disastrously, this falls most harshly on the mentally ill, who sometimes experience outcomes worse than poverty, homelessness, and incarceration. As we saw in Chapter One, people with untreated mental illness are *sixteen times* more likely to be killed during a police encounter. When we hear of a police shooting, we wonder if the person behaved in a manner that provoked the shooting. Sadly, with our current system, the outcome is often the same if the person is a vicious criminal or a desperately ill person meaning no harm. Since Black Americans with mental illness are less able to get care, and police rather than medical personnel are first responders for mental health crises, Black Americans are killed by police at nearly *three times* the rate of Caucasians, and *five times* the rate of Caucasians among those killed who are unarmed. These killings have consequences for Black Americans without mental illness, who well know and experience encounters with police who act under the assumption that they may have an untreated mental illness and might therefore be less rational and cooperative than White people.[45] As with Justin, whom we saw at the beginning of the chapter, for Black Americans, even those without mental illness, the arrival of the police may not signal an end to their danger, but rather, the beginning.

THE VALUE OF YOUR DATA VS.
THE VALUE OF YOUR HEALTH

As "consumers" of healthcare, our privacy is routinely disregarded. I receive multiple faxes (remember those?) a day from pharmacies requesting authorization to refill patients' prescriptions. Under the Health Insurance Portability and Accountability Act of 1996 (HIPAA), Protected Health Information (PHI) like a patient's medications may be faxed between different "covered entities" such as health plans, healthcare providers, pharmacies, insurers, and their various business associates as long as reasonable privacy safeguards are taken, like ensuring the receiving fax machine is secure and private. Not a single pharmacy has ever asked if my fax is secure or private. Many of these refill requests are not needed and are generated automatically to boost sales. Sometimes they are for medications the patient is no longer taking or for someone no longer under my care. What am I to do with them? Ignore them, or spend time tracking down my patient to see if the request is truly valid despite my chart records to the contrary? When I worked at a VA hospital I did not have a private fax and the number I listed on my state medical license was for the fax machine located in the administrative office of my department. Somehow, this number popped up in a pharmacy database. Pharmacies of vets who received their medication(s) from outside of the VA and those of my private patients sent their requests for refills to this fax machine, where their information spilled out into a very public room where secretarial staff and visitors congregated. Multiple calls to the pharmacies did not stem the tide. A complaint to my state's board of pharmacy asking what could be done was met with a shrug.

Healthcare systems now routinely share your health information with tech giants like Microsoft and Google.[46] Even wearable devices and health apps sell your data. Since your health is business, your PHI, which formerly was viewed as sacrosanct and held to the highest standards of confidentiality and privacy, is now business data and as such is bought, sold, traded, and stolen just like any other valuable commodity. Why would a corporation pay to know that you have diabetes, hypertension, or depression? It's all marketing, to know whom to target for sales, and how to pitch their product, and importantly, whom to avoid. Healthcare companies collect, buy, sell, and trade your PHI to other businesses by calling it "business data" or "consumer data," thereby skirting rules about sharing PHI.

As an example, Carrot, a leading vendor of data recently acquired by Unite Us—a network of health and social service providers—brags that it sells analytics that contain "up to 5,000 individually certified variables for every adult in America."[47] In 2022, IBM sold off its MarketScan family of databases that includes medical records on over 80 percent of the US population for $1 billion to the private equity firm Veritas Capital. Veritas then resold the records to two investment firms, Hellman & Freedman and Bain Capital.[48] Not a single one of those more than 270 million patients had consented to their data being sold. Did you? These deals skirted HIPAA regulations because privacy "rules apply only to the health entities that initially collected the data, not the commercial companies that compile and re-deploy it in search of profit."[49,50] While much of the data is supposed to be "de-identified," using multiple data points to "triangulate" and identify an individual is easy with these large databases. (Triangulation is where data points in various databases can be combined and cross-referenced to uniquely identify someone. For example, one database might identify you by your initials, your date of birth, your diagnosis of depression, and the doctor you see. Another database might identify you by your name, date of birth, medication you take, and the doctor you see. Combining the databases links your name to your diagnosis and medication.) Even carefully controlled hospital data is vulnerable to re-identification with triangulation. A 2018 study found that one-third of patients can be re-identified from released hospital data.[51]

As patients, our rights to privacy and confidentiality are routinely ignored. Pharmacies sell information about what we are prescribed (and who prescribed it) to health information clearing houses like IQVIA (formerly IMS Health) and SDI (formerly Verispan). In 2022, internal documents showed that IQVIA regularly shared personal health data with Experian, the multinational credit reporting agency, without doing required regular privacy reviews. Financial data from Experian were combined with IQVIA's healthcare information, such as patients' prescriptions, diagnoses, and doctor's visits, and used to market products such as glucose monitors and drugs to treat mental illness.[52] In 2021, Athenahealth was fined $18 million for using personal data as part of a kickback scheme to market their electronic health record (EHR) product.[53]

Using publicly available data, researchers found that between 2010 and 2017, 176.4 million health records had been reported breached (hacked and stolen), and these are just the ones that were reported.[54] (Breaches of PHI should be reported to the U.S. Department of Health and Human Services, and the individuals affected, but who ensures that this is done? Many breaches undoubtedly go unreported.) In 2023, a record 133 million Americans were impacted by stolen or breached healthcare data.[55] We are supposed to own our health information. If it's being stolen and sold, why is someone else getting the profit?

As a result of this lack of privacy, even when it is available and financially attainable, there are powerful disincentives to getting mental healthcare. Aside from stigma, there can be future economic and opportunity consequences to using mental health services: exclusion from jobs, organizations, certificates, health, and life insurance. Many application forms include a question to the effect of, "Have you ever been diagnosed with or treated for a mental illness or substance abuse problem?" Do you need to ask what happens if you answer yes, as my patient Lara discovered when she applied for life insurance and had been on Prozac many years earlier? The price she had been quoted suddenly doubled.

I find that most people are worried that information that they sought treatment for a mental disorder could harm them later. Many of my patients, if they can afford it, prefer to pay out of pocket and not file for insurance reimbursement as a way to keep their PHI truly private. Some request that I treat them under a pseudonym. A 2023 study published in the *Journal of the American Medical Association* (JAMA) found that more than 98 percent of hospital websites used at least one tracker, with a median of sixteen trackers per site.[56] The prior year, The Markup, a nonprofit that investigates how institutions use technology, found that a third of the nation's top hospitals used a Meta Pixel tracker on their websites. Making an appointment in their system prompted Meta Pixel to send the data to Facebook, often including information like the doctor's name, the medical condition that prompted the appointment, and the user's IP address, which could then be linked to the specific individual or household.[57]

As a 2021 study found, even something as seemingly innocent as visiting a hospital or telehealth company's website means health information about you is being harvested and shared, such as the health conditions you inquire about.[58] Similarly, telehealth companies have been found to widely share PHI, such as medications and illegal drugs you take, with big tech companies like Facebook and Google.[59] For example, the online therapy company BetterHelp was caught selling PHI to Facebook and fined by the Federal Trade Commission (FTC) because this violated their advertised claims of privacy. But BetterHelp was not charged with a HIPAA violation because, as a business rather than a healthcare company, they are not considered a "covered entity."[60] Shenanigans like these by the online healthcare industry finally prompted a Senate probe into their monetization of PHI in 2023.[61]

Sadly, your PHI is now worth more than you or your health and well-being because it is fungible; someone else can buy and sell it, without your knowledge or permission. There are myriad ways your PHI can be used. Insurers can avoid insuring you, or jack up the charges, as with Lara or a patient of mine who had contracted (and fully recovered from) Lyme disease years earlier. Annoyingly, you will also be targeted for ads and other unwanted forms of marketing.

Today, rather than being a closely guarded secret, your PHI is a valuable commodity. Why are some corporations exempt from the usual rules of medical privacy? Paradoxically it's worth more to healthcare businesses if you are sick than if you are well since they can use the information to avoid insuring you, or deny claims, and more accurately target you for drug and medical equipment sales. Shouldn't the opposite be true?

Personally, I prefer it when my patients are well.

CHAPTER THREE
Restricting Care

A FOCUS ON BILLING AND COSTS—NOT HEALTH

Healthcare corporations are just like other corporations. They are not charities: they exist to make money. In fact, like all corporations, they have a legal obligation to maximize profits for their officers and shareholders. To this end, as the healthcare industry embraced for-profit priorities, large corporations with deep pockets and vast resources flexed their muscles, assuming an ever-increasing role in how healthcare is delivered. Healthcare organizations that formerly adhered to more ethical goals were squeezed out. For example, the initially nonprofit Blue Cross insurance group was forced to shift to a for-profit model to compete with insurers who could exclude costly customers, those who might be a drain on profits. To remain competitive, companies "cherry-pick" healthy and wealthy customers, those who are likely to stay employed, pay premiums, and need little, if any, care, and "lemon-drop" (exclude) unprofitable people like the severely mentally ill from their plans. This chapter will examine how some of these general policies affect patient care; subsequent chapters will focus in more detail on how the delivery of mental healthcare has been corrupted.

As a first step to insure profitability, companies institute restrictions on costs they pay out. This is understandable and necessary, but since healthcare companies cannot know every patient or their circumstances, these restrictions are implemented through heavy-handed policies that globally restrict care, or "benefits" in industry lingo. These restrictions include limiting access to types of care (such as specialist treatment, laboratory tests and imaging studies, preventive procedures like colonoscopies), duration of care (including restricting physical therapy to six sessions), and medications they will and won't pay for. This chapter will look at some of these restrictions and other consequences of placing profits first.

Recently, a cardiologist colleague described to me how he and other physicians working for Sutter, a local "nonprofit" healthcare organization, will face a dressing-down and threats to not renew their contract if they refer patients to specialists outside of the organization. This is the case even if that specialist is the best doctor for the patient. Why would a nonprofit healthcare company want to deliberately keep their patients from seeing the best doctor for their situation?

Medicine used to be guided by two overarching patient-centered principles. The first was that physicians must *always* place the needs of their patients above their own. The second was the commandment *"Primum non nocere,"* or "first, do no harm." Now, these formerly inviolable rules are regularly ignored. An obvious recent example is the opioid crisis, where many in the healthcare industry, including some doctors, profited while patients died. There are myriad other examples where profit is placed before care. Some are more subtle, but have equally devastating results.

The Sutter restriction is not unusual. As healthcare companies achieve market domination in a particular geographic area, they can not only exert control over prices and access, they become what is known as a monopsony, with the power to control and squeeze workers, and how they practice their profession. Caregivers, who used to swear to serve their patients, are now beholden to these companies and face gag rules, as my colleague did, forbidding them from providing open and honest information to their patients. Often they face multiple restrictions, such as their ability to order diagnostic tests, prescribe the best medications for their patients, or refer them for appropriate specialty care when needed.

One way healthcare companies can mold clinician behavior is through what are euphemistically called "incentives." In the example above, Sutter was merely providing my colleague with an incentive to cease referring to any non-Sutter physicians. Not all incentives are punitive. Another psychiatric colleague of mine could count on finding a pair of highly desirable (and costly) tickets to the local NBA team's games under his office door the morning after admitting a patient to the hospital since that patient's hospitalization would bring in tremendous revenue. A 1998 study examining financial incentives in managed care systems concluded, "Incentives that depend on limiting referrals or on greater productivity apply selective pressure to physicians in ways that are believed to compromise care."[1]

As a resident (four years of specialty training after medical school) in psychiatry in the 1980s, we had a rule: when someone was admitted to the hospital, we would not start them on medication unless patient or staff safety required it. That way, the doctors who took over their ongoing treatment in the hospital would have the opportunity to evaluate them without the interference of medication, and allow the care team to chart a treatment course only after a more thorough evaluation was completed. More often than not, by the next day the patient seemed so much improved that the treating team would wonder whether the person had needed admission at all. Derisively referred to as the "three hots and a cot" phenomenon (three warm meals and a safe place to sleep), people did look and feel remarkably better the next day. What had happened? Simply put, people respond to care. Safety, food, and comfort matter to health. Regrettably, this cannot happen today. Insurers decline to pay for someone's hospital costs if they are not receiving "active treatment," which generally translates to medication.

As a result, now people are loaded up with medication immediately upon admission, often while still in the ER. In the morning, everyone smiles at how effective the drugs have been in improving the patient's symptoms, even though we know most psychiatric medications take weeks to work. Once someone has been started on medication(s) and feels better, we are loath to discontinue them, so we have sentenced them to a long-term treatment course even though they might have done well, perhaps just as well, without. Due to economic constraints and the dire shortage of available psychiatric beds—a 95 percent decrease between 1955 and 2005, as we saw in Chapter Two—waiting lists are the norm and hospitalization lengths have dramatically decreased. The average psychiatric hospitalization now runs somewhere between four and ten days, with many lasting just two or three days. With this intense pressure to medicate people in the hospital, followed by rapid discharge, we miss out on being able to truly assess just how well an individual responds to medication or to plan for effective care after discharge. For the hundreds of thousands of people with a serious mental illness in our country, like Dennis and Benny seen in Chapter One, revolving door treatment is the best to be hoped for. For many, there is no door at all.

Both clinicians and administrators can be squeezed into making economically based decisions, ones that may help the organization's bottom line but adversely affect patient care. As a physician with organizational responsibility at a hospital I was once directed by top administrators to disseminate an "executive decision." This was bureaucratese to mean I was being ordered to transfer valued personnel who helped with patient care to non-clinically related duties that served the administration's wishes, like scheduling meetings and writing reports. I knew these people well, and they did not want to be transferred. Further, losing them would compromise patient care by adding additional tasks to already overburdened clinical staff. But I also knew refusing would mean that the administration would just order someone else in authority to make the announcement, and I would be punished in subtle but real ways later.

RESTRICTING THE CLINICIANS SCHEDULE

It's a basic fact that to thrive in the marketplace a business must sell its product or service in the greatest volume and at the highest price possible. In healthcare this has grave consequences for both patient and societal health. Healthcare delivery companies have learned to bill for interventions, such as giving injections or ordering tests and medications, whether they improve health or not. Often it is a toss-up whether a health intervention is beneficial or not; making them financially advantageous can tip the balance when a physician considers ordering them, or a company crafts recommendations that push their use. Thus, these interventions become the goal, rather than good health. The focus of care delivery becomes selling billable transactions based on single encounters, with less responsibility or concern given to ongoing health and well-being of patients. Since a patient's relationship is with the company, not an individual practitioner, what is touted as a team approach means, in reality, that no one person takes responsibility for the person's ongoing care and health. People often end up seeing a different clinician each time they come in for care, particularly if it is an urgent matter, since the clinic rather than the doctor or nurse handles scheduling.

Patients with physical illnesses generally want their emotional concerns addressed too. A 2023 study of persons with diabetes found that the majority reported symptoms of anxiety and depression, as well as lowered self-esteem associated with the illness. Yet 57 percent reported that their diabetes team had never raised the topic of mental health. The overwhelming majority stated the best thing their diabetes team could do to help them was to simply ask about their mental well-being.[2]

Seeing a stranger and having to convey important elements of your health history, all while ill and in distress is unpleasant at best, but also results in crucial information being overlooked. Yet this is now the norm. When Zachary, my patient with bipolar disorder and alcohol abuse, entered the hospital recently for a depressive episode, he was placed on *four times* his usual dose of clonazepam, a benzodiazepine sedative. No one from the hospital called me or his family for information or assistance, and since Zach's phone had been confiscated he could not call us. Seventy-two hours later, groggy but no longer complaining of suicidal ideation, he was discharged, again with no discussion with his family or me, with no follow-up arranged.

Zach's care is an example of how, as healthcare's priorities changed, doctors' time came to be treated as costly and to be rationed, while the time of patients is treated as limitless and without value. Doctors used to wait on patients for hours—women in labor, an ill child—and home visits were a regular part of patient care. Now patients must wait, sometimes for hours, to obtain a brief audience with the doctor, who in all probability will be someone they have never met before. Healthcare workers now joke about the need to perform a "wallet biopsy" (determine the patient's ability to pay for services) as the first test before beginning treatment. This sometimes results in the potentially fatal diagnosis "no insurance coverage," which can exclude someone from treatment. Once our healthcare relationship is framed in economic terms, the adversarial elements of a business transaction enter the treatment room. When our lives are at stake, most of us want to be more than a negotiated transaction.

Perhaps even more egregious, many healthcare organizations require caregivers to sign "noncompete" clauses forbidding them from continuing to treat their patients if they leave the company, even if they are terminated, as if the company owns the patients and their lives. A 2023 report found that almost two-thirds of all physicians in this country were currently working under a noncompete clause.[3] To put this sort of restriction in perspective, the American Bar Association (ABA) ethics rules forbids noncompete clauses for attorneys since they limit an individual's right to choose legal representation. Since ABA ethics are ratified by state bars, attorneys and law firms cannot enter into these noncompete agreements. [4] These sorts of business practices are irreconcilable with medical ethics and the caregiver-patient relationship, but are now routine in our healthcare system. Fortunately, states are now enacting legislation forbidding them in healthcare, but individual clinicians are still loath to enter a complex and expensive legal battle against a healthcare company's legion of lawyers, despite what the law may say. Finally, in April of 2024 the FTC announced that it was banning noncompete agreements for most US workers. [5] However, the changes may not take effect for years—if they ever do—because the contentious rule will almost certainly be held up in litigation. And as STAT health news reports, "Crucially for the health care industry, the noncompete ban does not apply to nonprofit companies, as the FTC determined it only has jurisdiction over for-profit companies." This "means the ban likely won't apply to most of the country's hospitals, the majority of which are nonprofit, and some of the country's biggest health insurers," [6] and, in an important exception, companies will still be able to force doctors who sell their practices to sign noncompete agreements, meaning they wouldn't be able to leave the company and continue to work in the area.

Other financial "cat and mouse" games are common too, especially in mental health where it can be difficult to determine just what care is needed, and for how long. In this void, economic goals are substituted for clinical goals. As described by the author Maggie Mahar, beginning in the 1980s, National Medical Enterprises (NME) and other for-profit healthcare chains were unloading general medical/surgical hospitals and buying psychiatric and substance abuse facilities because they were particularly ripe for these manipulations, and hence were exceedingly lucrative investments. By 1991, NME owned eighty-six such facilities. By locking up the market, these chains could institute standards like their "continued stay" policy, where a patient's length of hospitalization would be determined not by need but by how much insurance the patient had available. Patients whose insurance paid less than 30 percent of billings were to be bounced out within ten days, while those with at least 60 percent coverage were to be confined for a minimum of twenty-eight days. [7]

On a side note, it's an odd quirk of history how the standard of twenty-eight days of inpatient drug rehab (rehabilitation) came to be. It had nothing to do with what worked. Twenty-eight days happened to be the standard maximum length of stay in the hospitals that insurers used to pay for. Guess what? Hospitals decided that twenty-eight days was the optimum length for inpatient treatment for everyone. Of course, insurers soon wised up and put stricter limits on the time people could spend in the hospital or drug rehab. The result is the well-known "revolving door" of drug rehab. Who doesn't know of someone who has cycled in and out of drug rehab, their care determined by financial constraints rather than what might be optimal care, especially for that individual? As the *New York Times* outlines in "The Evidence Gap: Drug Rehabilitation or Revolving Door," many programs fail to even use scientifically validated evidence-based care, and some do not even have a doctor on staff, both of which could cut into profits. [8]

In linking healthcare with the ability to pay exorbitant prices, healthcare is, in turn, tied to insurance, employment, and wealth. Thus, those most needing treatment are least able to access it. Individuals with a serious long-term illness (euphemistically called a "pre-existing condition"), or those unable to work and obtain insurance through an employer or unable to pay expensive premiums are left out—intentionally. Even when people are able to obtain insurance, perhaps through family, "cost sharing strategies" to reduce insurers' costs unfairly hit the seriously ill. A $40 co-pay or $1,000 deductible is discouraging if not prohibitive of care for many poor Americans. Those with real healthcare needs and most especially those with mental illness are out of luck.

ROADBLOCKS FOR MEDICATION

As we saw in Chapter Two, other physicians and I are deluged with faxed refill requests from pharmacies, all trolling for refill authorizations so they can sell more drugs. Many of these faxes are triggered automatically, even when the patient is no longer taking the drug. It's not uncommon for patients, when I ask them to bring in their medications, to show me a shopping bag full of pill bottles, most still full of pills. Insurers, who end up bearing the brunt of the cost for these surplus medications have countered with their own tactics, like the time-consuming prior authorization request forms (PARs). These are forms that must be submitted to an insurer (or their representative) to request permission to treat someone or use a certain medication which takes time (unreimbursed) away from patient care, and if not completed, and approved, will block care. These blocking strategies, and PARs in particular, have been so successful, insurers now outsource them to dedicated companies.

Just a few days ago, in the middle of a busy day, I received a fax from Express Scripts, the gargantuan pharmacy benefits manager (PBM), a subsidiary of the health insurance giant Cigna. PBMs are for-profit companies that act as administrators to manage *prescription drug benefits* on behalf of health insurers. They are inserted between patients and their insurance company and assume the role of processing prescription drug claims for the insurer. PBMs make money by pocketing a percentage of the drug discounts they negotiate, and kickbacks they can extract from drug companies. They choose drugs not for how well they work, but for how much profit they can extract. Express Scripts was refusing to approve a prescription refill I wrote, demanding that I complete a PAR. Paul, the patient involved, suffers from panic disorder, having rare but disabling episodes of fear and the sense he is having a heart attack, that started while rock climbing. His attacks have been successfully stopped with a single low-dose capsule of the medication venlafaxine taken once per day. He has been on it for years with excellent results and no side effects.

The wholesale price for this widely used generic drug is 6 cents a capsule, or $1.80 per month. Invariably, completing an Express Script PAR involves multiple faxes and phone calls involving long waits and multiple representatives to extract from them the information they want me to provide. It's a protracted game of "guess what I'm thinking" such as whether we have tried any of their "formulary" drugs (medications they want me to substitute for venlafaxine). However, they don't provide a list of these medications. The fact that the vast majority of PARs that doctors submit are ultimately approved demonstrates how unnecessary they are from a care perspective. [9]

A 2017 American Medical Association (AMA) survey found that physicians and their staff spent an average of 16.4 hours per week on PARs and that 84 percent of those surveyed found the burden "high" or "extremely high." [10] Physicians are not the only ones affected by these insurance hurdles. A 2021 AMA survey found that 51 percent of physicians reported that they knew of situations where the delay caused by having to get prior authorization had "interfered with a patient's job responsibilities and 34 percent said prior authorization led to a serious adverse event." [11] These PARs are now a cost of doing the business of healthcare, paid for in time by physicians and their staff.

Express Scripts has been fined numerous times for escapades like what they pulled on Paul and me, including obstructing patients' access to medication, manipulating medication they will supply in order to reap rebates from manufacturers, operating without a state license, and other kickback and drug-switching schemes. [12, 13, 14] These fines are just a relatively minor cost of business to giant companies like Express Scripts, dwarfed by the tremendous profit they reap from these strategies. But where does that leave Paul when his medication is interrupted, or refused, and what of the patients that I am unable to see while I spend time jumping through useless paperwork hoops? As David Balto, a former FTC policy director who represents a coalition of consumer groups announced: "PBMs are able to inflate drug costs and deny consumers the drugs they need because they exist behind a cloak of secrecy."[15] In fact, in 2021, more than 70 percent of Medicare Part D dollars spent on forty-five common generic drugs went to gross profit for these intermediaries.[16] In May of 2022, the FTC voted unanimously to investigate several of the largest PBMs, prompting a furious lobbying blitz by the PBMs. In the first three quarters of 2023, seven of the eleven most heavily lobbied bills in Congress were those relating to PBMs.[17] All told, the PBMs spent over $15 million on lobbying in 2023, putting them behind only the Pharmaceutical Research and Manufacturers of America (PhRMA), which spends more on lobbying than any other industry in the country.[18] In early 2024 attorneys general from thirty-nine states sent a letter to House and Senate leaders urging legislation to curb PBM abuses.[19] Meanwhile, the FTC reported that their investigation had been stymied by the industry's stonewalling of requests for information,[20] and by late February 2024 had given up on their attempt to reform the industry.[21]

Price gouging by pharmaceutical companies, insurance companies, and PBMs have spawned a new branch of healthcare business, one to battle these marketing manipulations. For example, GoodRx is a company that acts as a clearinghouse to help patients find which pharmacy offers the best price for their medication, and what discounts might be available to them. And specialized pharmacies are now springing up to sell drugs directly to patients, without involving their insurance company or PBM. Most famous is Mark Cuban's Cost Plus Drug Company. Some small pharmacies are also setting up their own alternatives to sell generic drugs for less cost directly to customers without involving insurance companies at all. These pharmacies can undercut the price patients have to pay out-of-pocket for drugs, even without insurance payments, by bypassing the profit-harvesting restrictions insurance companies and PBMs impose.[22,23]

To get an idea what all these market manipulations cost, let's compare what we humans pay for our medications as compared to those for our pets, where the vast majority of drug purchases are out-of-pocket and do not involve insurance. A 2022 JAMA study found that the average retail price of drugs was *five and one-half times* greater for humans than for pets, for the *identical* generic medications. [24] Middlemen like GoodRx might save individuals money, but in the overall picture these companies add one more layer to the complexity of healthcare, which ends up costing us all more in the end. And they add other complications. In 2023 GoodRx was fined $1.5 million by the FTC after it was found to have been sharing private information about users' prescriptions and illnesses with third parties such as Google and Facebook for advertising purposes, in violation of their own privacy policies. [25,26] (As a "business" rather than healthcare provider they were not charged with a HIPAA violation.) Why should these middlemen be needed? Those lucky dogs!

THE PRICE OF ADMINISTRATION

A generation ago, administrators were relatively minor figures in medicine, their roles generally handled on a part-time basis as a side job by a few physicians and nurses. Today, the largest sources of waste in healthcare are administrative costs, which make up 20 to 30 percent of the United States healthcare bill, far higher than in any other country. [27,28,29,30] A *Harvard Business Review* analysis found that from 1990 to 2012 the healthcare workforce grew by 75 percent, but 95 percent of these hires were administrative staff. [31] The ratio of doctors to other healthcare workers in our country is now 1:16, but of these sixteen, "only six are involved in caring for patients . . . The other ten are in purely administrative roles." [32] Another study concluded, "Nearly every industry in the US has experienced substantial improvements in productivity over the last fifty years, with one major exception: health-care . . . A typical US services industry (for example, legal services, education, and securities and commodities) has approximately 0.85 administrative workers for each person in a specialized role (lawyers, teachers, and financial agents). In US healthcare, however, there are twice as many administrative staff as physicians and nurses . . . "[33] These people all need to be paid, of course, and are part of our healthcare bill.

Growth of Physicians vs. Administrators

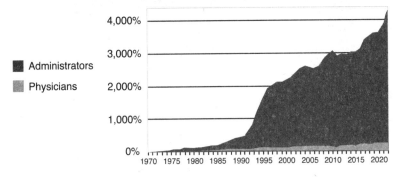

Relative growth in the number of physicians vs. administrators over the past fifty years.

At the pinnacle of these ten extra administrative workers are insurance executives, and healthcare system and hospital administrators. According to a 2014 analysis performed for the *New York Times*, the average salary was $386,000 for a hospital CEO, and $237,000 for a hospital administrator, compared with $165,300 for a family practice doctor, and $61,900 for a staff nurse.[34] These numbers almost certainly understate the payment gap, since executives frequently earn the bulk of their income in non-salary compensation. By 2021, things had dramatically changed, for the worse. The median income of healthcare industry CEOs was $30 million, the highest pay for CEOs in *any* sector of our economy,[35] and more than sixty-four times that of their average employee. In 2022 the ten highest-paid healthcare CEOs made a combined $1.4 billion.[36]

Overall Administrative Costs Per Capita United States & Canada, 2021

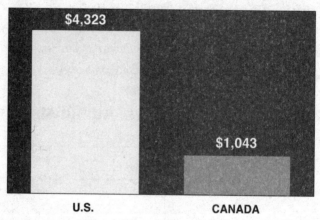

Administrative costs per capita US vs. Canada.[37]

Just who are these executives making life-and-death-decisions affecting all of us? A 2023 study examining board members of highly ranked US hospitals found that 44 percent came from the financial sector, representing investment funds, real estate, and other entities. Fewer than one in six were healthcare workers.[38]

These costs are escalating, even among the so-called nonprofit organizations. Healthaffairs.org, considered by the *Washington Post* to be the "bible of health policy," found that from 2005 to 2015, the average compensation of major nonprofit hospital CEOs rose by 93 percent, from $1.6 million to $3.1 million, while average hospital worker wages increased by a measly 8 percent over the same period of time. For example, in 2018 Kaiser's CEO earned more than $18 million and in 2017 the organization had thirty-six executives making over $1 million,[39] totaling over $54 million. This is the same Kaiser that has been repeatedly fined by the state of California for failing to provide timely and adequate mental healthcare,[40] and in 2023 was forced to spend $150 million to improve mental health services under a settlement agreement with the state.[41] This is not atypical. In 2019,

Forbes used IRS 990 informational forms to determine the breakdown of salaries for the top executives at nonprofit hospitals. They found that thirteen organizations paid their top earner between $5 million and $21.6 million, sixty-one organizations paid their top executive between $1 million and $5 million, and only eight organizations paid their top earner less than $1 million. These bloated "nonprofit" salaries all contribute to our high healthcare costs.

Far removed from multimillion dollar salaries, at the bottom of our system's financial priorities, lies mental healthcare. As we've seen, since insurance companies often restrict what services will be reimbursed, I, like about half of all psychiatrists, refuse to contract with any health insurers. But I do collaborate with a specialized billing service that I refer my patients to if they wish. For a small percentage of the reimbursement, the woman who provides this service, May (not her real name), will submit my invoices to their insurer on their behalf. She is good, and she gets results. While my patients and I find the billing process arcane and confusing, she knows it inside and out. Still, the circuity of the billing process established by insurers—one which neither I nor my patients could navigate alone—requires yet another administrator between my patients and insurance reimbursement. I think the insurers know my patients and I will just give up in frustration often enough to make the barriers worthwhile. Most medical practices hire dedicated personnel to handle billing. Think of the good that could be harvested and the healthcare dollars saved if May and all these other billing personnel were to devote their time and talents to caring for people rather than fighting over money.

An even greater source of waste is the time clinicians must now spend on electronic health records (EHRs). I remember the digital revolution in medicine well. Starting in the 1980s, VA hospitals utilized what later became known as the EHR. Initially, it was wonderful! In an instant I could pull up on my computer screen my patient's health problems, active and resolved, laboratory tests and medications prescribed, current and historical, the notes and thoughts of other physicians treating them, as well as important personal and demographic information. I recall sharing a laugh with a patient in California after congratulating him on his daughter's recent graduation from college in Florida. While attending her graduation he had received care at a VA facility in Florida for a minor ailment, and there the information was, at my fingertips.

Now this dream has become a nightmare. Once serving purely essential clinical needs, EHRs have been hijacked to serve multiple administrative functions, including scheduling, workload and productivity tracking, billing, diagnosis and procedure coding, compliance, administrative and clinical "reminders," "care plans," etc. Do you ever wonder why your blood pressure is checked when you see your dermatologist? It's a procedure which can add to insurance reimbursement, and the EHR prompts your doctor or nurse to do it. EHRs are packed with checklists and drop-down menus, which must be completed before one can continue, despite the all-too-frequent situation where none of the choices is truly accurate. Medical and especially psychiatric conditions often do not fit neatly into a box, since they occur in the context of a complex human being. When entering information in the EHR, the clinician can either ignore the deception they are being asked to perpetuate or spend considerable time filling in a "free form" narrative which serves no useful care function, and is unlikely to actually ever be read. EHRs are now filled with "note bloat," overly long notes which are cut and pasted from earlier notes, growing longer with each iteration, but obscuring the clinically important information under a mountain of billing verbiage.

A surgeon colleague was surprised recently to find that he could not obtain long-term care insurance until he underwent a neurological evaluation. The reason: his medical record shows him to have the diagnosis of "tremor." When he performs extremely exacting micro-surgery like reattaching severed fingers (and their vascular and nerve connections), he will sometimes take the common antihypertension drug propranolol to suppress the normal very fine shaking that is present in us all. Epic, the EHR system, wouldn't let his doctor prescribe him propranolol without a diagnosis, hence he now officially suffers from "tremor."

A 2020 study of physicians and medical trainees found that among those experiencing burnout, 75 percent identified the EHR as a contributor. But EHRs themselves are not the problem, it's how they've been repurposed from clinical use to billing and other administrative tasks. A 2018 study found that EHR notes in the US were nearly *four times* as long as in other countries that used the same EHR system (Epic).[42] Another study in 2021 found that outpatient doctors in the US spent an average of one to two hours of personal time each night doing computer and other clerical work, most of this on the EHR.[43]

It used to be that typing while sitting with a patient was considered rude and disrespectful, the height of insensitivity and ineptitude. Now it's standard practice. As Rani Marx writes in *The Journal of Patient Experience*: "The EHR kidnapped my formerly focused, clever, and empathic doctor: she spent more and more time gazing at her computer, speaking to the screen, repeating questions, tapping keys, muttering to herself, and retaining less and less about me, her patient of many years."[44]

Even worse perhaps is how the EHR can be used to divert care by encouraging or blocking certain clinical choices. Remember how as kids we learned to *tell* our parents our plans, rather than ask permission, when we wanted to play at a friend's house? We learned that most of the time they wouldn't bother to override what we wanted. EHR makers use the same trick, inserting default choices that channel clinicians to make choices that boost the EHRs and their affiliated healthcare companies' profits. Choosing a different option would mean having to deliberately take extra steps, adding time and effort to a harried clinicians' documentation tasks. A $145 million criminal fine was recently levied against EHR maker Practice Fusion after it was found to have made a secret deal with opioid makers. In exchange for "sponsorship," which allowed the company to give their EHR to clinicians for free, Practice Fusion placed embedded pop-up menus about pain in the program, nudging doctors toward prescribing opiates.[45, 46] A 2022 JAMA study demonstrated that when a default choice was placed in the EHR, such as how many doses of oxycodone to give (meaning that to order different dosing would take extra steps), the average number of opiate doses given to adolescents and young adults after undergoing a tonsillectomy could be manipulated.[47] Something as seemingly innocuous as a different default setting can alter patient care and increase company profits.

So where does this all leave us? Healthcare workers have historically worked long and difficult hours. During the COVID crisis doctors and nurses risked their lives working back-to-back shifts without adequate PPE (personal protective equipment). Considering the workload and amount of training these professionals undergo, they could choose more lucrative professions. Most in healthcare chose their profession because they wanted to do good, not because they wanted to become wealthy. People who view work as a calling rather than just a source of income tend to be more productive, do higher quality work, and have higher levels of satisfaction in both their job and their lives. This attitude depends on the sense that one is part of a community, that they are performing a task that enhances the well-being of the group. It internalizes a larger mission. Most of my colleagues went to medical school hoping to emulate the likes of Albert Schweitzer, Jonas Salk, and Frederick Banting, none of whom made fortunes from their care and discoveries. None of my colleagues had the ambition to be like the Sakler brothers, the physicians instrumental in promoting the opioid crisis.

CHAPTER FOUR
The Impact
of Language

REFRAMING PATIENTS

Throughout history, civilized societies have recognized the vulnerability and suffering of the ill and accordingly granted them special rights and protections, as well as a unique designation: "patient." This is changing. In the 1990s, when I was involved in negotiating managed care contracts for a community mental health center, I was surprised when insurers insisted that contracts use the term "client"; "patient" would not be allowed. Why were they so insistent? How much does a name matter? As it turns out, a whole lot.

George Lakoff, Professor of Cognitive Science and Linguistics at UC Berkeley, describes how the words we use frame how we think about and act on important matters.[1] As we shall see, referring to someone as a client rather than a patient profoundly shifts how we think about them, the rights and protections we offer them, and how we treat them. To this end, in service of the new economic paradigm, the healthcare industry sought to reframe patients as clients, and used similar mercantile terms to free themselves from the legal and ethical responsibilities historically associated with the care of patients.

Consistent with this shift, those seeking mental healthcare and addiction treatment are now most frequently referred to in business terms like client, customer, or consumer. The cynical use of these euphemisms was part of a deliberate effort to change the frame, as I found out in the negotiations for the community mental health center. Client brings to mind someone in need of a haircut, not someone facing illness. Paradoxically, this shift was actually promoted by a well-meaning humanistic movement in psychotherapy. Central to the doctor's code of ethics is to put a patient's needs above their own, not so with a businessperson selling their wares or services to a client. For example, it is standard business practice to sell a product to a client, but it is considered unethical for a doctor to do so to a patient. What was conceived as an empowering concept served instead as a linguistic Trojan Horse, bringing business interests into the treatment room, while stripping patients of rights and protections that had been accorded them since the time of Hippocrates.

CLIENTOLOGY

While healthcare corporations use commercial terms like client almost exclusively, it is only in psychotherapy and addiction treatment that clinicians themselves have embraced this term. I think this reflects the profound stigma with which our society views being a mental health "patient." The first to popularize it was Carl Rogers, who pioneered "client-centered therapy" in the 1940s and '50s. He chose this euphemism as an alternative to "patient" in an attempt to alter how those seeking therapy viewed themselves. With it he sought to foster a form of therapy that showed sufferers that they had within themselves the resources to figure out the answers to their troubles. Psychotherapists embraced this change for many reasons. Primarily, it served to distance them and their craft from the unpopular asylums, and from MDs who treat the severely mentally ill, as we'll explore further in Chapter Six. While well-meaning, it was in large part a marketing decision, a way to attract paying "clients" to psychotherapy, avoiding any association to severely mentally ill "patients." Rogers later recognized his error, admitting "the term client does have certain legal connotations which are unfortunate . . ."[2] and abandoned its use, rebranding his treatment "person-centered therapy."

Another influence came from social workers, whose core mission is to assist those seeking help from social service agencies, and appropriately refer to those they help in that context as clients. But working for the woefully underfunded CMHCs and other social service agencies was frustrating, and many social workers branched out into the practice of psychotherapy. Still, most continued to use the term they were trained to use, especially for those they helped with both social work and psychotherapy. Similarly, when Marriage, Family and Child Counselors (MFCCs) became Marriage and Family Therapists (MFTs) and were permitted to bill health insurers for individual psychotherapy, most continued to use the term from their prior "counseling" identity. (Counseling differs from psychotherapy in being short-term and focused more on external problems affecting an individual like employment difficulties or housing issues. It is more akin to coaching.) Psychotherapy when properly practiced focuses, like other areas of medicine, on the individual and his or her internal symptoms, experiences, and reactions.

The rapidly growing numbers of women psychotherapists saw use of the term "client" as a feminist issue, a way to rectify the imbalance in power between (historically male) psychiatrists and psychologists and their (primarily female) patients. However, there are now roughly equal numbers of women and men practicing psychiatry, and women outnumber men in psychology (59 percent), social work (83 percent), and among MFTs (60 percent). I find it curious that an area of healthcare where women now predominate should embrace the mercantile "provider-client" contract rather than the more compassionate and intimate healer-patient relationship. I think this may represent a wish to present a more assertive image to a field that has been criticized, much as have women, for being too caring and soft.

Some advocated the use of business terminology as a way of opening the practice of therapy to non-MD professionals. However, this idea is based on an erroneous assumption. A patient is one who receives care from *any* healthcare practitioner or healer. Midwives have patients, as do nurses, dentists, and oral hygienists. *Physio*therapists have patients, why should *psycho*therapists have "clients"? Veterinarians have both patients and clients, the former being the one they treat, the latter the one who pays the bill.

PATIENT, CLIENT: WHAT'S THE DIFFERENCE?

The Merriam-Webster dictionary defines "patient" (noun) as "a person who receives medical care or treatment."[3] It derives from the Latin "pati," meaning to undergo, bear, or sit with pain. It is related to the adjective "patient," as in "to endure." Whether the patient suffers from the pain of a broken bone or depression, the caregiver helps the person withstand, endure, or conquer their suffering. Its dual meaning is referred to in the Bible when Luke, the physician apostle, counsels, "In patience possess ye your souls." (Luke 21:19. The Bible, King John Version.)

In contrast, "client" is defined as: "1: One that is under the protection of another: Dependent, 2: *a*: A person who engages the professional advice or services of another -a lawyer's *clients*-, *b*: Customer - hotel *client*-, *c*: A person served by or utilizing the services of a social agency -a welfare *client*-."

Client comes from the Latin "cliens" (plural "clientes"), meaning follower or retainer, related to "cluere"—to "listen, follow, or obey." In today's world, retail or service businesses have clients; the term is used interchangeably with consumer and customer. While there are analogies between clients and patients, notably that money changes hands in both, there are also crucial differences. One fundamental distinction is that a client pays for a product or service to defend them against problems in the *external* world. Thus, lawyers have clients, banks have clients, and social workers have clients, and they help their client manage a specific external problem such as a legal threat, their financial affairs, or a lack of income or housing, respectively. Important tasks, to be sure, but what the term "client" leaves out that the term "patient" includes is the intimate bond dedicated to the avoidance and relief of *internal* suffering. While a client is passive, and provided with a service or product, a patient is a partner in treatment, which emphasizes and reinforces their strength as a person, rather than their weakness. At its core, "client" signifies the monetization of a relationship, whereas being a patient, at least as the relationship should be, is defined by empathy and collaboration, traits often absent in a financial transaction. For example, businesses themselves are frequently clients of other businesses, but they are never patients.

The term client suggests that patients are mere customers, or consumers. After all, the words are interchangeable. Most patients I've worked with do not want to be seen as consumers, yet many psychotherapists are puzzled, or offended, if I point out that client and consumer are interchangeable terms. Most I've queried about their use of client just shrug and say that they've never thought about it, it's just what they've learned and what is accepted. They feel it would be odd for a non-MD to use "patient," and they might even be ostracized, since to many, patient is associated with medical illness and doctors' arrogance. Others take overt offense. A friend witnessed the outraged rant by a fellow therapist who had heard another therapist call someone she treated a "patient." She thought the term disrespectful and demeaning. Still, it is odd to hear psychologists refer to themselves as "doctor," a term dictionaries reserve for those who practice medicine, yet refer to the people they treat as clients. Just who are these shifts in terminology serving? How did this view come to be in vogue?

Wondering about this, my (non-MD) colleague and I wrote an op-ed piece questioning the use of client in psychotherapy for publication in a local therapy institute's newsletter called "Viewpoint," a venue for exploring views and opinions. After a lengthy editorial process it was approved and scheduled for publication. At the last minute the institute's board of directors stepped in and refused to allow its publication, saying therapists would find it too offensive. Why would merely exploring the factors lurking behind a word's usage prove so threatening, especially to a group entrusted to care for others? Its use, I think, sits at the core of therapists' identity, their immersion in the world of the suffering, and how society marginalizes the notion of mental suffering. "Client" sanitizes the shame associated with mental suffering, and reinforces the distinction between who is suffering and who is providing the service.

For the vast majority of therapists I've talked to, use of the term client is pure habit. They heard it used by their teachers and continue to hear it used by their colleagues, and don't want to be thought of as odd by varying from convention. But in calling healthcare seekers "clients," psychotherapists use the term in an idiosyncratic manner. I don't think many intend to treat those they care for as mere customers or consumers. "Client" in this context is not generally recognized as appropriate by the fields of ethics and the law. They may mean well but haven't stopped to think about the ramifications of their language, how they have been unwittingly co-opted by business interests. For example, a client or consumer would "consume" healthcare services, but most people enter treatment to maintain or improve their health, not to consume these services. But words matter, they affect our behavior and expectations. It puzzles me why psychotherapists, whose primary tool is words and their meaning, think so little about the consequences of their own use of language. I suspect many therapists use the term because they are beholden to the healthcare organizations and insurers who write their paychecks and know they need to toe the corporate line. But some in private practice seem to embrace the entrepreneurial spirit of being a small businessperson and feel the need to promote their practice by using "client," which they employ, falsely, as an empowering term. One MFT colleague of mine stubbornly insists on exclusively using client rather than patient. Indeed, this otherwise kind and thoughtful man consistently puts the financial aspects of care, such as who pays for therapy, insurance or the "client," and how much, foremost in his work. He seems to have lost track of what his work should be: a collaboration to relieve suffering. Sadly, but not surprisingly, disillusioned and suffering from burnout, he decided to retire years before expected.

Use of another business term, "provider," has been widely promoted by healthcare corporations. But most of us want more than a "provider" when we need help. Surveys show that what people seeking healthcare value most is an ongoing collaborative relationship with a trusted individual professional. As with "client," "provider," the now widely used term for clinicians, is confusing and ambiguous when used in the healthcare context. It implies that their caregiver merely provides a pre-packaged product and thus is interchangeable, and healthcare a fungible commodity rather than a personally crafted and delivered treatment. While convenient for the healthcare company, since they can substitute different clinicians at will, even those less well-trained or experienced, it diminishes professionalism and ignores specialized training and experience the treater may have that makes them a good fit with the patient. Most of all, it erases the relationship between the patient and who is caring for them. Like client, it is ambiguous. Is the provider the organization delivering healthcare (insurer, pharmaceutical maker, hospital, clinic), or the individual treating a person?[4]

In fact, the term "provider" did not appear in English-language medical articles until 1965, and then primarily in reference to group practices, hospitals, and networks, not individual healthcare clinicians. Yet, as a 2021 study looking at adoption of the term in the medical literature found, its use has skyrocketed. While only 193 medical articles used "provider(s)" in their title during the decade of the 1970s, that number increased more than sixty-fold, to 12,256, in the 2010s. Moreover, the researchers found this was largely a US phenomenon: its use was far less common in the United Kingdom. The researchers also pointed out a chilling historical precedent to the imposition of the term "provider" on its workers by the healthcare industry. In 1938 the Nazis revoked the licenses of Jewish pediatricians. Instead of being called "Arzt" (i.e., "doctors"), they were called "Krankenbehandler," illness treatment provider. This term was ultimately applied to all physicians of Jewish descent to delegitimize them and take away their professional identity.[5] Hannah Arendt describes in her classic book *Eichmann in Jerusalem* how Adolf Eichmann, a key architect of the Holocaust, relied on his use of "amtssprache" ("office talk," or "officialese") and his overuse of clichés to justify and explain his contemptible actions.[6]

Ultimately, in the treatment room trust and comfort are the top priorities. I've used various terms over the years, including client, and I'm fine calling patients whatever they prefer. I don't quibble over what they call me, as long as it isn't overtly disrespectful. In my work at the Department of Veterans Affairs I found that many appreciated being called "sir," in deference to their age, life experience, and service to our country. I find that most people I see prefer patient, unless they've been taught to use client by a psychotherapist, and are just trying to be cooperative and polite. Surveys of care seekers in a variety of (non-mental) healthcare settings find that ". . . when quantified, considerable antipathy amongst recipients for the 'client' terminology has been observed, with 45 percent of respondents either 'strongly disliking' or 'disliking' the term on a Likert scale rating, as opposed to 14 percent feeling similarly for the term 'patient.'"[7] Here is the issue in a nutshell: People are comfortable in the role of patient when seeking care for a physical ailment, yet many recoil at using the term when the care is for mental distress.

BUSINESS TERMINOLOGY
AND PATIENT'S RIGHTS

Some say that using client helps dismantle the hierarchical medical paradigm and is less stigmatizing than patient. Why do we think a destigmatizing euphemism is needed? Is there shame in seeking healthcare, an activity we all do at one time or another? We are all patients from the time we are born, and every time we get a checkup, a vaccination, or have our teeth cleaned. The sexual orientation and gender identity movements have made great strides in visibility and acceptance in recent years (although there is clearly a ways to go) by embracing formerly disparaging terms, like gay and queer, rather than trying to hide behind sanitized euphemisms. Seeking healthcare does expose our vulnerability. Changing the name does not alter the reality that there is a certain inequality inherent to the healer-patient relationship, but this inequality is exactly why people seek healthcare—when we face illness or death we want help from someone with specialized skill and knowledge, but also compassion. This inequality in the relationship is precisely why healthcare demands a moral and ethical stance in the healer, far above that of a business transaction; referring to healthcare seekers as clients obscures these crucial elements in the relationship. As we shall see, referring to people as clients only makes this inequality greater by contractually limiting rights and protections.

Wendy Mariner describes overarching differences in how the law regards "clients," or "customers," as opposed to "patients": "In general, businesses are not legally bound to meet professional standards of care in their relationships with customers. Businesses may be liable for negligence, strict liability in the manufacture of their products, or misrepresentation. However, customer service does not include a legal duty to protect the customer's best interest or well being." In contradistinction, a caregiver *does* have the duty to protect their patients' best interest. Reframing patients as clients places contractual limits that "may force individuals to forfeit their rights as patients in order to obtain consumer benefits." This has been borne out in a number of unfortunate legal cases where insurance companies were held not responsible for injury and death caused by their denials of claims since the offending decisions could be framed as a business or contractual dispute with a client, not as the withholding of care to a patient, as in the case of Mr. Kuhl described in Chapter Two. [8]

As far back as the 1970s, concerns were voiced about the erosion of the rights and protections of patients under profit-seeking companies. The American Civil Liberties Union published a cautionary handbook entitled, "The Rights of Patients," whose author, George Annas, later summarized that: "The key to understanding patients' rights in managed care is to understand managed care's attempt to transform the patient into a consumer. . . ." [9] He enumerated crucial rights that patients, but not clients, are provided under the law. Central to these rights is the concept that the law treats "the doctor-patient relationship as a fiduciary or trust-based relationship, not as an arm's-length business relationship." (Businesses have fiduciary responsibility to their investors, not their clients.) Other patient protections Annas describes include the right to informed consent, privacy and confidentiality, and autonomy. This latter right, autonomy, has come to stand for the ". . . *proposition that the Constitution limits interference by the state in the doctor-patient relationship* . . ." which formed the legal underpinning of the *Roe v. Wade* decision. [10] As we all, including pregnant women, shift from patients to clients, it paves the way for initiatives like SB 8, the 2021 Texas anti-abortion law that makes it legal for citizens, not just the government, to interfere in the formerly protected caregiver-patient relationship. Seeing patients as clients makes it easier for not only financial interests to dictate medical care, but also religious and political ones.

When the US Supreme Court leaked that it planned to overturn *Roe v. Wade* in May of 2022, the American College of Obstetricians and Gynecologists, the American Medical Association, the American Academy of Nursing, the American College of Nurse-Midwives, and more than twenty other health professional organizations submitted an amici curiae brief to the court arguing against the decision. In the brief they made the points that the decision "undermines the patient-physician relationship . . . (which is) critical for the provision of safe and quality medical care, . . . (would) threaten the medical profession's integrity, (and) violates the ethical principle of respect for patient autonomy."[11]

The eventual announcement that the court had overturned *Roe v. Wade* in June prompted nationwide outrage and protests. In a bit of cynical humor, the humorist Andy Borowitz published the bogus headline, WOMEN DECLARE THEMSELVES CORPORATIONS TO FORCE SUPREME COURT TO GRANT THEM RIGHTS AS PEOPLE. He further explained, "The Supreme Court decided in 2010 that corporations are people, so all we want is to be treated like corporations. . . ."[12] Yet while massive protests erupted across the nation to defend the patient-physician relationship during pregnancy, one has to ask: where is the outrage, the protests, when the mentally ill are deprived of patients' rights, or turned into criminals as the Supreme Court is doing to pregnant women? Why is it OK to deem the mentally ill clients and exclude them from the protection of long-standing rules of medical ethics? Is pregnancy more of an "illness" than schizophrenia? Is the healthcare of a pregnant woman medical, but not the healthcare of someone with schizophrenia?

Another important distinction is that businesses have no obligation to their client other than to deliver a product or service. They do generally find good customer service useful since it increases the likelihood of future business. A healer has the opposite goal; their aim is to decrease the likelihood that their patient will need future care. In mental healthcare, as in all medical care, the patient-caregiver relationship is more analogous to that of the student-teacher, and assumes a level of trust and respect not generally expected in a business transaction. It is a partnership designed to effect *internal* change—for example seeing oneself as more capable or feeling less depressed—with the bulk of the work done by the *patient*, and the final outcome, or product, not assured. For most in the healing professions it is the relationship, the warmth, empathy, and mutual respect shared with their patients that inspires them, not the money. In a business transaction money serves as a substitute for trust, signifying that the reciprocal obligations of the contract have been met and are now terminated. In contrast, the caregiver-patient relationship usually continues after the treatment episode is completed; it is an ongoing commitment for care when needed.

The use of business terminology also facilitates the transfer of racial disparities to mental healthcare. Binyamin Appelbaum, a writer on business and economics, articulates how racial inequality is entrenched when we accept economic priorities. In his book *The Economists' Hour* he points out that ". . . economic discrimination—not just tolerated but celebrated as 'meritocracy'—was itself a powerful and durable proxy for other forms of discrimination."[13] When psychotherapy is couched in economic terms, where the ticket for entry is money, not medical need, the poor, who are more frequently of color and who face more social challenges, are squeezed out of the very care they are more likely to need, as we will delve further into in Chapter Six. The philosopher Michael Sandel crystallizes sentiments lurking under our economic meritocracy: "If my success is my own doing, their failure must be their fault."[14] This line of reasoning is known in psychology as a "fundamental attribution error." When bad things happen to other people we are more likely to believe that they are personally at fault, but when they happen to us we are more likely to blame the situation and circumstances beyond our control. We can be comfortable and justified in knowing, as Anatole France put it: "The law, in its majestic equality, forbids the rich as well as the poor to sleep under bridges, to beg in the streets, and to steal bread."

Use of client in our radically business-oriented America is now so widespread that even some in business and the law, fields historically linked to the term, are uncomfortable with its overuse. Client has become a cliché. Even school administrators (most often at for-profit schools) and my yoga instructor now use the term, eschewing the term "student." John Boiler, CEO of a top advertising agency, describes "Five Reasons You Should Quit Using the Word Client." He points out that client is frequently used in conjunction with a complaint, to signify a problematic person, and that it only serves to distance oneself from them, thus avoiding empathy for their situation.[15] While empathy may not be important in business, except as it may assist in boosting marketing and sales, it is central to healthcare. Using terms like client in applying the business model lessens empathy and the import of healthcare, and the need for protection when we are most vulnerable.

ERODING ETHICS AND DISTRACTING FROM SUFFERING

In yet another example of how economic priorities have subsumed medical ethics, doctors in the past were advised that "advertising is not resorted to by honorable, upright, and self-respecting members of our profession."[16] Today, the AMA offers online training for physicians to "create and market" their own "brand."[17] When I started out in psychiatry, it was considered déclassé to run even a small name-only listing in the yellow pages. People were expected to seek care when they felt they needed it, and find the best psychiatrist for them through reputation and referral by trusted people in their lives, not through advertising. Today, therapists routinely pay to be listed in *Psychology Today* and pay for advertisements and favorable placement on Yelp, Google searches, and other sites. Some ask clients to place favorable results online, and even pay for fake reviews, as a *Washington Post* investigation found.[18] Some even include testimonials from their "clients," a practice that, with a patient, would have resulted in scorn and even sanction in the past.

This language split is perhaps most absurd and hypocritical in our treatment of substance use. Substance abuse *is* physical. The ingestion (or injection or use of another mode of entry) of substances directly disrupts our physiology. Drugs of addiction cause measurable and

lasting changes in the brain (and other parts of the body), and we have
effective medications to manage and treat addiction. The National
Institutes of Health's National Institute on *Drug Abuse* (NIDA) and
the National Institute of Alcohol Abuse and Alcoholism (NIAAA),
as well as other major organizations concerned with substance abuse
proudly insist that addiction is a disease. Yet those who seek addiction
treatment are most commonly referred to as "clients." I think a major
reason for this is the fact that so many clinicians who work in addiction have themselves struggled with addiction and wish to avoid the
stigma associated with mental illness, the shame of being a patient with
a disorder of the mind. But being a client denies the physical aspects
of their disorder and implies that their problems, as well as their treatment, are a matter of choice and motivation.

Laws and ethical rules guiding healthcare workers and their con-
duct with patients are (or at least used to be) far more stringent than
those guiding the behavior of other professionals and industries—if
they exist at all in those industries. A basic tenet of the Hippocratic
Oath is that, above all, a healer must do no harm to their patients. An
individual may ask for a potentially harmful service or product, like
cigarettes for example, and a businessperson will sell it to their client.
However, it would be considered unethical for me to recommend that
a patient of mine smoke or for me to provide high doses of an opiate
when not needed, even if my patient asks and is willing to pay for it.
What industry has pledged to do no harm to its clients? Certainly not
our healthcare corporations.

Framing people as clients can cause healthcare professionals to
forget these ethical duties to those they treat. The subjugation of
ethical responsibilities to patients in the service of marketing to clients
recently caused the American Psychological Association (APA) considerable embarrassment. Vying for military contracts, some psychologists
were eager to market themselves as experts on torture, or, using another
euphemism, "enhanced interrogation," and obtained the support and
approval of the APA. With no relevant experience or training, these

psychologists advised and assisted at CIA "black sites," Abu Ghraib prison, and the Guantanamo Bay "detention camp" (other cynical euphemisms). When this shameful dereliction of professional ethics came to light, the APA characterized it as the work of a couple of rogue psychologists. Later, an independent investigation found that, in fact, the association's leadership, led by the APA's director of ethics, was at the heart of the effort. For those interested, I heartily recommend M. Gregg Bloche's *The Hippocratic Myth*, which explores the theoretical and ethical issues behind this scandal.[19]

However, their tactic was successful from a business perspective. In response to the APA's support, the Assistant Secretary of Defense for Health Affairs issued instructions prioritizing the hiring of psychologists as advisers over the hiring of psychiatrists. He specified that the APA's "clear support" for the use of psychologists in interrogations "influenced our thinking."

Prior to this debacle, the APA had ludicrously declared that the terms client and patient were interchangeable. The subsequent investigation brought to light the fact that, in their role as experts on torture, the psychologists' clients were the Department of Defense (DOD) and the CIA, not those being tortured. Following this fiasco, in 2018 the APA passed a resolution stating: "Therefore be it resolved that the American Psychological Association henceforth will freely use, when appropriate, the term patient (rather than client) in all of its publications, policies, rules, and public relations and news releases. . . ."[20]

Even the California Association of Marriage and Family Therapists, a group that almost universally uses the term client, specifies in their legal articles that sex with patients is prohibited, without mention of sex with clients.[21] "Patient" is unambiguous and does not allow for these sorts of ethical obfuscations.

A psychiatrist mentor of mine once told me that if someone used the word "unfair" more than three times in their first therapy session it predicted a poor treatment response. Life *is* unfair, very unfair, but what can we do to mitigate this but play the hand we are dealt in life well? Experienced psychotherapists know that real progress in therapy begins only after a client becomes a patient, when they acknowledge that their troubles lie, at least in part, within themselves, which gives them the power and incentive to change. Therapy conducted with a "client" can reinforce a person's dysfunctional attitudes and fuel resentment against an unfair world. It can cause them to dig in rather than work on internal changes to be a more productive and contented individual and member of the community—which may include working to remedy real unfairness in the world.

The psychoanalyst Alice Miller describes in her classic book *Drama of the Gifted Child* how ". . . I prefer to use the word patient instead of 'client,' which is more frequently used by therapists today. It was not until I experienced myself as a patient, as a suffering person, that I could find my way out of the trap of repression and help myself. As the client of (seemingly) 'good therapists,' I could find only their knowledge, something which was of no help at all in my quest for healing."[22]

The use of business euphemisms facilitates the corruption of healthcare priorities in the interest of profit. Barry Farkas, a geriatrician and family physician, perhaps said it best: "The term 'provider' for clinical caregivers, like the term 'client' for patients, depersonalizes and commodifies that which is neither and so very much more. The more we use these commercial terms to refer to intimate and personal care, the more that care becomes commercial and impersonal. Such is the power of language."[23]

CHAPTER FIVE

Business Models and the Practice of Psychiatry

THE MIND AS A SECOND-CLASS CITIZEN

M edical care in this country is now so expensive that without insurance coverage, most cannot afford it. Thus, health insurance became crucial for maintaining ones health. As states and the federal government discontinued providing mental healthcare by closing the asylums and defunding the CMHCs, health insurers saw both a threat and an opportunity. Not wanting to pick up the considerable costs of caring for those with a mental illness, or lengthy and time-intense psychoanalysis, they found, as we've seen, they could instead contain costs and bolster profits by enacting policies that limited access to mental healthcare. Framing mental health treatment as distinct and separate from medical treatment was a crucial rationale to minimize or even disqualify it from insurance reimbursement. This has had profound consequences for mental healthcare, leaving those needing care out on their own, which will be explored in this and the following two chapters.

Since mental illness is viewed askance by society, and persons with mental illness tend not to advocate well for themselves (and families often shun advocacy due to the stigma and shame of a mentally ill relative), insurers knew they would get little pushback if they minimized or eliminated coverage of mental healthcare. When questioned, they employed the justification that the severely mentally ill could rely on government programs, like Medicaid, or the CMHCs. These, of course, helped few. Medicaid served only the very poor (who were unlikely to have private insurance), and there were few psychiatrists who accepted Medicaid anyway. President Kennedy's National Plan for Mental Health in 1963 was never adequately funded or staffed. Insurers' exclusionary policies were so effective that, as a 1981 study based on twenty-five years of Kaiser Healthcare data found, *60 to 90 percent* of primary care medical appointments were prompted by stress or psychological problems rather than medical illness.[1] It's unquestionable that a lot of these primary care visits were a result of patients being unable to find mental healthcare, especially not care that their insurer would cover.

This abandonment by insurers has had many consequences, effectively making mental healthcare unobtainable for many Americans, even those with health insurance. Even when mental health coverage is offered, insurers reimburse clinicians at a lower rate for mental healthcare than for physical healthcare. Milliman, an actuarial advising company, analyzed claims data on thirty-seven million Americans and found that in 2017 insurance reimbursements were 23.8 percent higher for primary care (physical health) than for behavioral care (mental health) appointments. In eleven states they were more than 50 percent greater. But these data obscure an even greater discrepancy. They grossly underestimate the magnitude of physical versus mental discrimination since so many more mental health visits are paid out-of-pocket by the patient or their family without involving their insurance company, and thus were not included in the data. Even our government's Medicaid program, on which many uninsured mentally ill depend, reimburses psychiatrists on average at only four-fifths the rate of the already too low Medicare rates.[2]

Studies show that people seeking mental health treatment spend far more on out-of-network care,[3] meaning they seek help more often from physicians who don't contract with their insurance plan. *And,* insurers pay a smaller portion of the cost of care or refuse payment outright for physicians who are out-of-network. As we saw in Chapter Two, the percentage of visits to psychiatrists that are *entirely* self-paid is more than *fifteen times* those to primary care physicians, and increasing. Further, a Milliman report found that substance abuse inpatient facilities were accessed out-of-network more than *ten times* as often as medical-surgical facilities and office visits *nine and a half times* as often.[4]

These discriminatory policies have affected psychiatric reimbursement overall, not just those involving insurance companies. According to the Medical Expenditure Panel Survey—the most complete source of data on the cost and use of healthcare and health insurance coverage—the average payment for a psychiatric office visit in 2016 was $159, lower than for any medical specialty. The payment for cardiology, for example, was $335, and $419 for orthopedics, despite these visits generally being much briefer.[5]

Claims for mental health treatment are simply denied more frequently by insurers than those for other diseases. As reported in the *New York Times* in 2019, ". . . a federal judge in Northern California ruled that a unit of UnitedHealth Group, the giant health insurer, had created internal policies aimed at effectively discriminating against patients with mental health and substance abuse disorders to save money."[6] In 2021 United Healthcare finally agreed to pay over $15 million in fines for violating federal and state laws for imposing more restrictive limits on coverage and treatment for mental health and substance abuse disorders than it imposed on physical health conditions.[7] The bottom line is that insurers often just won't pay for mental healthcare, or pay so little that insurance is effectively useless. In 2020, Milliman analyzed insurance claims for twenty-one million people and found that: "behavioral health treatment was meager, accounting for a fraction—*4.4 percent*—of total (insured) healthcare costs."[8]

Over the past few decades there have been attempts to rectify this prejudicial care and require health insurers to offer equivalent coverage for physical and mental care, called "mental health parity." All have failed miserably. Insurers flagrantly flaunt these attempts, the 2021 United Healthcare settlement being a rare exception. Even measures such as the much praised Wellstone-Domenici Mental Health Parity Act (MHPA) of 1996 have done little to reverse discrimination. Moreover, the MHPA only affected employer-based policies, which few people with severe mental illness are able to obtain. Even the Health Insurance Portability and the 2010 Mental Health Parity and Addiction Equity Act (MHPAEA) and the Patient Protection and Affordable Care Act (ACA, or "ObamaCare") enacted the same year have rules to ensure equivalency in coverage for physical and mental disorders, but have done little, if anything, to fight prejudicial insurance coverage.[9] Insurers successfully skirt the rules because, as former APA president Bruce Schwartz points out, insurance companies "counted on [stigma] so that they could continue to discriminate against the care of the mentally ill, because no one was going to complain, or complain effectively."[10] A 2022 report to Congress by the Departments of Labor, Health and Human Services and the Treasury on the effectiveness of the MHPAEA concluded that insurers were still "failing to deliver parity in mental health coverage as required by law." Of 1,000 government requests for parity analyses sent to health plans, "we unfortunately did not receive one we viewed as sufficient."[11]

In August of 2022, 2,000 Kaiser psychotherapists in California went on strike, accusing their employer of ignoring the mental health needs of hundreds of thousands of patients, making them wait weeks and even months for care. Yet the supposedly "nonprofit" Kaiser earned $8 billion in profits the prior year.[12] This, despite a 2020 California law legislating that insurers can be fined for failing to provide coverage for mental healthcare equal to what they provide for physical healthcare. A 2022 Bloomberg Law study found that California insurers "regularly" denied mental health claims, which, when contested, were overturned by regulators two-thirds of the time.[13] Insurers merely view these fines (when and if levied) as a relatively minor cost of doing business, and far cheaper than paying for mental health treatment. For them, it's a simple cost-benefit business decision. After the strike, in late 2022, the California senate passed SB 858, which increased the maximum penalty for prejudicial coverage from $2,500 to $25,000. It remains to be seen if this will be enforced, and if so, how effective it will be.

Clinicians themselves feel trapped. Signing an insurance contract to be an "in-network provider," agreeing to be on an insurer's "panel," can in some ways offer security, especially for clinicians starting out in practice. You know you'll have a steady stream of insured customers, and you can avoid unseemly (but important) discussions about your fees, especially with patients who will have to pay out-of-pocket. Most physicians are more comfortable discussing a patient's bowel movements and sex life than asking them exactly how much money they earn, and exactly where that money goes. It's relieving to avoid awkward discussions about the financial aspects of treatment, especially with someone in distress, and leave it to the insurance company to manage that facet of care. But the result is that both caregiver and patient are restricted by constraints dictated by the insurer, constraints guided by financial rather than health priorities. As a consequence, paperwork and billing have come to demand more time and effort than care of the patient. Physicians now spend about eight minutes face-to-face per patient visit, and, ironically, more than twice that amount of time on the computer and its EHR as we saw in Chapter Three,[14] affording little time for the caregiver-patient relationship.

What frequently results is a "shotgun wedding" brokered by the insurer between a reluctant caregiver and an uncomfortable patient, both wishing they had other options. There are no negotiations available for patients or caregivers under these insurance contracts. These are "take it or leave it" contracts with no wiggle room to account for severity of illness, financial hardship, or distance required to travel for care. They are "one size fits all," which is "fair" under a business model, but a ludicrous concept when dealing with the complexities of human life experience and health.

Since psychiatrists are reimbursed by insurers at lower rates for the same services than other MDs, I, like many of my colleagues, refuse to sign on to these nonnegotiable binding contracts.[15] I feel I can be more efficient and give more effective care by working directly for my patient, not their insurer. Instead, I negotiate a rate with my patients based on their ability to pay, and provide them with paperwork so they can seek reimbursement from their insurer, if they so desire. Still, insurance companies routinely restrict what medications they will make available to my patients, and reimburse them for my services at a rate less than that charged by local plumbers, contractors, and auto mechanics, and one-quarter that of local attorneys. What of a patient who is treated under insurance whose benefits run out, or who loses their job? My duty is to the patient, but the entity that is supposed to pay for their care has walked away. Often my only choice is to treat them for free, or a nominal fee, because their only other option is no care.

Epidemiologic studies show that mental illness causes more suffering and disability than virtually all physical ailments.[16] As we've seen, in 2022 we lost roughly 300,000 people to suicide, excessive alcohol use, and overdose,[17, 18, 19] more than we lost to COVID (244,000)[20] which dominated the news and public discussion. Compounding this, the mentally ill and substance abusers tend to be high utilizers of medical care. Yet we know that proper treatment of psychiatric illness and substance use reduces the need for medical care, whereas lack of treatment results in a vicious cycle that worsens both, and increases overall health costs.[21, 22, 23, 24, 25, 26] The barriers to care that our healthcare system erects are certainly an important factor. As a 2021 study in New Zealand found, those with physical illness benefited from mental health intervention, which in turn *lowered* overall healthcare costs,[27] and that in the US untreated mental illness results in a substantial financial burden on society.[28] Depressive symptoms increase overall mortality,[29] and serious mental illness is associated with a ten to twenty year reduction in life expectancy. In 2024 it was shown that for patients with coronary artery disease or heart failure combined with anxiety or depression, those receiving mental health treatment were about 75 percent less likely to be rehospitalized, have an emergency department visit, or die.[30]

Even the young (ages twenty to twenty-nine) with a mental disorder have been found to be 58 percent more likely to have a heart attack.[31] Studies in 2021 and 2022 showed that people with depression or schizophrenia have far worse COVID outcomes, including higher rates of hospitalization and death.[32, 33, 34] If mental health needs were treated along with the physical, the lives of many Americans could have been saved or improved, and healthcare costs reduced.

LOSS OF PSYCHIATRIC CARE

This strangling of resources has resulted in an acute shortage of psychiatric care, as we learned in Chapter Two. A full 60 percent of US counties do not have a single psychiatrist. Because of the acute shortage of psychiatrists in this country, the vast majority of Americans who receive psychiatric medication get their prescriptions from non-psychiatric doctors such as family practitioners, internists, and other medical/surgical specialists. In fact, over 80 percent of antidepressant prescriptions in this country are written by non-psychiatric doctors.[35] While these doctors, of necessity, have become familiar with prescribing common antidepressants, most will not treat the severely mentally ill. I get multiple calls a day from people seeking care. Running at full capacity, I can't come close to offering care to each of the tragic cases that call my office. Most often my colleagues are also too full to accept my referrals. When I can, I will squeeze someone in for a quick assessment and medication prescription. Then comes the harder part: finding a therapist I know to be a good match for them who has the time to take them on. I have to call in a lot of favors. Often, I do not succeed.

My experience mirrors a national trend. Prejudicial insurance coverage for mental health has had many downstream effects, including restricting access to care, and the very nature of that difficult-to-access care. In the 1990s, as psychiatrists became overwhelmed with the crush of patients and diminishing insurance reimbursement, they turned to more remunerative (on a dollar-per-hour basis) and more efficient (on a patient-per-hour basis) "med" (medication) visits: fifteen-minute brief encounters focusing on medication, with little time to truly understand the patient, the challenges in their life, or how they are actually functioning. The patient might be asked about their mood, sleep, energy level, and appetite, and might be asked to complete a self-assessment questionnaire (saving the harried clinician the time to ask these questions) like the popular nine-item Patient Health Questionnaire-9 (PHQ-9). But other important factors like the person's home being repossessed, their spouse's infidelity, or their child's suicide attempt might not come up in the perhaps nine minutes of face-to-face time, eight minutes of which the psychiatrist's face is buried in the computer screen. Questions about important life factors that might be exacerbating or ameliorating symptoms, impinging on medication effects, or consequences of their illness such as relationship problems or job loss remain unexplored and unaddressed. Meetings like these may result in a change of medication or dose, but little else.

Even the PHQ-9, touted as a valuable and validated screening tool, is problematic when examined more closely. It was actually developed by a marketer, Howard Kroplick, working for Pfizer pharmaceutical company, not a clinician. It was intended to encourage the prescription of its then-new antidepressant Zoloft® (sertraline) by busy primary care doctors who didn't have the time to properly assess psychiatric symptoms. Its purpose was to help these busy doctors identify patients who might be candidates for Zoloft.[36,37] While useful as a screening tool, when used as an alternative to an actual in-depth interview, it serves as a crutch and may result in the overprescription of antidepressants, instead of implementing other more appropriate and effective interventions like psychotherapy.[38]

As psychiatrists increasingly handled only medication issues, psychotherapy, which more fully explores the complexities of peoples' lives, became the domain of lower-cost non-medically trained therapists such as social workers and MFTs (this transition will be discussed further in Chapter Six). A 2022 study found that between 1996 and 2016 the percentage of visits to a psychiatrist that included psychotherapy and an adequate discussion of the life issues that person was grappling with fell by half, from 44 to 22 percent.[39] This suits insurers, who can get more patients into care for less money, even if this care is inadequate.

Non-MD therapists cost insurers less than psychiatrists, and, as we'll explore in Chapter Six, are more frequently on insurance panels. Since medications tend to work better in more severe cases of depression[40] and other severe mental illnesses like bipolar disorder and schizophrenia, it can be catastrophic for those with a serious mental illness when an insurer directs them to a non-MD therapist who can't provide medication that could truly help. Evidence also shows that combined care, where psychotherapy and medication treatment is managed by the same clinician, is often more effective than "split treatment," where these two treatments are divided between different clinicians, the psychiatrist (or more often a primary care doctor) prescribing medication and the psychotherapist providing talk therapy.[41]

PITFALLS OF ONLINE SOLUTIONS

The COVID-19 pandemic and the dramatic change to our routines, not to mention threat to our futures, brought heightened awareness of the vulnerability of our mental health and that of our loved ones.

Rates of suicide and depression have risen right alongside the physical
health effects of COVID. Almost everyone suffered in quarantine,
some more than others. COVID's threat also lowered long-standing
barriers to talking about psychiatric symptoms. As more people
sought care and were unable to find available clinicians, online entrepreneurs jumped in. The highly entrepreneurial technology industry,
always looking to serve a need (and make a buck), gladly entered the
breach caused by the shortage of mental healthcare, offering online
therapy and mental health apps. *Forbes* reported that venture capitalists (VC) poured $1.5 billion into mental health startups in 2020,
fueling an explosive growth known as "blitzscaling."[42] In 2023 the
VC firm Andreessen Horowitz published its annual startup ranking.
Their conclusion: "Mental health emerges as the fastest-growing
marketplace for startups, and it's not even close."[43]

While these VC firms invested billions funding these sketchy
enterprises that cater to those desperate to find mental healthcare, any
care, even paying out of pocket, they invested little in the development
of treatments that might truly help. Over the past decade these firms
poured *270 times* more money into developing new cancer drugs than
new treatments for addiction.[44]

As Tarun Galagali and Leonard Schlesinger of the Harvard Business School point out, these startups, which typically expect to make a
profit by going public in five to seven years, have not been able to overcome crucial systemic problems, like the shortage of licensed clinical
mental health therapists and the possibility of doing more harm than
good.[45] As the *Forbes* report cited above reiterates, "technology alone
won't solve long standing problems like low reimbursement rates and
provider shortages."

Mobile phone mental health apps have fallen flat, too, when they
have undergone scrutiny. A 2020 study in *PLOS Digital Health* synthesized results derived from 145 randomized controlled trials that
included 48,000 participants and "failed to find convincing evidence
of efficacy."[46] While it's true that a 2023 study of apps for depression

concluded that they were helpful, the study was funded by a pro-technology institute dedicated to "Secure and support the commer-cialization of core original technology. . . ."[47] I think the title of Molly Fischer's 2021 *New York* magazine article says it all: "The Therapy-App Fantasy: An overwhelming demand for counseling has spawned slickly marketed companies promising a service they cannot possibly provide."[48] An evaluation by *The Economist* reached the same conclu-sion.[49] Desperate mental healthcare seekers now pay (out-of-pocket since insurance rarely covers these services or apps) for "treatment" that is often unproven and offers no real relationship or commitment from the "provider." Our online world of social media and divisive political rhetoric, made worse by the pandemic, has fostered a profound sense of isolation, depression, and anxiety, as well as deep divisions in our sense of community. While online care offers many advantages, especially convenience and access to remote areas, it is a marginal substitute for connection with a real live person.

A tech-savvy ex-patient of mine who had moved to another state called me recently in desperation. After trying for months to estab-lish care with an online service he finally gave up. Frequent last-minute cancelations, repeated substitution of klutzy caregivers who spent most of the session going over finances and old history proved too frustrating. This was a common experience for online care seekers interviewed by *Forbes* and *The Economist*. Like my patient, they found long waits for care, and inconsistent and rapidly shifting providers. It is true that the convenience and relative anonymity of talking to someone through a company portal virtually may facilitate access for many. As a therapist who moved online during the pandemic I do find a certain intimacy in talking with someone when they're in their personal space, and learn things about them from observing their home surroundings. In an odd throwback to Freudian psychoanalysis where the analyst sat behind the patient as they lay on a couch, some patients are more comfortable revealing aspects of themselves when partially shielded behind electronic barriers.

But what these services can't overcome is the shortage of qualified mental-health professionals, and the few who have tried to work under this model rapidly grow disenchanted. High-tech solutions don't solve the problems of the "ghost networks," poor insurance coverage, or the "full" practices prospective patients encounter when trying to find an appropriate clinician. Talkspace, the largest of these new online therapy businesses, was valued at $1.4 billion in January of 2021 when it went public, but by November of the same year was valued at $315 million, and its stock dropped 35 percent after disappointing quarterly results and an exodus of its top executives.[50]

Erica Johnson, cofounder of the online mental health company Modern Health, filed a lawsuit in 2020 against her former company after being fired, she claims in retaliation for revealing that the company misrepresented its capabilities including the size of its provider network to potential customers and investors.[51] A 2022 Bloomberg investigation found that the fastest growing online mental health service, Cerebral, best known for being backed by SoftBank and promoted by the gymnast Simone Biles, utilized pseudonyms like "Eileen Davis" for a horde of "care coordinators" to make it appear as if they were the same person and care was consistent and coordinated. Employees described pressure to serve an overly large number of patients in an inadequate time frame, resulting in over-diagnosis and overprescription of medication, and generally substandard care.[52] Finally, in 2022 the U.S. Office of the Inspector General issued a special fraud alert regarding telemedicine companies. They described schemes where telemedicine companies intentionally paid physicians and non-physician practitioners kickbacks to generate orders for medically unnecessary durable medical equipment, genetic testing, wound care items, and prescription medications, including controlled substances.[53] These companies reaped profits through the sale of unnecessary and unneeded equipment and medication, and fueled the spread of powerful addictive drugs like stimulants.

As a business, online therapy services follow a business model and must serve their investors. This also means they solidify and promote existing economic inequities; they cater to the relatively wealthy, who can afford to pay out of pocket for the price of entry, and who can access and negotiate remote technology. Jail cells and tent encampments tend not to have robust computer resources or internet access. There is the previously mentioned case of the online therapy company BetterHelp evading HIPAA rules as a business, rather than a healthcare company, selling patients' confidential health information to Facebook. This resulted in an FTC fine but no prosecution for violating HIPAA regulations.[54] These new online therapy services are just another high-tech step in banishing those who can't pay top dollar, the poor and severely ill, from mental health treatment. These services are purely transactional; there is little if any reciprocal relationship, concern, or caring. I don't want my doctor following Facebook founder Mark Zuckerberg's motto: "move fast and break things." When applied to healthcare, it's people you are breaking.

Two other common tools of businesses have also proven to be a poor fit in healthcare: the client satisfaction survey and online consumer ratings. Healthcare systems and even individual clinicians now use satisfaction surveys or solicit favorable online reviews to use in marketing to attract and retain customers. In a further step, Medicare reimbursement rates to hospitals are affected by their score on a thirty-two-question patient satisfaction survey known as HCAHPS (Hospital Consumer Assessment of Healthcare Providers and Systems). As the *Atlantic* summarized in 2015: "When Department of Health and Human Services administrators decided to base 30 percent of hospitals' Medicare reimbursement on patient satisfaction survey scores, they likely figured that transparency and accountability would improve healthcare . . . They probably had no idea that their methods could end up indirectly harming patients."[55]

The business motto that the customer is always right does not translate well to medical care. Doctors give their patients unpleasant and even frightening news all the time, and must decline patient requests for inappropriate or dangerous care. Unwarranted care can and does harm, and may even kill. For example, a 2020 study found that individuals who received at least six opioid prescriptions in a year were more likely to rate their care satisfaction in the top quartile than those receiving fewer or no opioid prescriptions.[56] Another 2012 study of more than 32,000 patients over seven years found that while higher survey ratings of satisfaction with their healthcare provider were associated with less emergency department use, they were also associated with more hospitalizations, higher overall use of healthcare, higher use of prescription drugs, and a greater likelihood of dying.[57] Caring for someone properly means respectful honesty and frank information exchange, even if the patient doesn't like what they hear. Currying favor with people by whitewashing health problems and habits, and providing tests and drugs they may want but don't need, can and does do harm.

Online reviews fare no better. A 2020 study examining the relationship between online reviews of physicians and their patients' actual clinical outcomes found that reviews by those with chronic diseases had no correlation with the quality of care provided as measured by objective clinical outcomes like risk for hospital readmission.[58] In 2021, a *Washington Post* exposé showed that fake patient reviews found through Yelp and Google make it very hard to seek out quality medical help.[59] While the prevalence of fake or coerced reviews is hard to quantify, an expert estimated that 20 percent of businesses in the health care industry, including doctors, have suspicious review activity on Google and Yelp. A front-page 2023 article in the *New York Times* described the extent of fake online reviews but saw no easy solution despite the efforts of organizations like Fake Review Watch.[60]

I've received emails from companies like the one bragging that "Our program gets you consistent 5-star patient reviews on Google, Vitals, RateMDs, Healthgrades, WebMD, and other major review websites. Negative reviews are removed or buried down and positive reviews are published across the internet." I have no idea if their claims are valid, but their $345 per month charge certainly is real. I find it odd to look at the Yelp reviews of colleagues. Most psychiatrists and other mental health practitioners have at most a couple of reviews. These tend to be either ecstatically thankful and positive or furious about the care they received. After all, who wants to go online to publicly rate someone they tell their most intimate secrets to, in the process potentially revealing they are receiving mental healthcare, unless they have a strong incentive? In contrast, some practitioners have fifteen to twenty reviews, or more, generally very positive but bland and formulaic. What drives this wide disparity? I doubt that many practitioners are paying for these reviews, but somehow there must be some enticement or pressure to go public. And just whom do these ratings serve, the rater, prospective patients, or the practitioner's business?

Anna Lembke, an addiction medicine doctor at Stanford, describes a dilemma physicians face when medical care is thrust into the public eye. She quoted a colleague who told her, "'Sometimes I just have to do the right thing and refuse to prescribe them, even if I know they're going to go on Yelp and give me a bad rating.'" She went on to explain, "His 'sometimes' seems to imply that at other times he knowingly prescribes opioids to abusers because not doing so would adversely affect his professional standing. If that's the case, he is by no means alone. Healthcare providers have become de facto hostages of these patients, yet the ultimate victims are the patients themselves, who are not getting the treatment for addiction they need and deserve."[61]

The specter of a bad Yelp review can sway a clinician to give a patient what they want, even if it is not in that patient's best health interest. Like Dr. Lembke, I, too, practice addiction medicine, and like her, people come to me to get off opiates. Still, I've had patients who are so confused that they can't recall what medication they took that day, often doubling or tripling what they should take, yet refuse to enter a hospital (which might bankrupt them even if they were willing). The possibility of a review by such patients puts us in a tough position. Do we treat these complex patients who very much need care, or avoid them and the aggravation and bad reviews they bring? Moreover, these negative public comments can disconcert people, especially those needing care but already ambivalent about seeking that help. Given the nationwide shortage of psychiatrists, one has to ask: why invite trouble and wasted time when there are so many other needy individuals, ones unlikely to cause trouble and more likely to respond to treatment through better compliance? This dynamic causes problems for patients too, who may feel they must be "nice" to their clinician, and bite their tongue when they are unhappy or disagree with care offered lest they be cast out of care and be unable to find a replacement. This can put a damper on frank discussions, which are a necessary part of quality healthcare.

A DUBIOUS ALLIANCE

In the forty years I've practiced medicine, the blurring of patient and corporate interests has become so prevalent that practices physicians once thought unacceptable are commonplace. Many clinicians no longer seem to question this shift. In 2012 I recall attending a lecture given at my medical school by a young schizophrenia researcher who admitted, with some embarrassment, that he had been required to submit his slides for review by the talk's pharmaceutical company sponsor. When I pointed out that this amounted to censorship and violated medical education rules, my colleagues seemed more embarrassed by my calling attention to the issue than by the breach in scientific integrity. As one told me, "I'm not exercised by this sort of thing." Sure enough, a couple of years later, an ethics scandal (not involving this researcher) involving research conducted by his department, including the suicide of a subject, hit the news.[62] But the interdependency between psychiatric research and drug companies, as well as the general squelching of medical ethics by money has kept people silent, people I know to be kind and caring physicians.

To remain profitable in an increasingly competitive marketplace, insurers are constantly seeking ways to tighten the belt. As we've seen, insurers impose increasingly tough restrictions on the cost of psychiatric care. In the 1990s, as this trend accelerated, embattled physicians, especially psychiatrists, allied with another healthcare player chafing against insurance restrictions: the pharmaceutical industry. Pharmaceutical companies, colloquially known as "Pharma," realized that a physician's endorsement could bolster their product's credibility, as well as foster a promotion-and-prescribing partnership. Doctors who talk up a drug tend to prescribe it more, putting their money, well, actually their patients' money, where their mouth is. Pharma tracks prescribing data and well knows that physicians who help promote a drug tend to be large prescribers, and can be pied pipers to their colleagues. Pharma also began recruiting physicians to lend their name and advice (and prestige) to Pharma-sponsored clinical trials. But in reality, many papers detailing the research were ghost-written by the pharmaceutical company (or an outside PR shop) and then published under the name of the physicians and their prestigious university partners.

These universities lacked the experience or infrastructure to bring a drug to market and promote it, and the pharmaceutical companies lacked the scientific labs and brainpower to develop these drugs. So, initially, their collaboration seemed to be a match made in heaven, and cash-strapped academic institutions jumped at this opportunity. A random sample of five hundred drug trials published between 1981 and 2000 found that the percentage of drug trials that were industry-sponsored went from 26 percent to 62 percent over this period—a 2.4-fold increase. [63]

This influx of Pharma money into medical research also caused a wholesale shift in the emphasis of this research, from basic science designed to discover the causes and cures of illnesses, to clinical trials of drugs for symptomatic treatment. The focus of American medical research shifted away from seeking to understand and cure diseases and toward the testing of drugs that merely ameliorate symptoms and could be rapidly moved to the marketplace, giving a quick return-on-investment. In reality, these "new" drugs were often not much different from those already available, known in the industry as "me-too" drugs.

As Marcia Angell, former editor of the *New England Journal of Medicine*, calculated, of the 415 new drugs that received FDA approval from 1998 to 2002, only 14 percent were truly innovative.[64] Also, industry sponsorship of clinical trials tends to skew the reporting of study results. As one 2006 analysis[65] found, in 90 percent of published Pharma-sponsored studies comparing antipsychotic drugs, the reported outcome was in favor of the sponsor's drug. They found that the industry-sponsored studies contained multiple sources of bias, including improper dosing, biased selection of study subjects, biased statistics and methods, and inaccurate reporting of results and wording of findings. In other words, the stated study findings were frequently not in agreement with the study data. And this was just the published studies. Most often, if a study went unfavorably for the sponsor, it would not be published, effectively burying it.

Another powerful impetus driving medical school and academic physicians' collaboration with Pharma was the Bayh–Dole Act of 1980. This law gave universities intellectual property control of the inventions, including drugs, which they discover or develop from federally funded research. The vast majority of public and private universities and colleges are tax-exempt entities as defined by the Internal Revenue Code Section 501(c)(3) because of their educational purposes and because the bulk of their, and NIH, research is supported by tax dollars, which means it must be publicly shared. But this is rarely the case. The Bayh–Dohl Act lets these entities reveal their discoveries to private for-profit companies, exclusively, to get a cut when these companies sell the products. So the companies get research discoveries for free, and might kick a tiny bit back to the universities when they make a profit. The act backfired in another way. Rather than spur new drug development, Pharma pressure squelched the development of new and better drugs and encouraged universities to focus on me-too drugs that could be brought quickly to market but offered no advantage over existing ones already on the market. The result is we pay for the drugs twice; up front for the research, and again for the expensive product that the research they funded delivers.

In 2020 a *Science* investigation found that the Food and Drug Administration and National Institutes of Health routinely ignore rules requiring transparency and let companies keep clinical trial results secret, information that could save lives.[66] In just one recent example, an advocacy group filed an ethics complaint with the University of Texas MD Anderson Cancer Center for their refusal to share results of a sixteen-year-old clinical trial on the treatment of metastasizing brain tumors,[67] results that could advance treatment and save lives. By selectively revealing data, hiding evidence about what works (and just how well it works), and what doesn't, corporations can "spin" the perception of just how much benefit their drug provides and how serious its side effects may be, meaning that marketing rather than effectiveness drives their use.

When Frederick Banting and his colleagues were awarded US patents in 1923 for their discovery of insulin, they sold them for $1 to the University of Toronto so that their discovery could benefit all. Jonas Salk, inventor of the first polio vaccine, refused to patent it, instead asking: "Could you patent the sun?" In 1847 the founders of what was to become the American Medical Association (AMA) adopted a code of ethics stating that it was "inconsistent with beneficence and professional liberality" to patent a medicine or to prescribe a medicine that was patented.[68]

Today's reality is different. It was you and I, through our tax dollars, who funded development of COVID vaccines. In all, it's estimated that the US government spent nearly $40 billion on COVID vaccine development, yet private companies profited wildly from this research. In 2021, the vaccine producer Moderna sued to avoid sharing patent rights with the National Institutes of Health, whose scientists were key in developing the technology on which the vaccine was based,[69] and despite the fact that 100 percent of the $1 billion cost of developing the vaccine was paid for by our government.[70] Also in the midst of the pandemic, Merck charged the government $712 for a five-day course of molnupiravir, a drug used for the emergency treatment of COVID.

But this drug was actually developed at Emory University with government funding and costs only $18 to produce a five-day course.[71] In fact, a 2020 investigation by the Institute for New Economic Thinking found that *every single one* of the 356 pharmaceutical agents developed and approved in the prior decade had depended on taxpayer-funded research.[72] Yet the median price for a year's (or standard course of) treatment of drugs new to the market has skyrocketed from $2,115 in 2008 to $180,007 in 2021.[73]

Hiding behind a maze of patent laws lets companies fend off competition and jack up prices for up to twenty years, the life of a patent. Some companies are now manipulating FDA requirements to fend off competition even longer. By modifying the recommended dosing schedule in special populations for their on-patent antipsychotic Iloperidone (Fanapt®) which costs around $2,000 per month, Vanda Pharmaceuticals is hoping to block generic competition for another fifteen years.[74] Of course one can always use the generic drug risperidone (approximately $300 per month), which is virtually identical and shown to work just as well.[75] But that hasn't stopped the company from peppering medical journals with multi-page ads for Fanapt®, knowing that some well-fed but perhaps not so well-read doctors will be prompted to use it. Finally, in late 2023, Congress and the FTC are stepping in and challenging inaccurate or improper patent listings, and introducing legislation to fight Pharma's use of "patent thickets" to protect their market exclusivity as cases like Humira discussed in Chapter One.[76,77]

Over time, university-Pharma collaborations and funding became the norm, and academic psychiatrists and their departments came to depend on this collaboration for their survival, even as that dependence led to a blurring of the line between commercial and medical interests. Some were flagrant in the use of their positions of privilege. Charles Nemeroff, former chair of psychiatry at Emory University, received over $960,000 from GlaxoSmithKline (GSK), for personal use, all while conducting research projects on their drugs, and declaring only

$35,000 of this income to the university. He typically made at least $3,500 per talk, speaking about GSK's products.[78] During this time he was also receiving money from Janssen, Eli Lilly & Co., Merck, and others. Three prominent psychiatrists from Harvard's Massachusetts General Hospital were found to have collectively received over $4 million from the drug industry and neglected to report the majority of this income to authorities. One of them, Joseph Biederman, presented a slide to solicit further funding at a meeting with Johnson & Johnson executives, which offered to run a trial of their powerful antipsychotic drug Risperdal® for bipolar disorder that "will support the safety and effectiveness of risperidone in this age group." The age group he was referring to was preschoolers; the favorable results he promised were for an experiment that had not been done.[79]

In 1995 I was invited by the maker of Zyprexa® (olanzapine), an antipsychotic used to treat schizophrenia, to be a consultant on a special panel of psychiatrists meeting to discuss the soon-to-be released drug. Since I had considerable experience in the use of Clozaril® (clozapine), Lilly's earlier atypical antipsychotic on which Zyprexa® was modeled, they offered to pay me to fly to a fancy resort in Florida to discuss my experience with clozapine and how Zyprexa® might fit into clinical practice. To my naive shock, the "conference" rapidly devolved into a hard-sell marketing show. Meaningful discussion about the drug was discouraged, mindless praise encouraged. During the wrap-up meeting the speaker, a psychiatrist, tried to whip up excitement in the audience like an auctioneer, exhorting the crowd to yell out ways Zyprexa® could be used. We could have been at a circus sideshow with a charlatan hawking his patent medicine of a hundred years ago. The company had no interest in hearing our impressions about the drug (good or bad), but only in getting us on board to spread the word: prescribe. I had been lured to the meeting on false pretenses; it seemed clear to me their intent was to exploit my and my colleagues' reputation and influence.

What rapidly became evident was that I was being groomed to be a key opinion leader, or KOL, a speaker who delivers speeches, prepared by the drug company, at fancy resorts and restaurants to other physicians. These "speaker programs" lure physicians by offering continuing medical education credit (CME), a requirement for physicians to maintain licensure. Pharma uses professional representatives—the aforementioned KOLs—for one reason: they work. And, yes, Pharma collects data to show how well they work. Although it is not widely known, pharmacies in the United States sell data on the medications they dispense, including who receives the medications and who wrote the prescriptions. This lets Pharma monitor how the prescribing habits of attendees change after a CME conference, providing direct evidence[80] of the marketing effectiveness of the KOLs and CME programs. By 2007, Pharma sponsorship of CME had grown to a $1.2 billion enterprise.[81] A particularly biting 2021 commentary in the *British Medical Journal* outlined the harm caused by industry sponsorship of CME: the opioid crisis and the overuse of inferior and overpriced medications in the US being merely two of the more obvious consequences.[82]

Restrictive reimbursement of mental healthcare by insurance companies may partially explain why psychiatry has historically topped the list of medical specialties taking payments and other gifts from the pharmaceutical industry.[83, 84] Recently, with the prominence of lucrative devices and prostheses on the marketplace, psychiatrists have been bumped to second place. From 2013 to 2022, pharmaceutical and device companies made more than eighty-five million payments totaling $12.1 billion to approximately 826,300 physicians. Orthopedic surgeons received the largest amounts at $1.36 billion, followed by neurologists and psychiatrists at $1.32 billion. Pediatric surgeons and trauma surgeons received the lowest sums—$2.89 million and $6.96 million, respectively.[85] Interestingly, advanced practice clinicians, like nurse practitioners, physician assistants, and nurse-midwives are actually slightly more likely to accept these kickbacks from the pharmaceutical industry than physicians, although the amount taken tends to be less.[86] (Advanced practice clinicians are non-MD clinicians who undergo alternate medical training and are permitted to prescribe medication.)

Pharma also recognizes the influence of non-prescribing psy-chotherapists. In multidisciplinary clinics where I've worked, non-MD therapists such as social workers and psychologists seem to embrace these free drug company lunches and gifts even more than psychiatrists. While these psychotherapists can't prescribe medica-tion, Pharma is aware that they can strongly influence prescribing practices in a clinic setting by making suggestions to patients and managing their expectations. If a patient's therapist recommends to them that they take Lexapro®, a commonly used antidepressant, rather than, say, Zoloft®, another very similar antidepressant, and the patient relays that request to their psychiatrist, it will mean an unpleasant and time-consuming conflict to disagree. It's hard to refuse a patient's request for a specific medication unless it is unsafe. Perhaps non-MD therapists feel especially deserving of these drug company gifts (much like their psychiatric and advanced practice colleagues) due to their lower pay, while not appreciating that it is ultimately their patients who bear the cost of these "free" lunches through higher drug prices and inappropriate prescriptions.

Why do otherwise smart and well-intentioned people drop their ethics at the sound of "speaker fees" or "free lunch"? I recall carpooling home after work with a friend. He was bemoaning the fact that he had to don his three-piece suit immediately upon returning home and drive an hour to a restaurant where he was to give a CME lecture to other doctors about a newly released drug. When I asked him why he chose to do this rather than have dinner at home with his wife and children, he grew testy and replied: "There is perhaps a 6-month window of opportunity while this drug is new, and I don't want to miss it." Sure, the drug company would pay him at least $500 for a one-hour talk, provide him with a script and ready-to-show slide set, and he would get a free dinner to boot. But even though he was a true expert in the specific area the drug targeted, or perhaps because of this, he would need to spend hours reviewing the company's PR info, as well as the legitimate data on the drug (in case anyone asked challenging

questions). When you add up the time spent, including an entire eve-
ning with commute, treating patients would have been just as lucrative
and probably more satisfying. I think there are more powerful factors
than money at work here.

By giving the CME lecture, my friend would be seen as an expert on
the drug, burnishing his reputation, and join a team of elite researchers
at the vanguard of care, introducing a new and hopefully revolutionary
treatment, an exhilarating position. It would put him at the front of
the line for promotion of subsequent drugs. So what if he had to spin
his talk (and ethics) a bit. He was doing so in the name of progress
against a terrible illness. Hippocrates and experts in medical ethics
throughout history have recognized these temptations, and urged
physicians to put their patients' needs first.

Even psychiatry's "bible," the *Diagnostic and Statistical Manual* (DSM)
produced by the American Psychiatric Association (APA), which
serves as the standard guide for making psychiatric diagnoses—and
perhaps most important, provides specific disease codes required for
billing—was, like most psychiatric practice guidelines, written largely
by industry KOLs. In fact, for DSM-IV, issued in 1994, 100 percent
of the members on the panels that determined the diagnostic criteria
for the "Mood Disorders" and "Schizophrenia and Other Psychotic
Disorders" sections had financial ties to drug companies. Industry
conflicts in its 2022 update, DSM-5-TR, were little diminished,
with contributors taking more than $14 million from the pharma-
ceutical companies,[87] and has been met with blistering criticism. Since
no major advances have been made in our understanding of the causes
of psychiatric illness, their diagnosis, or their treatment since DSM-IV,
one must question why a new manual is needed.

The original edition of the DSM in 1952 described 106 mental
disorders, whereas the DSM-5 contains 298. However thin the science
behind DSM's latest update, it is turning out to be a huge money-maker
for the APA. DSM-IV is reported to have brought in $120 million,[88]
and DSM-5 at $199 in hardcover and $149 in paperback appears to

be even more profitable. As Jennifer Kingson, a reporter at the news outlet Axios reported in 2022, "The 'psychiatrist's bible' is suddenly a bestseller" as people facing the dearth of mental healthcare are buying up the DSM for self-diagnosis.[89]

Until the Affordable Care Act's "Sunshine Law"—named in honor of Supreme Court Justice Louis Brandeis's famous statement "sunlight is said to be the best of disinfectants"—mandated that Pharma's payments to physicians be made public, the industry spent only 15 to 17 percent of their income on research and development of new drugs, but *two to three times* that much on promotion. Further, a 2021 report by the House Oversight and Reform Committee found that Pharma also spends more on stock dividends and pay for executives than it does on research, which could develop more effective medications. But these more effective medications might decrease profits by better treating or actually curing illness, which might decrease demand for their drugs.[90] Under our profit-driven healthcare model, promotion, dividends to shareholders, and executive bonuses are more important than developing more effective drugs. In another example of where pharmaceutical companies' priorities lie, between 2012 and 2022 the industry spent $87 billion more on buybacks and dividends to shareholders than on research and development of drugs.[91, 92] From free CME, to lucrative speakers panels, to advertising directly to "consumers" (prospective patients), the industry has, like any successful business, figured out what works.

Somewhat ironically, the lucrative payments to KOLs are referred to as an honorarium, although some feel "dishonorarium" would be a more appropriate term. We also have a term for gifts given to government officials and jurists to change their behavior— a bribe. It saddens me that we don't hold doctors to the same lofty ethical standards as lawyers and politicians. Finally, in 2020 the government took action on this front. Citing the Federal Anti-Kickback Statute [42 U.S.C. § 1320a-7b(b)], the Office of Inspector General for the Department of Health and Human Services recently issued a "Special Fraud Alert" highlighting the "fraud and abuse risks associated with the offer, payment, solicitation, or receipt of remuneration" relating to KOLs and these industry-sponsored speaker programs. Recently there have been a number of large fines levied against pharmaceutical companies and their physician collaborators.[93,94] (You can find out whether your doctor takes Pharma money at Propublica's online database, Dollars for Docs: https://projects.propublica.org/docdollars/ or The Centers for Medicaid & Medicare Services (CMS) Open Payments database: https://openpaymentsdata.cms.gov/search/physicians/by-name-and-location.)

The fact that pharmaceutical companies now spend more on both administrator bonuses and marketing than on research (and that research focuses more on drugs that can be rapidly brought to market, rather than innovative ones that might actually work better) has resulted in a virtual standstill in improvements in the treatment of mental illness. I hear drug industry administrators complain that the cost and complexity of running clinical trials in order to get a new drug approved justifies the exorbitant prices they charge. While this is partially true, independent investigations show that the industry greatly exaggerates their costs. Their claims skirt an underlying truth. These drugs just aren't better than the old ones, and therefore huge trials with hundreds or thousands of subjects are needed to show that they meet "statistical significance" for improvement, even as this improvement may be clinically trivial. A truly new and better drug wouldn't need the sort of gargantuan studies we see today; its benefit could be made clear by a much more modest well-designed clinical trial. This is just one more consequence of industry's focus on "me-too" drugs that can be rapidly brought to market rather than taking a longer view and working to develop truly better treatments.

There is a saying in psychiatry: "hurry up and use a new drug while it still works." The sad truth is that most effective psychiatric drugs we have today were all developed before the much hyped "decade of the brain" (1990–1999 as designated by President George H. W. Bush) and "biological era" of psychiatry. Far and away the best medication for managing bipolar disorder is the element lithium, which was first used clinically in 1948. Our most effective agent for schizophrenia is clozapine (Clozaril®), developed in 1956 and first sold commercially in 1972. The most effective anti-anxiety drugs are the benzodiazepines, which have been in use since 1960, and imipramine, first marketed in 1957, is at least as effective as any of our current antidepressants, albeit with greater side effects. A Goldman Sachs report recently warned against the pharmaceutical industry developing cures for illness as this would hurt long-term profits. It cited Gilead Sciences, a pharmaceuticals company, "as a case in point, where the success of its hepatitis C franchise has gradually exhausted the available pool of treatable patients . . . In the case of infectious diseases such as hepatitis C, curing existing patients also decreases the number of carriers able to transmit the virus to new patients, thus the incident pool also declines."[95] In our healthcare system, chronic diseases are chronically profitable, and it is through avoiding cures, effective marketing, high prices, and squelching competition that real money is made.

A GROWTH OF DIAGNOSES—AND DUBIOUS INTERVENTIONS

When evaluating an ill patient physicians used to follow the time-honored tradition of developing a "differential diagnosis," a reasoned inventory of the most likely conditions the patient is facing. The differential diagnosis acknowledged the limitations and ambiguity of medicine, the tentative nature of some treatments, and the need to continuously assess and modify interventions as more information becomes available. Now, clinicians must give a diagnosis and billing code at the first visit, and any change can bring unwanted scrutiny and paperwork. This is one of the reasons the DSM has expanded its list of diagnosable mental disorders with each update, as well as softened the criteria needed to make a diagnosis for many of the disorders.

In mental health especially, diagnosis can be tricky and susceptible to subjective interpretation, and may take time to determine. There is an adage in psychiatry: patients come into treatment "pleading guilty to a lesser charge." I've found it to be a valuable guide. People will come in asking for help on things that they genuinely want help with, but they hold off on revealing their most sensitive and important issues, their most closely guarded secrets, until trust has been established. That's why it's so important not to jump to reassurances such as "there, there, that's not so bad," which is a sure way to stop someone from proceeding on to share things that they worry you might find "so bad."

As part of the ongoing battle between healthcare systems, clinicians, Pharma, and insurers, professional medical groups, government agencies, and disease societies have produced "expert consensus" guidelines to standardize and optimize care, as well as justify treatment regimens to insurers. If a panel of experts recommends that disease X should be treated with medication Y, an insurer is hard pressed to deny care, no matter what the cost. Seeing an opportunity, Pharma helped to fund many of these initiatives, and panel members were often on the companies' payroll. Even the state-sponsored and widely cited Texas Medication Algorithm Project (TMAP) became embroiled in controversy over conflicts of interest among its panel members. Texas sued Johnson and Johnson (J&J) for paying kickbacks to the project's director Dr. Stephen Shon to move Risperdal®, produced by J&J's subsidiary Janssen, up the list of recommended drugs. Janssen and other drug companies had paid the state more than $1 million to help promote the plan.[96] In Pennsylvania, a state official instrumental in implementing TMAP in his state was convicted of "felony conflict of interest" for taking payments from Janssen and other pharmaceutical companies.[97] A critical commentary concluded that often these "expert consensus" guidelines were neither.

To hedge their and their patients' bets, doctors and healthcare delivery systems have learned to use the guidelines strategically. They may upcode, or choose a more serious and therefore more reimbursable diagnosis code among various options to justify treatment, as well as claim a more lucrative procedure code, which defines the intervention performed and determines reimbursement. For example, a clinician might choose to bump someone's diagnosis from "Adjustment Disorder with Depressed Mood" (icd-10 F43.21), which signifies the development of emotional symptoms in reaction to identifiable psychosocial stressor(s), to "Major Depressive Disorder, Single Episode, moderate" (icd-10 F32.1), indicating a more serious and often more persistent illness in order to secure insurance support for more intense and longer-lasting treatment.

But upcoding from F43.21 to F32.1 can conflate worry with illness, and might change the intervention used. The initial clinician might be tempted to suggest medication sooner to justify the diagnosis, and someone, once carrying the F32.1 diagnosis, might be channeled by another clinician in the future toward medication and away from psychotherapy, which would generally be the preferred initial intervention for someone carrying an F43.21 diagnosis. This chicanery can take many forms. In 2012, the federal government implemented an initiative aimed at reducing the use of antipsychotic medication in nursing homes where they were often used to quell agitation, especially in understaffed facilities. But these drugs carry serious health risks, especially in the elderly. The initiative mandated that facilities' use of the drugs was to be publicly reported unless the individual had an underlying medical reason (diagnosis) for their use, such as schizophrenia. Over the ensuing twelve years the diagnosis of schizophrenia in nursing homes increased by 70 percent.[98] With proper and ethical medical care, diagnosis generally drives treatment. In our profit oriented healthcare, it is often just the opposite.

Jumping to a diagnosis can upset the therapeutic alliance too. The mind, and its distress, is subjective. Forcing a label on suffering can change more than just the interventions employed. I've had patients take offense at my telling them they were suffering from an "adjustment disorder," feeling it trivialized and dismissed their level of suffering, while others took offense at the diagnosis of "major depression," feeling that the label was stigmatizing and that their circumstance justified their emotional reaction. Are they wrong? There are reasons that effective medical care requires a close caring relationship and trust.

As a specialist in mood disorders I am referred many people with the diagnosis of bipolar disorder. This devastating illness currently has a certain cachet owing to a number of celebrities who have "come out" publicly, claiming to have the illness. People find comfort in an explanation for their pain, particularly if it is shared with the likes of Virginia Woolf, Robert Schumann, Britney Spears, Ted Turner, Kanye West, and Carrie Fisher. However, while the people I see are all in distress, only some truly have bipolar disorder. Others may have an anxiety disorder, or depression, or an emotional personality style, or be misusing drugs, or a combination of these conditions. The pressure to prescribe them medications for their diagnosis is immense. If I refuse, they may well just seek out another physician who will give them what they want. But these medications are not benign, some having rare but potentially lethal side effects, or lifetime consequences like involuntary muscle movements, diabetes, and heart disease. A frank discussion with a patient usually works, but not always. I have had people leave my care in anger when I decline to prescribe drugs they want. Most often, if the risks are low, I comply. It gives us time to work together, for me to learn more about them and for them to trust me and to see if by chance the medication helps. A young attorney recently asked me to prescribe Vyvanse®, a new and very expensive stimulant to improve her attention and concentration. Friends of hers had raved about its positive effects, saying it was like a "vyvasm." She didn't find it helpful and soon discontinued it, but because I prescribed it, her trust and our treatment alliance was strengthened. She felt I was on her side and took her concerns seriously.

Since medical care and its reimbursement are now determined by diagnosis and procedure code, not necessarily by the symptoms or needs of the patient, in psychiatry especially, whatever you are feeling we now have a billable diagnosis for it. As D. J. Jaffe, executive of Mental Illness Policy Org., a think tank that provides policy analyses, points out in his wonderfully illuminating book *Insane Consequences*, "While it is common for someone to go to a medical doctor with a physical complaint and be told nothing is wrong, the same is not true for those who visit psychiatrists. If you walk in the door, you will get a diagnosis and, likely, a prescription."[99]

As profits increasingly drive services, aspects of health "care," such as spending time actually talking with the person, conferring with family and other care givers, and helping patients access social services are neglected. These care activities, which are difficult to quantify and therefore poorly reimbursed, have been replaced by discrete and more quantifiable and billable "procedures." The treatment of mental illness has historically had few procedures, and those few, such as the lobotomy and electroconvulsive (ECT, or electroshock) therapy are controversial and rarely used. Responding to the need for specific billable procedures, the use of discrete mental health interventions or procedures has increased, especially ones involving physical manipulations, elaborate protocols, or big and flashy machines. Highly ritualized, manualized (and trademarked!) psychotherapies have flourished, such as eye movement desensitization and reprocessing (EMDR), which borrows from the trance-inducing swinging pocket-watch of the hypnotist of yesteryear, and various variants of cognitive behavioral therapy (CBT) like dialectical behavioral therapy (DBT), which are based on the teachings of the Stoic philosophers of two millennia ago. Many of my patients find the most useful book on CBT to be *Meditations*, written by the Roman Emperor Marcus Aurelius between 161 and 180 B.C.E. [100]

We now have an unfettered explosion of these trademarked behavioral and somatic treatment procedures. Repetitive transcranial magnetic stimulation (rTMS) and other stimulation technologies that are hugely popular today employ large and loud electrical machines that are reminiscent of the electrical "cures" of the late nineteenth century. Elliot Valenstein, in his 1986 classic *Great and Desperate Cures: The Rise and Decline of Psychosurgery and Other Radical Treatments for Mental Illness*,[101] as well as Andrew Scull in his 2022 book *Desperate Remedies: Psychiatry's Turbulent Quest to Cure Mental Illness*,[102] describes the popularity in the late 1800s of "electrotherapy," or electrical stimulation of the nervous system, for the treatment of neurasthenia (a popular diagnosis then) and depression. Valenstein quotes from a 1901 textbook: "Neuroses are, par excellence, the kind of nervous disease in which favorable results are obtained from electrical treatment."[103] The author of this chapter, Morton Prince, goes on to describe how the noisy "static machine" could have "suggestive power" on patients, and advised exploiting this unconscious benefit.

I myself was involved in a nationwide study of the effectiveness of the new and popular treatment rTMS on veterans with treatment resistant depression (depression not responsive to standard antidepressants). rTMS uses a large, loud, and expensive (in the neighborhood of $100,000) machine that pulses a magnetic field through the skull into the brain. Our study, however, employed a clever "sham" (placebo) treatment arm. All subjects (who were made aware that they might receive sham treatment) were subjected to the same elaborate, loud procedure, utilizing the same impressive machine, and were stimulated on the forehead with a small electric shock to mimic the sensation of the actual treatment. However, only the "active" treatment group received the magnetic stimulation. The treatment was remarkably effective: 40.7 percent of those receiving the active treatment had a remission of their symptoms. This sounds great, until one notes that 37.4 percent of those receiving the inactive (placebo) rTMS also remitted, a difference of about 3 percent. This trivial difference is well within the statistical margin of error, and also explainable by the likelihood that some subjects could discern the difference between real and sham treatment, which would diminish the placebo effect.[104] Nevertheless, the study was touted as evidence of rTMS's effectiveness and the VA, bending to requests for the treatment from desperate people caught up in rTMS marketing hype, now offers it, much as the VA bowed to patient and family pressure to offer lobotomies seventy years ago. Subsequent studies of rTMS have been more positive, but these have been conducted by adherents of the lucrative technology. Scientific findings are generally considered preliminary and not valid until they have undergone *independent* verification and validation.

Ted Kaptchuk, an acupuncturist and professor of medicine at Harvard, has done extensive research on the placebo effect. It is far more than just a sugar pill, but a true, measurable effect due to often ignored aspects of treatment involving our many senses and cognitions. These include hearing, sight, touch, taste, and smell, and the even more difficult to measure factors, such as the perception of care, authority, and expectation. We certainly want to utilize the placebo effect to good effect, but we should distinguish it from other therapeutic interventions to avoid confusion about just what is benefiting someone. We need to be clear about when and how each intervention should be implemented, and billed for. [105] In 2012, *Scientific American* took an in-depth look at the widely popular (and wildly promoted) EMDR and summed up the case for EMDR as, "What is effective in EMDR is not new, and what is new is not effective." [106] While there is evidence that EMDR works, this should not be a surprise since it borrows from a number of other treatments for post-traumatic stress disorder (PTSD), like prolonged exposure and imagery rehearsal, that also have been shown to work. But one must ask: would treatments such as rTMS and EMDR be as widely promoted if they didn't include flashy elements that scream bling and exclusivity to justify billing that enriches those who promote their use? In an intervention-driven system, practitioners become "providers" of a product (healthcare), and thus become self-promoters, sometimes encouraging unneeded, overpriced, or unhelpful interventions.

After forty years of seeing supposedly revolutionary treatments promoted to great fanfare, only to disappear later in a cloud of smoke,

I take a more circumspect view. Two recent books, Jesse Singal's *The Quick Fix: Why Fad Psychology Can't Cure Our Social Ills*[107] and Satel and Lilienfeld's *Brainwashed: The Seductive Appeal of Mindless Neuroscience,* [108] effectively show the foolishness in grasping at the latest shiny object in mental health treatment be it high-tech "neuroscience," the latest re-discovered psychedelic drug, or talk-based therapies. These treatments *should* be studied, but when financial interests and marketing are driving new treatments rather than science, we need to take note. People's motivations are always complex, a mixture of impulses including intellectual curiosity, altruism, and desire for fame and fortune, among others. We want medical advances to be made by those wanting to improve the human condition; we don't want to chase bogus cures sold by a self-promoting huckster. Worshipping financial priorities makes discriminating between the two difficult. Scientific findings are only considered valid after they've been independently confirmed. Two studies, both done by people with a financial stake in the outcome, is not independent verification. We want the results to reflect a products' health benefit to patients, not its financial benefit to the maker or clinicians using it.

CHAPTER SIX

Business Models and Psychotherapy

THE REJECTION OF THE MEDICAL MODEL AND NON-MD THERAPISTS

Just as psychiatrists fled the widely reviled asylums and their unpopular inhabitants for the cities and analytic institutes, nonmedical psychotherapists like psychologists, social workers, and MFTs (called marriage, family, and child counselors or MFCC back then) sought to distance themselves from the seriously mentally ill. Invoking mental illness, such as diagnosing someone with depression, brings judgment, not only on the sufferer, but also the caregiver, as we'll explore further in Chapter Seven. While most of us are comfortable assuming that someone with a mild fever and sore throat is likely to have the flu, many hesitate at saying that someone who is overcome with sadness and thinks about death is depressed and could have an illness. This is not new. Throughout history the mentally ill were treated differently than those with a more overtly physical illness. People with behavioral and emotional trouble have long been scorned, tortured, and imprisoned, all before we had an inkling of bacteria, viruses, endocrinology, physiology, or any other cause of physical illness.

Compounding this, most psychotherapy training focuses on the treatment of less severely ill patients, ones not needing medications, which they cannot prescribe. Thus, they embraced psychotherapy more as a treatment for those, especially the relatively healthy and wealthy, who might be going through a rough period in their life but would recoil at the thought that they might have a mental illness.

More than any other area of healthcare, psychotherapists embraced a business model, eschewing their role as a healer treating patients in lieu of one as an entrepreneur catering to "clients," as we saw in Chapter Four. In the process however, they segregated the seriously ill from those with more minor complaints as well as affirming a mental-physical divide. In no other area of healthcare would we have, for example, one clinic for "patients" with lung cancer, another for "clients" with bronchitis. Many therapists I know overtly state that they do not want to align what they do with the "medical model," which focuses on the treatment of those with an identifiable illness such as diabetes, schizophrenia, or depression, and sees illness as rooted in measurable physiological or behavioral (in the case of mental illness) processes. Of course, all "medical" illnesses have environmental/behavioral components, so the distinction is always somewhat muddy, and some argue that the split has roots in western society's ancient concept that the church owns our minds.

While the attack on use of the medical model in mental health was championed by the psychiatrists R. D. Laing, who denied the very existence of mental illness, and Thomas Szasz, who claimed that mental disorders were merely metaphors for "problems in living," psychiatry as a field for the most part held to its identity as physicians. In fact, psychoanalytic institutes barred non-MDs as members until a lawsuit forced them to admit "non-medical candidates" like psychologists in 1988. It was many of these non-medical psychotherapists who rejected the medical model wholesale, often citing its hierarchical nature, due no doubt in part to the greater reimbursement given to MDs over psychologists, and their previous exclusion from analytic institutes.

Psychotherapists' rejection of the medical model as applied to the brain and mind has had far-reaching consequences, a prime example of good intentions gone awry. In rejecting the medical model they embraced the archaic and discredited Cartesian concept of "duality," that of a separate and distinct mind and body, and the Judeo-Christian belief that while we have a body, our mind belongs to God. This latter belief has fostered another split, that between faith and psychotherapy as determinants of happiness, as if they are in competition rather than complementary. I don't think psychotherapists adequately anticipated the consequences to their patients that this stance allowed in the financial battlefield that the evolving healthcare marketplace would become, one in which their anti-medical stance would facilitate insurers' ability to lower or outright deny reimbursement for mental health treatment. For example, if someone's sadness is not caused by an illness, then health insurers can more easily claim it does not fall under their responsibility.

But attacks on our healthcare system's over-focus on physical factors like infection or elevated blood pressure or temperature are valid. Medical care in the US often ignores complex psychosocial factors, or Social Determinants of Health (SDOH), such as financial stress, unstable housing, or marital problems, which results in simplistic and inadequate understanding of a person, their illness, and the interventions needed. It reduces people to an easily quantifiable checklist of symptoms rather than viewing them in the context of their overall life. Likewise, it assumes that the only treatments available are medications or "procedures," quick interventions that are more easily quantifiable and billed for, but which may carry risks in themselves, and may not meaningfully improve quality of life. For example, a 2021 study found that among Medicaid insured youth, those in foster care were treated with psychiatric medication more than three times as frequently.[1]

Yet another study by the Office of the Inspector General found that among youth in foster care who were medicated, more than a third do not receive treatment planning or medication monitoring.[2] However, the needs of these kids, many of whom are the victims of or witnesses to violence and other trauma are many, and unlikely to be remedied with a pill. A 2022 study found that adverse SDOH were significantly correlated with youth self-harm,[3] yet the Physicians Foundation's 2022 Survey of America's Physicians found that 61 percent of physicians felt they have little to no time or ability to effectively address their patients' SDOH. Of these doctors, seventy-three percent cited a lack of reimbursement for screening for or addressing SDOH.[4]

It is important to recognize that this bias is not a result of the medical model. These non-physical factors are given short shrift in our system because they take time to identify and evaluate, and in our healthcare system time is money, not because of any inherent limits of the medical model. Proper care under the medical model should always examine relevant identifiable factors affecting illness. But insurers are simply not going to pay, or healthcare systems tolerate, lengthy evaluations to ferret out the subtleties in someone's life story. People don't readily volunteer disturbing yet important aspects of their life, such as an abusive spouse or a financial crisis, in a ten-minute appointment. In truth, the medical model, as it should be employed, depends on truly knowing one's patients and all that affects them. Sir William Osler famously observed that "The good physician treats the disease; the great physician treats the patient who has the disease." Ignoring psychosocial aspects of suffering runs counter to medicine's goals of beneficence and to do no harm.

When I was a medical student (medical students' time is cheap since they pay to be there, not the other way around), I was asked to evaluate a Cambodian woman in the neurology clinic who continued to suffer from severe headaches despite multiple trials of medications. I obtained a translator and slowly, over time, a gruesome story unfolded. A decade earlier, she had returned to her village one afternoon to discover that it had been completely wiped out. She found the dismembered bodies of her husband and children near where their hut had stood. She was quickly relocated to a refugee center and then on to a large US city with a small Cambodian population, but knew not a soul from her former life. With time and patience (and a good translator) she was able to convey that her "headaches" were not what we generally call a headache, but psychic pain from her trauma and loss. No pills were going to take that away, and only caused her unpleasant side effects.

Also, it bears noting that this "medical model," with its focus on science and the development of effective medications, vaccinations, physical and social interventions, and particularly public health measures, has worked miracles in improving our physical health. It has doubled our life expectancy, eradicated polio, and smallpox, and contributed to a greater than 90 percent reduction in infant and maternal death rates over the last century—successes eclipsing those seen in the treatment of mental health. Ultimately, separating mental from physical illness implies that mental problems are not real illnesses with real medical treatments. And this has left the field of mental health relatively stuck as compared to physical healthcare for the last fifty years. Let's examine some of the many consequences of separating treatment of mental illness from the rest of medicine.

A FALSE MIND-BODY SEPARATION

First off, if one creates a fundamental division between how mental and physical health and their treatment are viewed, where do you draw the line separating them? As the anthropologist Grinker laments, "Descartes set the stage for mental illnesses to be stigmatized by isolating the "mental" from all the other factors that shape us . . . to say that body and mind always influenced each other was still to accept that they were two distinct entities."[5]

Arguments pitting biological versus behavioral aspects of suffering have always been absurd; the two are inextricably intertwined. My patients with depression, mania, and anxiety often describe their symptoms as feeling *physical*, and may even disavow emotions and thoughts linked to these physical symptoms. A frightening situation, such as a near-miss automobile accident, can evoke the "fight or flight" response, raising epinephrine (adrenaline) and norepinephrine levels, as well as the heart rate. Similarly, giving someone an injection of these neurotransmitters will raise the heart rate, and may induce anxiety. People describe a panic attack as feeling like they *are* having a heart attack, and may be unaware of any source of anxiety other than the belief that they are having a heart attack. One can't ignore that the racing heart and elevated blood pressure of a panic attack can precipitate an actual heart attack in a vulnerable individual. It has been shown that both selective serotonin reuptake inhibitor (SSRI) medication and CBT, which focuses on the interrelationship between thoughts, behavior, and emotions, can cause similar changes in the brain activity and behavior of people with obsessive-compulsive disorder (OCD).[6]

This artificial duality fosters other deceptions. We prefer concrete, palpable, simple, physically measurable answers to complex questions of the mind. Years ago it was reported that magnetic resonance imaging (MRI) could measure anatomical differences between the brains of gay and straight men. This was debunked later of course, but at the time a patient who had heard of the study came to me asking for an MRI to determine whether or not he was gay. Giving credence only to aspects of our existence that we can physically measure ignores the depth and breadth of human experience, and those aspects of life that matter most. When we do admit to emotional troubles, we tend to couch them in terms like "stress" or "tension," since stress and tension are seen as arising from external situations such as job, financial, or family pressure, not from our own mind. As Oscar Levant, the famous pianist-comedian once said, "My doctor told me my illness is all in my head. What a terrible place for it to be."

I believe this craving for simple answers to complex questions of the mind is one reason (aside from the prevalence of trauma in our world) that PTSD has become so popular. As the anthropologist Grinker describes it, ". . . PTSD has, to a large extent, become an all-purpose diagnosis, an equalizer of sorts that mutes biographical and cultural differences, and offers a relatively non-stigmatizing diagnosis by blaming an environmental stressor rather than an individual's distinctive personality and history." It is something that is done to you, you may be a victim, but you are not mentally ill, and in fact carry a badge of courage. As William Shakespeare put it in *As You Like It*, "Sweet are the uses of adversity, which, like the toad, ugly and venomous, wears yet a precious jewel in his head. . . ."

But why must someone have to say they have PTSD to be heard, or to access care for psychological distress?[7] The treatment of "trauma" has become a cottage industry, blurring the boundaries between PTSD and what might be an unfortunate but expected and manageable reaction to life events.[8] Concerns about overreach of the diagnosis were validated in at least one elegant and ingenious study that examined people requesting pharmacologic treatment of depression. Of these, 78 percent had a history of trauma and met criteria for PTSD. However, the researchers found that an identical percentage of those who did not report trauma also met criteria for PTSD. In other words, trauma was not a predictor of who would have symptoms of PTSD.[9] Fear and panic, a racing heart, and nightmares are normal psychological and physiological responses to a frightening event. Do we refuse to care for physical illnesses until they come to define or disable the person? The mind-body split and our fear of mental illness just fosters these sorts of deceptions and evasions which serve to further stigmatize and marginalize mental illness. Viewing emotional suffering as stemming solely from the external world can trivialize true mental illness, and deflect from internal work to build personal strength and resilience. PTSD has become a sanitized, destigmatized catchword for psychological suffering in our society, all while this same society fails to adequately address the causes of this distress: violence, xenophobia, isolation, child abuse, sexual predation, and war.

HEALTH INSURANCE AND CATERING
TO THE HEALTHY AND WEALTHY

There are other unintended consequences of rejecting the medical model. As the psychoanalyst Mark Ruffalo notes: ". . . in the past 50 years, and especially the past 30, we have witnessed the concept of psychotherapy applied to a host of endeavors unrelated to the treatment of psychopathology . . . there is a tendency to see psychotherapy as a process wholly unrelated to the concept of mental illness (i.e., not as a form of treatment for illness, but rather as an endeavor undertaken for other reasons). . . ."[10] Following the lead of the anti-psychiatry movement, this demedicalization framed psychotherapy as a tool to manage what were considered normal and expected reactions to societal pressures, but not real illness.

Moreover, as Ruffalo goes on to point out, with demedicalization, "Psychotherapy becomes devalued relative to other forms of psychiatric treatment, despite its proven effectiveness for a range of mental disorders." Thus psychotherapy becomes the belittled stepchild of the already disparaged field of mental health despite studies showing that in many situations it is as effective as medication.[11] Access to psychotherapy as a treatment for severe mental disorders becomes more difficult as fewer therapists choose to specialize in treating psychiatric patients and instead become focused on other more lucrative forms of therapy or counseling, those that cater to the relatively well and well-heeled.

Finally, demedicalization allows training requirements for psychotherapists to loosen, so many graduating therapists have had little to no exposure to patients across the psychiatric diagnostic spectrum. But, with this drop in training standards, there has been a commensurate drop in the value (and reimbursement) of psycho-therapy for serious mental illness, further inducing psychotherapists to pursue private practices catering to the healthy and wealthy paying out of pocket.

This last point is important. Mental health, the area of health-care which concerns itself with the brain, the most complicated and least understood organ in the body, has, under economic incentives, become the only area of healthcare where practitioners with a two-year degree can practice independently, that is without the oversight or recommendation of a doctorate-level trained clinician. Most non-MD independent healthcare practitioners (advanced practice nurses are an exception in some states) who treat other parts of the body, like dentists, podiatrists, and optometrists, must have gradu-ated from a four-year post-college (doctorate) program. Not so for those who treat the brain. Most masters-level psychotherapists I know are excellent therapists, but the question remains: Why the double standard?

Of course it comes down to money, not what is best for the patient. Back in 1986 MFCCs were licensed by state, not nationally, and were officially recognized in only eleven states.[12] Insurers for years had fought legislation that would allow MFCCs and other counselors with only two years of graduate (non-medical) education to bill as medical caregivers for their services, fearing the increased supply of practitioners would fuel demand to pay for their services. These same insurers later realized that MFCCs would perform therapy at far lower rates than MDs and psychologists, who undergo more extensive training, and reversed their position and advocated for legislation allowing MFCCs to directly bill health insurers as independent medical practitioners. As part of this change, MFCCs were rebranded as Marriage and Family Therapists (MFTs). On July 1, 1999, the state of California launched the Board of Behavioral Sciences,[13] specifi-cally to regulate masters-level trained psychotherapists like MFTs and social workers.

For the majority of MFTs, however, their opposition to the medical model, that is, to seeing emotional or behavioral problems as an illness, did not change. Moreover, the alliance MFTs forged with health insurers, who now allowed them to bill as medical caregivers, was a mixed blessing for them. Achieving licensure to practice and bill for psychotherapy did not guarantee them a living wage. According to the US Bureau of Labor Statistics, in 2022 masters-level psychotherapists like MFTs and social workers were paid a median wage of less than $24 per hour when employed by a healthcare company, which is less than *half* that of other masters-level healthcare practitioners like nurse practitioners and physician assistants who treat physical illnesses. Even registered nurses, whose licensing requires only a bachelor's degree, earn 50 percent more.[14] MFTs and social workers in private practice in the Bay Area charge self-pay clients, as they most often call them, between *four and six times* this median industry wage. With the acute shortage of psychotherapists and the pitiful wages they are paid by insurance and clinics, who can blame them? Thus, therapists who are on insurance panels and agree to accept insurance's paltry reimbursement tend, of necessity, to be at the very beginning of their career, with less experience. These therapists are willing to work for a pittance to build their practice and reputation so they can get off insurance panels as soon as possible. What results is a two-tiered psychotherapy system, one for the less-desirable insured (if they can even find care), and another for the preferred more wealthy ones who can self-pay. This only adds to the "othering" of people with serious mental illness since they rarely have the means to pay out of pocket for therapy.

Aligning with insurers has had significant demographic consequences for the practice of psychotherapy. For example, there is a stark racial divide in terms of who gets treatment. Ongoing therapy, which is more commonly utilized by those with more money and less severe illness, or those dealing with life's stressors—of which people of color have more than their share—is predominantly the territory of wealthy

Caucasians. On average, African Americans access mental health services of any sort less than half as frequently as White people,[15] and they receive antidepressants only half as often as White people with similar symptoms.[16] The fraction receiving psychotherapy is undoubtedly far less.

The fact that non-MD therapists are predominantly white adds another hurdle for persons of color. The CDC found African Americans are two times as likely as Caucasians to resort to obtaining their mental healthcare in an ER.[17] Moreover, African Americans are more likely to be brought to emergency rooms by the police, and once in the emergency department more likely to be physically restrained,[18] have longer wait times, held for longer evaluations (no doubt related to limited options for outpatient treatment and referral), and are less likely to be admitted or transferred to another hospital.[19] Even when people of color can access care, it tends to be inadequate and briefer. For example, Black people are prescribed buprenorphine for opiate addiction half as often as White people,[20] and when they do get medication treatment for addiction it is much briefer, even though longer treatment is known to improve rates of recovery.[21]

The hard truth is that it takes a certain degree of economic security, one less frequently found in minority communities, to afford six years of college and grad school to wind up earning $24 an hour. Surveys find that 88 percent of psychologists[22] and 95 percent of MFTs[23] identify as White, while only 2.6 percent and 1 percent, respectively, identify as African American.

Psychiatrists are somewhat more balanced in regard to race, with 69 percent identifying as Caucasian.[24] However, even this statistic hides a deeper prejudice against mental health. The same study found that nearly a third of all psychiatrist positions in the US were filled by doctors who graduated from a foreign medical school, likely because of the difficulty in filling positions with American trained doctors.[25] The sad reality is that in the United States we have a double double standard in healthcare, between mental and physical illnesses, and between persons of color and Caucasians.

TWO OPPOSING CAMPS:
PHARMACOLOGY AND PSYCHOLOGY

A common claim I hear among my non-medical psychotherapist col-leagues is that they are "holistic." Holistic means to treat the whole person, to take into account all factors, including mental and social ones. But, as discussed above, choosing to be anti-medical is exclu-sionary, not holistic, and restricts the focus to subjective symptoms (and treatments) of the mind while excluding those grounded in the measurable, observable world. This stance is limiting, and an evasion. Rejecting the medical model to avoid stigma has lessened the focus on the full spectrum of causes of mental illness, particularly physi-ological causes. This has led clinicians to over-focus on more generic and universal issues like the usual childhood struggles most of us have experienced. Thus psychotherapy has focused almost single-mindedly on behavioral and interpersonal causes of mental illness, from personal losses to misattuned parents.

The reality is that in today's healthcare environment, the small per-centage of those who can access psychotherapy through their insurer will see a non-MD psychotherapist who cannot prescribe medication. In contrast, someone who gets care from a psychiatrist is unlikely to receive psychotherapy, despite evidence that medication and psycho-therapy usually work better together than either alone.[26, 27, 28] How did this unhealthy split come about?

Since our for-profit medical system is driven by billable units of service delivered, care is defined by a procedure rendered. These units can be, for example, a physical examination, stitching up a laceration or draining an abscess, or procedures that focus on the disease or injury (or potential disease) being treated. The specific individual undergoing treatment is essentially irrelevant, aside from their insurance status. The private circumstances that led to the laceration or the festering abscess are not addressed. The result is that people feel dismissed and unheard, their individual needs and personal suffering ignored.

When feeling unheard by the medical system, understandably, people look elsewhere for help. Unfortunately, this has often led to an uncritical acceptance of "alternative" or "complementary" medicine. Many of the remedies alternative practitioners offer are based on anecdote or folklore, and we just don't know which of these might work, or what harm they might cause. Individuals and companies promoting these treatments such as homeopathy, cleanses, chelation therapy, or naturopathy have not demonstrated their effectiveness and safety since, as many are natural products, they are difficult to patent, and would be unlikely to be profitable enough to justify the expense of clinical trials to prove their effectiveness.[29] This all begs the question: What do you call alternative medicine that's been shown to actually work? Medicine. Moreover, these treatments are rarely covered by insurance, further burdening the patient financially.

As healers, we make hard decisions all the time, such as what we believe is the best course of action to recommend, and what should be avoided, even if it challenges patient (and treater) assumptions. People want to talk with someone knowledgeable about what is troubling them and the best way to ameliorate it. Still, I find that psychotherapists are often reluctant to refer their patients who don't respond to psychotherapy to a psychiatrist for medication since this involves a shift to a more medical model. Rather than seeing this shift as a smooth integration of medical and behavioral treatments, they may view it as an admission of failure. Many MDs are reluctant to refer their patients for psychotherapy due to their own fear of and prejudice against mental illness and psychotherapy's unscientific "non-medical" assumptions, such as a reliance on unverifiable unconscious motivations.

When patients receive medication and psychotherapy from different clinicians, unneeded complications can arise. Individuals with severe mental illness have difficulty engaging in psychotherapy until their symptoms have been brought under control with medication. Yet comfort and compliance, as well as the effectiveness of prescribed medication, are enhanced if the patient has a close relationship with the prescriber, as occurs in the context of psychotherapy. I recall receiving a phone call from a psychotherapist I know asking how I thought her patient was responding to medication. I had to tell her that I had no idea, since I had never met this person. Her patient had been telling her that she was meeting with me regularly, but was too embarrassed to admit her fear and deception. Further, psychiatrists tend to prescribe medication more readily for those with whom they do not have a close ongoing psychotherapeutic relationship, perhaps because they are eager to at least offer help of some sort.

Clinicians engaging in these "split" treatments have been found to collaborate poorly, often not communicating adequately, or at all.[30] This has been my experience. When a patient I treat is seeing a psychotherapist who I have not worked with before, often the therapist is surprised when I call to coordinate care. They tell me that getting a call from a psychiatrist is highly unusual. I suspect the fact that time spent on coordinating care is generally not reimbursed, and takes time away from another deserving patient, dampens clinicians' enthusiasm for this kind of communication.

In my practice as a psychiatrist I find that medications, when combined with a comprehensive care plan that includes appropriate support and psychotherapy, are extremely effective, and the data backs this up.[31] This often means mobilizing family and social support, and examining lifestyle and relationship choices. It's true that for some patients I do have to look for small victories, like convincing my hesitant patients to get vaccinated, or just keeping someone from getting worse so they don't need hospitalization or end up on the streets. But these interventions can make a major difference in peoples' lives, and the lives of their loved ones, and are no different than what we do in the management of chronic physical illness, like guiding someone with coronary artery disease away from unhealthy dietary choices. With the young it sometimes feels like all I can do is hold their hand, and get them through to young adulthood without making any disastrous life choices. This is less likely to happen in a primary care visit with all of eight minutes of actual face-to-face time.

A LACK OF CHECKS AND BALANCES

Rejecting the scientifically based examination inherent to the medical model leaves psychotherapy vulnerable to what is known as the "Dodo bird verdict," a critique of psychotherapy dating back to 1936, but equally valid today. The name is taken from Lewis Carroll's classic children's book *Alice in Wonderland*,[32] in which contestants run around a lake, but neither speed nor distance are measured. When the Dodo is asked who won he replied, *"Everybody has won, and all must have prizes."*

This line of criticism points out that comparisons of various forms of psychotherapy tend to find roughly equivalent, vaguely defined outcomes regardless of the specific approach.[33] As in *Alice in Wonderland*, where everyone wins, there are a multitude of psychotherapies which seem to produce equivalent results, none being more effective than another, making choice of treatment more dependent on the therapist's beliefs and training than the patient's needs and wishes.[34] If a depressed patient goes to a therapist who is an adherent of psychodynamic therapy, the therapy will focus on the psychological roots of emotional suffering, particularly those stemming from past relationships even if CBT, which examines negative or inaccurate thinking, might be more effective.

When psychotherapy falls outside of the medical model, it misses many of the checks and balances that apply to other healthcare. Framed as a non-medical business endeavor, psychotherapy avoids the same legal, scientific, and ethical oversight applied to physical medicine. It's true, for example, that California has an effective Board of Behavioral Sciences, but why is treatment of behavior separated from that for the rest of the body? Why do we hold treatment of our brain and mind to different standards? We don't have a separate Board of Lung Sciences. Unlike with medication and medical devices, there is no equivalent of the Food and Drug Administration (FDA) to evaluate and monitor the efficacy and safety of psychotherapeutic treatments or guide their use. And clinical studies of psychotherapy done outside of academic institutions largely evade the oversight or scientific scrutiny for effectiveness, safety, compassion, or ethical boundaries that studies of pharmacological and other medical treatments must comply with. This can expose people to useless and even harmful treatments.

As with any health intervention, psychotherapy properly applied can do good, but when mis-applied it has the potential to do harm. Examples of this are cringeworthy, like the debacles of the "recovered memory," "satanic panic" cults, alien abduction, multiple personality disorder, and sexual conversion therapies.[35] Yet these supposed "treatments" were promoted as valid and effective treatments of real disorders. Once the self-promoting hype surrounding multiple personality disorder, alien abduction, and satanic cult brainwashing was questioned it was found that far from being common, these "disorders" do not exist or are vanishingly rare, and their "treatments" did serious harm. In the case of gender identity, this is a very real issue that our country is still struggling with, but sexual conversion therapy unquestionably has harmed many people. But even more mainstream psychotherapies have the potential to cause harm, as examined in psychologist Scott Lilienfeld's 2007 article "Psychological Treatments That Cause Harm." Lilienfeld concludes that despite the relative lack of oversight in behavioral health, "the field of psychology has been reluctant to police itself. . . ."[36] While it is true that any health intervention that helps may also hurt, in the case of medications we call this "side effects" or "adverse effects," and in fact, almost all interventions do both. We want the former to outweigh the latter. With the growth of economic incentives, the self-examination and self-policing that weighs these competing factors in psychotherapy has diminished.

When presented as a business endeavor, a product or service is not required to meet scientific or objective standards, as is required

of medical care. For example, NPR listeners will likely remember
Lumosity, the popular "brain-training" program that was wildly promoted as an incentive for larger donations during NPR's on-air fund
drives. Lumosity's claims were unsubstantiated and ultimately shown
to be false, yet trusted NPR personalities uncritically attested to its
effectiveness—"proven" they said—in maintaining and improving
memory, as well as warding off dementia. The FTC ultimately fined
Lumosity $2 million for false claims (a business offense), but only after
years of successful promotion.[37] Because psychotherapy is divorced
from medical care, it obeys the more illusory rules of commerce. As
long as someone is willing to pay, overblown claims for psychotherapeutic interventions can, and generally will, continue.

The prioritization of fame and fortune over patient benefit has had
consequences. Prominent findings in behavioral science, and especially
behavioral economics, have of late suffered from what has been called
a "crisis of reproducibility," with multiple failures to replicate formerly
widely accepted studies, and charges that researchers failed to follow
accepted scientific methods. And now, outright charges of fraud are
being leveled at some of these prominent researchers.[38, 39, 40, 41, 42]

The treatment of mental illness has historically been littered with
examples of truly bizarre, if well-meaning, interventions, like removal
of teeth and organs (especially the uterus), lengthy ice baths to induce
hypothermia, as well as outright bad behavior. Eliot Valenstein's classic
Great and Desperate Cures[43] as well as more recent books like Jeffrey
Lieberman's *Shrinks*,[44] Anne Harrington's *Mind Fixers*,[45] and Andrew
Scull's magnificent and wrenching 2022 book *Desperate Remedies*[46]
tell the sad tale of just how wild and far-fetched treatments of mental
illness have been. Since people with serious mental illness may lack
insight and judgment, and resources, they are particularly vulnerable to
exploitation. The vulnerability that mental illness can cause is why the
field should require more, not less, oversight than is expected of other
branches of medicine. Certainly it should not be left to lax business
ethics and "market-driven solutions."

In the Bay Area where I work, self-appointed practitioners of mental health are common, although they may couch their work in terms like "coaching," "empowerment," and "life skills." These practitioners often have no legitimate training or oversight for the "counseling" they offer. Some incorporate spiritual ceremonies and folk remedies (especially the use of herbs) from other cultures, as if such treatments were on par with those that have undergone rigorous scientific testing. Quack mental health interventions abound, often using psycho- and techno-babble terms like "neurolinguistic programming" or "chelation therapy."[47] While some interventions seem to work for some, without scientific evaluation, we don't know which truly offer a benefit, which offer only a placebo response, and which might cause outright harm. We can't evaluate anecdotal evidence without objective scrutiny. Worse, some therapists, as well as psychiatrists and psychologists, have lost their professional licenses due to unprofessional (translate: repugnant and damaging, like rubbing their genitals against their patient or outright engaging in sexual intercourse) behavior, only to continue to offer services as unlicensed counselors. Practicing medicine without a license is a crime in all fifty states. Apparently not when treating the brain, since it's not medical. As above, people seeking mental healthcare are particularly vulnerable, which is why mental health clinicians should, if anything, have greater scrutiny than other areas of healthcare, not less.

The truth is, psychotherapy could grow, in both acceptance and effectiveness, if it embraced the scientific model. The scientific model does not exclude any modality, whether derived from the natural world, such as an herb, or synthesized in a laboratory such as an SSRI antidepressant. It can include behavioral approaches, such as psychotherapy, or physical ones, such as repetitive transcranial magnetic stimulation (rTMS), which might be of benefit. All it asks for is reproducible demonstration of evidence showing effectiveness. People are frustrated with our limited ability to treat all chronic illnesses, whether physical or mental. But the paucity of hard scientific evidence about which psychotherapeutic approach actually works leaves them vulnerable to spurious claims. Some forms of psychotherapy, especially those based on the cognitive behavioral model, known as CBT, have gained wider acceptance by establishing themselves as "evidence based." This means that they *have* been shown to be effective in controlled studies, in which they are compared to a placebo treatment or no treatment under "blind" conditions, where those rating its effectiveness do not know what intervention the subject received. Is this too much to ask when peoples' lives are at stake?

But even legitimate-appearing psychotherapy research can be tainted by hiding under the business umbrella and avoiding true scientific scrutiny. As Jennifer Steele, associate professor in the School of Education at American University points out: "The protections for human subjects" set out by the Department of Health and Human Services apply only to studies that are "designed to develop or contribute to generalizable knowledge . . . Because 'market research' is not meant to be seen by the public, the rules protecting human subjects are not generally applicable—and there are no equivalent federal protections for consumers whose behavior is studied by private organizations seeking monetary gain,"[48] leaving people vulnerable to quack interventions like Lumosity.[49]

Perhaps even more insidious, unlike published research on drugs and medical device treatments, authors of psychotherapy studies do not have to reveal financial conflicts of interest.[50] Not surprisingly, studies have found that protocol discrepancies and outright "spin" are common in psychotherapy outcome research,[51] and that the effectiveness of some of these "evidence based" psychotherapies is overstated in the published literature.[52] Lamentably, the "evidence" used to promote the use of some specific forms of psychotherapy are all too often generated by someone or some organization that stands to profit from its use, whether it was or was not truly effective, with no acknowledgment that this is the case. Sadly, today, rather than being guided by altruism, community solidarity, and science, too often psychotherapy and mental healthcare in general are instead guided by the trifecta of prejudice, profit, and promotion.

CHEAPER BUT LESS EFFECTIVE SUBSTITUTIONS

When financial enrichment is prioritized over what actually helps patients, low-cost programs that may lack evidence of efficacy are promoted over more costly ones that might be more effective. For example, there has been an explosion in programs promoting "wellness," offered by employers or healthcare corporations, such as those to increase exercise or improve diet. While these initiatives are not necessarily bad, and in fact may help some, their main attraction is their minimal cost to insurers and corporations. "Wellness" interventions do not have to undergo any sort of testing for their effectiveness as do true medical "treatments." Again, the situation in mental health is particularly fraught, where just what constitutes "well" or "happy" is difficult to quantify. It is true that, when offered *in addition* to proven health interventions, many physical health and wellness programs that encourage good health practices such as those for weight loss, exercise, and diabetes management, make sense. But in mental health, where proven treatments such as medication and individual psychotherapy are difficult or impossible to access, these programs end up as substitutes for rather than adjuncts to proven and effective, but more costly, treatments.[53] A "stress management" group is not an adequate substitute for someone with bipolar disorder or someone trying to escape an abusive relationship. These wellness programs and online health offerings often just provide a fig leaf of legitimacy for insurers and care systems.

A 2010 Rand study found that the majority of employers with at least fifty employees in this country offered some sort of "wellness" program.[54] The sad truth is that many of these programs have been found not to work. Though some early studies suggest economic and some health benefits to physical wellness programs, a 2021 *Washington Post* analysis pointed out multiple problems in these studies, perhaps most important that they examined individuals who *chose* to work on improving their health,[55] and would likely have improved their health through other available means even if the program had not been offered. Two 2021 studies found that when looked at over the long run, these programs had *no* economic or health benefits.[56, 57] A huge 2024 study of over 46,000 workers found similar results: People were no better off after participating in one or more of ninety different corporate wellness interventions than colleagues who did not. In contrast, workers who were given the opportunity to do charity or volunteer work did experience improved well-being.[58, 59]

Healthcare corporations now offer a range of wellness programs, while failing to provide adequate one-on-one visits with a psychologist or psychiatrist, a common program being "mindfulness meditation." While many have found mindfulness helpful in their lives, particularly in dealing with day-to-day stress, others question the way it is now being recommended for virtually everything that ails you. Ronald Purser's 2019 book *McMindfulness: How Mindfulness Became the New Capitalist Spirituality* traces how what was a "countercultural, antiestablishment practice" was leveraged into a lucrative industry. Buddhist monks generally practice mindfulness within a tight community; it is not a solo endeavor. In contrast, mindfulness in the US is largely a do-it-yourself stand-alone technique, where happiness is a skill and not really contingent on your environment and community. The practice focuses on attaining personal gains and builds on the ideal of self-sufficiency over community cooperation.[60, 61] There is evidence that mindfulness, when pushed on large populations, can do harm. Two studies in 2022 found that school-based mindfulness training programs in adolescents resulted in worse scores on risk of depression and well-being. Moreover, higher "doses" of the intervention were associated with worse social and behavioral functioning.[62, 63, 64]

Mindfulness, at least as espoused in this country by adherents like Jon Kabat-Zinn, author of the wildly popular *Wherever You Go, There You Are: Mindfulness Meditation in Everyday Life*,[65] is steeped in value-neutrality; it is non-judgmental, apolitical, and non-religious. But it also avoids any self-examination or evaluation of external conditions that may be affecting thoughts and emotions, such as an abusive boss, that might warrant attention and change. This may be most starkly demonstrated by Purser when he examines the military's use of mindfulness training to prevent PTSD in soldiers.[66] Just how does this application of mindfulness fit with its Zen Buddhist roots if the goal is to make people better killing machines?

Overhype about these self-help practices has flourished and fostered a cottage industry, derisively known as "woo-woo wellness" and the "wellness-industrial complex."[67] These programs reinforce the uniquely American belief in the rugged individual above all else. They suggest that the individual can, against whatever adversity, improve themselves without the need of help from others. In this paradigm, seeking the collaboration of a psychotherapist becomes a sign of weakness.

Rina Raphael writes in her 2022 book, *The Gospel of Wellness: Gyms, Gurus, Goop, and the False Promise of Self-Care*,[68] that the very thing that was supposed to help us heal ourselves, such as meditating twice a day, becomes another obligation. Most of these wellness initiatives make health treatment an individual's responsibility, offloading healthcare companies' responsibility to provide care. HMOs like Kaiser do now offer an impressive array of more mainstream groups, for everything from smoking cessation to addressing anxiety and depression. While these groups can be helpful, if someone needs individual care, or can't be available at the group meeting time, they are out of luck, and may face a six-month wait for skimpy, inadequate individual care. Would it be acceptable to place someone with diabetes in a diabetes management group and have them wait six months before initiating insulin or an oral hypoglycemic agent, and then only provide them with enough to take it every other week? It is for reasons like this that patients protested and Kaiser mental health staff went on strike in 2022.

A strong community connection, which can be misinterpreted as a lack of rugged individualism, can be deemed as pathological by American psychotherapists when they treat people from different cultures. An individual from certain Asian or Latino cultures that prizes community and family solidarity may be perceived as too dependent on what others in these groups think of them. Their sense of self-worth may be determined to a large extent on external validation, whether they are seen as valued and honorable by those around them. In these cultures this external validation is prized, while in America this is seen as a weakness, suggesting a lack of character. Yet, in my experience, those who feel well-connected and well-respected in their community tend to be quite satisfied with their lives. To address this discrepancy, a field called "cross-cultural psychiatry" has developed to examine and rectify exactly this sort of professional misunderstanding of those from different cultures. Which, ultimately, is healthier for the individual and society, strong community ties or individual autonomy, and how are these values reflected in our healthcare? We'll examine this more in-depth in Chapter Seven.

Regrettably, given the poor support for psychotherapy in our society, even some psychotherapists have embraced and promoted "wellness" and other highly speculative interventions, most often highly remunerative ones. These pre-packaged programs ignore the fact that real wellness and happiness are ultimately a personal judgment. As the British author Edward St. Aubyn observes: ". . . the American citizen's famous entitlement to the 'pursuit of happiness' was in fact a guarantee of unhappiness, since a person can only pursue something that is missing. . . ."[69] Recent studies suggest that, in contrast to enhancing community connection and overall satisfaction, ". . . valuing happiness could be self-defeating because the more people value happiness, the more likely they will feel disappointed."[70]

These one-size-fits-all wellness fixes tend to miss the mark for many: what satisfies one may frustrate another and do actual harm and leave sufferers blaming themselves for not benefiting from the program. One person might need help in improving connections to others in their life after the death of a spouse, while another, juggling multiple family and job duties, might benefit from more solitude. These programs not only reinforce the idea of mental illness as a personal shortcoming, but they also divert attention from our responsibility as a society to provide a safe and cohesive community with opportunity for all, a community that provides the structures that encourage and support health, mental and physical, and importantly, good healthcare.

CHAPTER SEVEN

Why We Maintain This Crazy System

"Am I my brother's keeper?"—Cain's evasive
reply to God when asked the whereabouts of
his Brother Abel, who he had just slain.
—Moses 5:34, Genesis 4:9, Bible, King James Version

UNDERSTANDING OUR MOTIVATIONS

So why do we cling to our model? We know we can't expect the corporations managing our healthcare to treat us with compassion and charity when we are ill. It would violate fundamental business practices. As Joel Bakan points out in his book *The Corporation;* "The people who run corporations are, for the most part, good people, moral people . . . The money they manage and invest is not theirs. They can no sooner use it to heal the sick, save the environment, or feed the poor than they can to buy themselves villas in Tuscany." Further, deferring the management of our healthcare to

businesses ". . . immunizes them to the effects of citizens' participation in the political process and leaves their control to an arena where
one dollar—not one person—equals one vote."[1]

Most in the healthcare business mean well, but to succeed they are
forced to do things that harm us and our communities. To ensure continued economic vitality in their sector, Pharma and healthcare spent
$295 million on lobbying in 2019, money that could have been spent on
treating patients, inventing better drugs, or returned to those in the
community who paid. This is more than is spent on lobbying
by any other sector of our economy, and almost *twice* that of the
second-place electronics/technology sector.[2] During the pandemic,
Pharma launched major lobbying blitzes to protect high prices and
exclusivity of COVID vaccines and treatments,[3] and a successful
$26.5 million push in 2021 to block Medicare from being allowed
to bargain with drug companies over drug prices.[4] In 2022, legislation
was passed that allows for a phase-in of Medicare's right to negotiate
prices on a small number of generic medications, but even this is
now under intense attack through a number of lawsuits and vigorous
lobbying, and threats against legislators like: "We'll do whatever we
can to hold them accountable."[5] Also in 2021, after learning that the
Michigan Attorney General was investigating Eli Lilly and Novo
Nordisk for charging "grossly" excessive prices for three different
insulin products, practices that "have caused serious disability and
even death in some patients," the companies' response was a lobbying
assault totaling over $10 million.[6] Is this how successful companies
want to be spending their profits, lining the pockets of politicians and
gouging on drug prices? I doubt it. I suspect they'd rather be spending
it on developing new drugs and giving themselves bigger bonuses. But
they have to do what works in our profit-driven system. And work
it does. In 2023 alone, new drug prices in the US rose 35 percent.[7]

Added to this is a reciprocal complication. As healthcare costs have
soared, so too have employers' costs to provide healthcare coverage to
their workers, leading them to cut back on pension plans and other

retirement benefits. As benefits were cut, workers had to shift their money to 401Ks and similar plans, whose growth depends heavily on profits from healthcare corporations. Americans are anxious about their financial future, especially given the cost of healthcare, so legislation that might rein in healthcare corporation profits is blocked to protect retirement accounts, especially through an army of healthcare lobbyists and their political donations.

For example, antitrust rules are almost entirely ignored in health-care; consolidation and monopoly (at least at the local level) are widely accepted, and even embraced, in the name of efficiency. Hospital mergers evade the usual antitrust laws by applying for a loophole called a Certificate of Public Advantage (COPA). Under a COPA the hospital agrees to state oversight of their prices and quality, but in reality, as the FTC states: "COPAs can be difficult to implement and monitor over time, and are often unsuccessful in mitigating merger-related price and quality harms." And, as a 2024 study found, the FTC just doesn't have the resources to rein in the industry's hunger for consolidation.[8]

The amount of oversight it takes to hold hospital monopolies accountable is burdensome for state health departments, and the political pressure for states to remove regulations is strong. After a while, many states repeal their COPAs, leaving the hospital monopoly intact with no regulations in place.[9] Yet evidence shows that costs sky-rocket and quality goes down as healthcare corporations consolidate and increase market share, and control the clinicians delivering care. After hospital system MaineHealth acquired Southern Maine Medical Center under Maine's COPA system, when the COPA expired the FTC found that prices at Southern Maine Medical Center increased by 50 percent, while quality of care declined.[10] In 2024, the Justice Department launched an antitrust investigation into UnitedHealth, the largest health insurer in the country and owner of Optum, which manages prescriptions and a network of doctor groups, employing about one in ten doctors in the US.[11]

While the intentions behind turning to a for-profit business model may have been well-meaning, we have to look at the results. We encouraged the business takeover of American healthcare, legally, legislatively, and culturally. Unfortunately, American free-market capitalism, a model that resonates—at least in theory—with many of our uniquely American ideals, turned out not to be so good at caring for our bodies and minds. Why is it that we maintain our current system when every other developed country has moved on? What are the forces that make change so difficult for us? By unpacking what drove us to build and maintain our current healthcare model, we have the ability to craft real solutions.

AVOIDANCE AND FEAR

I always approach a first meeting with a new patient with interest and respect, but also caution. I never know how someone will react to discussing intimate issues, the worries that drove them to seek my help. They may respond with relief, sadness, or any number of emotions. Most often it is a combination. It is never bland. Delving into our deepest fears is not something we relish, and we do so only when we can ignore them no longer. Seeking healthcare has an uncomfortable association with vulnerability, pain, and death. As a patient you may be poked, prodded, probed, and asked embarrassing questions. You could be given bad news, sliced open, or given disagreeable medications. And even when our health is perfect, merely assuming the patient identity reminds us that this will not always be so. Most frightening is to seek mental healthcare, to worry that our mind could be misjudging things, or managing our world sub-optimally.

Unlike a client conducting a business transaction, becoming a patient can be a lot of work. Although a surgery might last a couple of hours and getting an antibiotic prescription may take only minutes, as a patient your recovery will likely take weeks—or much longer. Some illnesses are lifelong, and they change our world forever. Thinking of our health as a business transaction that ends neatly with payment allows us to avoid acknowledging our long-term vulnerability, and ultimate death. It enables us to hold the illusion that money can buy health and happiness, and that death and illness, especially mental illness, are for "others" less fortunate or less deserving. Most important, it conceals the fact that the work of being a patient, taking care of one's body and mind, is a fulfilling part of a well-lived life.

Nowhere in health is this obscuring of the consequences of our policies greater than in mental health. Stigma in mental illness is real, and leads to discomfort and discrimination. People are particularly troubled by the mentally ill because their symptoms and behavior *are* disturbing. As D. J. Jaffe quotes from a 1961 federal task force, "Mental illness is different from physical illness in the one fundamental aspect that it tends to disturb and repel others rather than evoke their sympathy and desire to help . . . The reason the public does not react desirably is that the mentally ill lack appeal. They eventually become a nuisance to other people and are generally treated as such. This is what causes the public aversion. People will never tolerate bizarre, violent, psychotic behavior. Never have. Never will."[12]

Humans (and animals) show empathy to members of their own group, but not to those they view as outside of their community. Those viewed as "other," especially those who cannot, as the philosopher Michel Foucault put it, "get a grip on their inner lives," are not afforded the same concern as those we can more readily identify with. Behavioral economists actually make a distinction between what they call a "statistical life" as opposed to an "identified life." As the quote, attributed to Joseph Stalin, bluntly puts it, "The death of one man is a tragedy. The death of millions is a statistic." The amount we are willing to give to a charitable organization so that it may save a child's life on the other side of the world as compared to how much we are willing to spend to save our own child's life is, literally, worlds apart. We have empathy for those we identify with, less for those we don't, like the seriously

mentally ill (SMI). In fact, only a paltry *1.3 percent* of philanthropic
giving in our society goes toward mental health, reflecting our avoidance and lack of empathy for the mentally ill.[13] The personal narratives
that would humanize them are rarely told. They are de-identified in our
society, faceless, segregated to the streets, encampments, or prison. We
don't imagine that we or a loved one could be struck down by mental
illness, despite statistics that firmly say otherwise. Framing decisions
in economic terms makes it easier for us to avoid these uncomfortable
realities, to assuage our lack of empathy for their suffering. Excluding
someone from care because they cannot afford it, or can't sustain
employment, or can't cooperate with that care, is more palatable to most
of us than admitting we won't help them because their illness disturbs
us. That would feel barbarous and cruel.

The stigma attached to mental illness often leads people to downplay
the seriousness of mental illness, and to fail to advocate adequately
for themselves or ill loved ones. I vividly recall being called to the ER
in the middle of the night to see a frightened family with the concern
that their father was "nervous." Further probing revealed that "nervous" meant that he had boarded up the windows in their house to
keep poison gases out, smashed their five gallon glass water dispenser,
believing it was poisoned, and the previous night had climbed onto the
roof, naked, in a rainstorm with a machete to hack down the telephone
and power lines to their house. Fortunately he was not electrocuted.
Their shame made them delay seeking help, and then to minimize the
severity of his illness when they eventually sought help.

Stigma and prejudice against mental illness extends beyond the
individual, to others associated with them. It acts as essentially guilt
by association. There is even a term for this: "courtesy stigma," where
"public disapproval (is) evoked as a consequence of associating with
stigmatized persons."[14] From *The Cabinet of Dr. Caligari* to *Silence of
the Lambs* to *What about Bob?*, movies, TV shows, and literature are
littered with portrayals of inept or malignant psychiatrists and psychotherapists, with only rare exceptions. As psychiatrist and Director of

the Program in Ethics in Science & Medicine at University of Texas John Sadler succinctly described in 2005:

> Any discipline that would dare to address, in the aggregate, the politically oppressed, the socially marginal, the sexually deviant, the worried well, the intimately abused, the morally dubious, the unpredictably irrational, and the emotionally labile must be controversial. Psychiatry, by the nature of its subject matter, is destined to be esteemed and loathed, scrutinized and dismissed, overlooked and debated. Psychiatry accepts many of the messy truths that almost everyone else would like to ignore or deny.[15]

Andrew Scull, a sociologist at University of California San Diego who studies the history of medicine puts it thus: "Mental illness haunts us, frightens us . . . Ironically, the stigma that surrounds those who exhibit a loss of reason has often extended to those who have claimed expertise in its identification and treatment. Of all the major branches of medicine, psychiatry, throughout its history, has been the least respected, not just by those to whom it ministers but also by physicians and the public at large."[16]

There is an interesting historical parallel to this aversion in the historical distinction between physicians and surgeons. Prior to the twentieth century surgeons were the disparaged cousins to physicians. Like psychiatry, surgery was messy and scary, associated with feared events like accidents, trauma, and war, and left people disfigured. But in reality, until a hundred years ago, physicians could offer little aside from reassurance and bloodletting, which did more harm than good, whereas surgeons could sometimes actually save lives and limbs. In a curious nod to history, my current California medical license accredits me as a "Physician and Surgeon."

Carl Jung observed, "Everything that irritates us about others can lead us to an understanding of ourselves." We cringe at the aberrant and sometimes abhorrent behavior of the mentally ill. Behind our reaction is the fear most of all that mental illness could afflict us, or a loved one. Denying the reality of mental illness, hiding behind business terminology and contracts, failing to fund and provide adequate treatment, all help us to avoid thinking about this possibility. Throughout history, societies have concealed or cast out the mentally ill. Keeping mental illness out of sight and out of mind is how societies have operated for centuries; the for-profit model of medicine has merely provided a cleaner and more efficient means to extrude people with a mental illness from society, banishing them to the hidden margins of our world, to prison, homeless encampments, or death. We don't even have to think about it. Our healthcare system does it for us.

A HARMFUL IDEAL—INDIVIDUALISM OR COMMUNITY

As Americans, we are steeped in the myth of the "rugged individual," a term coined by Herbert Hoover during the 1928 presidential campaign, when he said that it defined his political ideology.[17] Merriam-Webster defines rugged individualism as "the practice or advocacy of individualism in social and economic relations emphasizing personal liberty and independence, self-reliance, resourcefulness, self-direction of the individual, and free competition in enterprise."[18] President Truman later backed away from the myth, after the great market crash. As he pointed out, "Rugged individualists drove us to the brink of ruin in 1929 . . . The country brought to social and economic disaster, was promptly left to shift for itself while the rugged individualists hid under the bed."[19] Never dead, the myth has had a resurgence in recent decades, whipped up by Hollywood films, popular fiction, a pro-free-market business environment, and populist politicians.

Horatio Alger-esque ideals of upward financial mobility, self-sufficiency without need of collaboration with others, and rationality are in our blood, and now more popular than ever. A 2017 Pew Research poll found that 57 percent of Americans disagreed with the statement that "success in life is pretty much determined by forces outside our control," a higher percent than in any of the other (European) countries polled.[20] These beliefs are so ingrained that a 2018 TD Ameritrade survey found that even among millennials, the famously demoralized generation whose median wealth is lower than any other of the past thirty years, almost two-thirds believe they will be millionaires someday, and one in five believe they will get there before the age of forty.[21, 22]

But the myth has especially damaging consequences when applied to healthcare. In 2009, *New York Times* foreign editor Roger Cohen distilled the absurdity of using rugged individualism to guide our healthcare succinctly: "I can see the conservative argument that welfare undermines the work ethic and dampens moral fiber. But it's preposterous to extend this argument to healthcare. Guaranteeing health coverage doesn't incentivize anybody to get meningitis. Individualism is more 'rugged' when housed in a healthy body."[23]

The problem with idealizing individualism is that it becomes elevated over community benefit. Even clearly beneficial endeavors, like healthcare for all, get pushed aside. People strive to enrich themselves rather than work to make life better for everyone. Most of us would agree that it is good to be relatively self-sufficient, but working for individual gain to the exclusion of common good isolates us, and fosters a lack of trust and caring. Life can become, increasingly, a struggle for individual survival and advancement. Does moving from a seven- to an eight-figure investment portfolio enhance one's life more than say, an investment that betters one's community? And this sort of self-focused behavior leads others to behave similarly, in ways that are less likely to benefit us all.

Further, an over-focus on self-sufficiency leads us to avoid and even disparage the expertise of others. Authority is seen as suspect, bent on our subjugation. But the reality is that we can't be experts in everything. The world is a complicated place and we need trusted experts, like lawyers, car mechanics, appliance repairmen, teachers, and accountants. Life would indeed be difficult and lonely if we had to accomplish everything by ourselves. The English philosopher Thomas Hobbes famously postulated in 1651 what life might be like without a central government around which a community could coalesce: "No arts; no letters; no society; and which is worst of all, continual fear, and danger of violent death: and the life of man, solitary, poor, nasty, brutish and short."

Today we lionize wealthy entrepreneurs and underpay workers such as teachers and social workers toiling to improve the lot of the less fortunate in the community. As the reverend Dr. Martin Luther King Jr. pointed out in 1968, "This country has socialism for the rich, rugged individualism for the poor." This statement aptly describes our healthcare industry, where corporations benefit from government funding, like drug research and protective policies, like restricting Medicare's right to negotiate drug prices, while individual citizens are quite literally on their own.

Being ill, especially mentally ill, where self-sufficiency and rationality may be impaired and one may need the help of others, runs counter to our individualistic ideals. This creates cognitive dissonance, which we resolve by putting the possibility that mental illness could touch our lives out of our minds. We don't like to think about unpleasant health realities that don't immediately endanger us which leads us to defer hard decisions. We ignore the broader community effects of our priorities and policies, like failing to provide preventive healthcare or invest adequately in scientific research to prevent and cure diseases, rather than simply manage their symptoms, or put needed equipment and planning in place to manage a future pandemic. Individualistic thinking leads us to ask why we should pay to develop medicines to help others, if we ourselves don't need them, or at least don't need them yet. For example, among care-givers of children reported to child protective services who have mental health or substance use disorders and were covered by Medicaid, less than half received counseling or substance use medication.[24] Just what do we expect will happen to these kids, and how it will affect our world? The dismal provisions we make for the elderly are another example of our denial of illness and vulnerability, and how community cooperation has benefit. Many of our nursing homes are costly, overcrowded, dismal waiting-stations for death. Do we think we'll never get old and become more dependent on others? Our short-sighted mentality lets us ignore the suffering of the elderly, and instead focus on what huge money-makers nursing homes are for the companies that run them, and for the funds that invest in those companies.

These attitudes played out in dramatic fashion during the COVID pandemic. Wearing a mask is annoying, but has been shown unequivocally to lessen the spread of COVID, which can kill others in our community, especially the elderly. Yet rather than being viewed as a health and safety issue, mask wearing became a symbol of authoritarian intrusion into our rights as an individual. Asserting one's autonomy became more important than protecting the lives of others.

The anti-authoritarian ideas that undergird rugged individualism also played a role in our abandonment of care for the mentally ill back in the 1960s. After deinstitutionalization, the SMI were met not with care and empathy, but instead with the misguided platitudes of that era's "be yourself" antiestablishment attitudes, that period's version of the rugged individual. This, coinciding with then-popular psychoanalytic theory that held that we are all a little crazy, as well as equally fashionable sociological theories that denied the boundary between sanity and insanity, fostered further demonization of mental healthcare. Caring for mental illness was framed as establishment oppression. Our individualistic model made needing care a weakness. While the '60s counterculture movement included communes, an extreme expression of community cooperation, it was anti-authority and anti-technology, rejecting even beneficial advancements like medical care, which they saw, not entirely incorrectly, as too hierarchical and patriarchal, and a well-rounded education that establishment institutions could provide.

Echoing psychoanalytic ideas, many in the idealistic '60s felt that if society could be made less stressful, mental illness would fade, and if parenting and our childhood experience were optimized, mental illness would not develop at all. The 1966 art-house film hit *King of Hearts* depicted inmates of an asylum set free due to the insanity of the "normal" world's war, and behaving with greater wisdom and kindness than those in the "sane" outside world. The movie's ending scene shows the "sane" protagonist acting as if he is crazy so that he will be accepted into the insane asylum. Like some of the anti-psychiatry followers of Szasz and Laing, the extremely popular social psychologist Erving Goffman discussed in Chapter One argued not only that psychosis was a normal reaction to an insane society, but that those who suffered from psychosis might have special insights into life, just as those who took hallucinogenic drugs felt they derived a deeper understanding of life. This stance was exemplified by the gonzo (a postmodern style of writing without claims of objectivity) journalist Hunter S. Thompson, a prominent chronicler of the '60s who famously said, "I hate to advocate drugs, alcohol, violence or insanity to anyone, but they've always worked for me." Attacks on the legitimacy of mental illness and its treatment were everywhere in the '60s and '70s, bolstered by the bogus Rosenhan "study" discussed in Chapter One.

The leaders of the anti-psychiatry movement did not fare well. Szasz, his recently divorced wife, and Thompson ended up taking their own lives. Laing abandoned his public claims that mental illness was a myth after his daughter developed schizophrenia, and later in life became increasingly bizarre, developing "rebirthing workshops" where participants would re-enact their struggle to break out of the womb. Goffman abandoned the derisive quotation marks he placed around "mental illness" after his wife, Angelica, died by suicide in 1964.[25] But their destructive legacy lives on. Their "myth" kills at least 300,000 Americans a year, takes years off our lifespan, and, as we saw earlier, makes those with the "myth" sixteen times more likely to be killed in a police encounter. Yet the anti-psychiatry tropes of the 1960s and 1970s that fostered the abandonment of the mentally ill persist.

A psychiatrist friend who sat on the ACLU's national board recalls a debate he witnessed in the 1970s. Bruce J. Ennis, then legal director of the ACLU, who was deeply wary of state intrusion into mental health treatment, was arguing stridently that the organization should endorse the legal position that civil commitment of the mentally ill was unconstitutional. The debate seemed to be going Ennis's way until a woman, one of the organization's state representatives, stood up and said, "If not for the state hospitals I would not be alive today." Yet today the ACLU is still fighting laws that could bring the most ill members of our society into treatment.

WHY WE RESIST CHANGE

Bill, whom I've seen for several years, is doing relatively well now. His panic disorder is under control and his panic attacks are now relatively mild and rare. Still, he lives in fear of an exacerbation of his illness, which in the past rendered him homebound. He is working at a job well below what he is capable of in terms of responsibility, challenge, and income. I see him only once a month now, his medication is stable, and he has learned techniques to manage his anxiety. I charge him only a little over what his insurance will reimburse him, less than half my standard rate. Still, despite my reassurances, he feels uncomfortable with the arrangement and worries what will happen if he has to move, or his insurance changes, or he loses it altogether. So he doesn't look for a better job or think about moving. It's not worth the risk to him. What if he were to lose his insurance? What if another job provided worse benefits, or required him to sign up with a (HMO) plan which would not reimburse him for my care? Bill is not willing to take that chance. So he sticks with his lousy but stable job.

Most of us are not so different from Bill. In fact, my practice is populated with many patients who have insurance through Kaiser, our local HMO giant. Kaiser is supposed to offer psychiatric care, but in reality patients will wait many months for even a brief meeting, and follow-up appointments will likely be yearly, or even less frequent. So these patients come to me, paying out of pocket for care. Yet they keep their Kaiser coverage for non-psychiatric care. One-half of our population obtains health insurance through employer-sponsored programs,[26] and we're loathe to give up what we have, especially without rock-solid alternatives. We hear of healthcare horror stories, like people entering bankruptcy due to healthcare debt, losing their home, or forgoing lifesaving care, so we cling to the meager coverage we have.

This self-protective feeling extends to our healthcare system overall. We tolerate a dysfunctional system because as humans we are "risk averse," and most often prefer hanging on to what we have—no matter how unsatisfactory it is—rather than take a chance on something new. Better the devil we know than one we don't, especially if alternatives like a national healthcare system are disparaged with inflammatory and inaccurate attacks by current healthcare players, on whom we depend, like the insurance and pharmacy companies, and the AMA. And paradoxically, the worse our situation is, the less likely we are to risk change. As Paul Starr points out, "Rising health costs and other problems with healthcare do not necessarily lead members of the protected public to accept the need for change: on the contrary, they may cling to the protections they have all the more tightly and insist that they not be taxed to pay for anyone else."[27] We may not like or trust our system, but we don't want to be left out in the cold.

Although we are afraid of letting go of what little safety net our current healthcare offers, most of us are uncomfortable with the current healthcare priorities. Look at where consumers place their trust. As an industry, health insurance companies rank at the bottom of forty-three industries ranked by the American Customer Satisfaction Index, ahead only of the much reviled Internet Service Providers (ISPs) and the Pay TV industry.[28] A recent KFF study found that Americans feel less favorably toward health insurers than even the widely disliked banking and airline companies, and rate the industry above only drug (another healthcare profiteer) and oil companies.[29] Interestingly, surveys also show that while people distrust the healthcare system in general, they do trust their personal caregivers. The fields of nursing and medicine rank number one (80 percent) and two (65 percent), respectively, compared to other professions in ratings of honesty and ethical standards, with positive ratings three to four *times* that of professions such as banking (23 percent) and businessmen (17 percent).[30] Yet these latter professions now make vital healthcare decisions for us.

Our healthcare system's abandonment of both individual and community benefit in the service of profits has cost it a devastating loss of trust. Public health measures, which have played such a huge part in objectively measured improvements in health over the last century, are based on community solidarity and trust. This lack of trust played out in our acrimonious COVID vaccine divisions. Science has clearly shown that getting vaccinated against COVID is overwhelmingly likely to benefit the person, their loved ones, and society. While it's true that many are too young to remember polio, measles, or smallpox, or the pre-antibiotic era, it's extremely rare today to find someone whose own life or that of a loved one has not been profoundly helped by modern medical care and public health measures. Why then are some so hesitant? I think it comes down to a lack of trust, not a lack of information.

In September of 2021, a report by The Covid States, a non-partisan study group, found that while 71 percent of vaccinated individuals had "a lot" of trust in hospitals and doctors to handle the coronavirus outbreak, only 39 percent of the unvaccinated did.[31] As consumer groups have charged, they know vaccine makers are reaping huge profits on vaccines developed with *their* tax dollars, hiding the technology behind patents to boost prices.[32] They know these companies prioritize profits over their health. Why would they trust vaccine mandates from politicians who rake in millions of dollars from healthcare lobbyists? It was discovered in 2022 that Eric Lander, the head of the Office of Science and Technology Policy that publicly promoted COVID-19 vaccination efforts, held between $500,000 and $1 million of stock in BioNTech SE, Pfizer's COVID-19 vaccine partner. Further, he held the stock for sixty-nine days after his confirmation, until it shot up more than $50 a share from two days prior.[33] Meanwhile, Pfizer's revenue rose to a record $100 billion that year, in large part on the basis of vaccine sales.[34]

That same year, 2022, shareholders of three of the world's biggest COVID vaccine makers, Pfizer, Johnson & Johnson, and Moderna, voted not to share their technology, technology that could save many thousands of lives in the US and poorer countries, lest it cut into their profits.[35] By deferring our health policies to profit-seeking investors or someone with no healthcare training and a seven-figure income to maintain, untethered from humanitarian motives and medical ethics, trust has been lost. A 2021 Department of Health and Human Services study found that strong vaccine hesitancy was significantly more common among those without health insurance, and increased over time during the pandemic.[36] No doubt feeling abandoned, people recognize that our government has abdicated its protective role and put corporate profit above its citizen's safety. When trust is broken, facts and statistics don't matter. Once trust is betrayed, it is hard to reclaim. Like my patient Bill we don't want to rock the boat to risk losing what modicum of healthcare we have.

WHO PROFITS FROM A BROKEN SYSTEM?

"It is difficult to get a man to understand
something, when his salary depends
upon his not understanding it."
—Upton Sinclair

Wednesdays were always a staff favorite at the busy downtown outpatient clinic where I worked in the early 2000s. They meant free lunch, always sumptuous, catered by a rotating cast of pharmaceutical representatives (reps). These lunches were a respite from the brutal clinical load, the tragic cases seen, a rare opportunity for the staff to feel appreciated and cared for. The reps were friendly, personable. They brought in small gifts, notepads, and pens. They became friends, like allies in a storm. But they also knew that with seven almost identical SSRI antidepressants and fourteen second generation antipsychotics (all with roughly equal efficacy) to choose from, the personal attention might sway which drugs the clinic would use. Especially since they knew a competitor would be providing lunch the next week. The reps were captives of the system too. To NOT provide lunch would be professional suicide. Patients, those who paid for the lunch through the price of their drug purchases, were not invited. As Senator Elizabeth Warren put it: If you don't have a seat at the table, you are probably on the menu.

It is important to appreciate that when viewed from the perspective of an employee, corporation, or investor in the healthcare system, wasteful medical spending is not a problem. In fact, it is the goal, since it means more income. Twenty-two million Americans—14 percent of our entire workforce—are now employed in the healthcare industry. While "healthcare workers" brings to mind doctors and nurses for most of us, this is not the case. Pharma reps are merely one other example. The *majority* of "healthcare workers" serve purely administrative functions, supporting the business side of healthcare rather than working to make people healthier.[37] Of the 9.8 million who are actually involved in healthcare delivery, a significant portion of their time is now spent on administrative tasks. Many within healthcare are trying to dismantle the money monster, but they face fierce resistance. Examples include advocacy organizations like Healthcare-NOW, physician organizations like Physicians for a National Health Program, and nursing organizations like the California Nurses Association (CNA). The CNA was a major force behind California's 2022 Single Payer legislation, AB 1400. Ultimately AB 1400 was defeated, but only after a furious lobbying campaign by healthcare interests, which unfortunately included the California Medical Association. AB 1400's fate may have been sealed by the fact that the vast majority of California physicians now work for healthcare corporations, like Kaiser and Sutter, rather than run their own practices. Kaiser and Sutter, who fear being squeezed out by single-payer plan, pay their physician employees' CMA dues. The threat that they might withdraw this financial support should the CMA support AB 1400 no doubt loomed large in the CMA's decision to oppose AB 1400, even as the physician members of the CMA were not included in this decision.

Moral licensing is a psychological term describing the process by which we excuse our bad behavior by justifying it with other good behavior. To this end, I've heard healthcare administrators justify decisions that clearly harm the mission of helping patients by arguing that no care would exist without the institution, so its health comes first. This view might hold some validity if our healthcare corporations' primary goal was improving patients' health, but it is not. Their primary goal is profit, hijacking the mission of healthcare and those working in it. As the institution's survival becomes primary, individuals' position in the hierarchy also takes on added importance, since their professional survival depends on how and where they fit into the organization, pushing patient needs even further down the list of priorities.

Putting a price on important issues like our lives and our health irreversibly changes how we view them. We are more likely to violate ethical norms if a situation is framed in economic rather than human terms. Deferring decisions to businesses is comforting since it allows us to distance ourselves from the ethical consequences of these decisions. We're happy to get a bargain on our clothing or our iPhone if we focus on price rather than the social cost of child labor in Asia. When we buy a product or service, we leave it to the provider (that word again!) to worry about how they acquire or produce it, essentially outsourcing our ethical dilemmas. Similarly, when we receive healthcare, we don't ask about who isn't getting care, and why they aren't. We ignore even those living near us, especially those on the streets or in jail.

These sorts of moral dilemmas and societal damage caused by handing our healthcare over to businesses were in fact predicted. At the beginning of the last century, courts in several states ruled that ". . . corporations could not engage in the commercial practice of medicine, even if they employed licensed physicians on the grounds that a corporation could not be licensed to practice medicine, and that commercialism in medicine violated 'sound public policy.'" These rulings applied to *all* corporations as the possibility that a business interest might be allowed to influence something as important as healthcare delivery was abhorrent. [38]

States now all have Corporate Practice of Medicine (CPOM) rules. [39] Most permit the formation and licensure of business corporations established as professional service corporations (but not a non-profit corporation) to practice medicine only if controlled by physicians but many vary in the exceptions they allow. Most forbid profit-seeking entities from controlling or interfering with a physician's clinical duties to put patients' interests first but healthcare companies today evade these rules in a number of ways. Many call themselves nonprofit, which often means only that they don't sell shares and instead rely on other forms of funding such as venture capital (VC) or private equity (PE) (often hidden behind shell companies).

Some PE firms conceal their ownership by claiming to only provide administrative support or hiding behind a sham physician figurehead known as a "straw doctor," who may have no say in the company's policies. [40, 41] Gretchen Morgenson and Joshua Rosner relate the example of Gregory J. Byrne in their book on PE, *These Are the Plunderers*. Byrne, an emergency physician from Houston, "owned" as many as three hundred medical practices for Envision HealthCare, a "staffing company" famous for their surprise billing schemes, which in turn is owned by the giant PE firm KKR. Sadly, they quote from a judge opining on a 1931 case: "There are certain fields of occupation which are universally recognized as 'learned professions.' The law recognizes them as a part of the public weal, and protects them against debasement, and encourages the maintenance therein of high standards of education, of ethics, and of ideals. A corporation, as such, has neither education nor skill nor ethics." [42, 43]

Physicians working for these corporations (three-quarters of physicians in this country are now salaried employees and half of all physician practices are owned by a hospital or corporate entity now) often sign strict noncompete and non-disclosure agreements and legislators by and large ignore CPOM rules, even granting corporations waivers, bowing to the tremendous lobbying clout of these companies.

How do we weigh the goal of community good against the goal of profit in an economically driven model? Seven of the ten most profitable hospitals in the US are classified as private and not-for-profit, which exempts them from federal as well as sales and property taxes. Nonprofit used to mean caring for the indigent, but no longer. Now it means that they are supposed to provide some vaguely determined "community benefit." But many give little back to their community, and their tax benefits vastly outweigh any advantage they provide to the community. [44, 45] In 2021 a Lown Institute study found that 72 percent of private nonprofit hospitals spent less on charity care and community investment than they received in tax breaks, [46] an assessment echoed by the *Wall Street Journal* in 2022. [47] Some have even taken to suing patients who are unable to pay their bills, the very people they formerly served, going so far as to garnish their wages and seize their homes.

One egregious example was outlined in a 2022 *New York Times* investigation. It found that Providence, one of the country's largest chain of nonprofit hospitals, was systematically shaking down impoverished patients as part of its "Rev-Up" program, which was created with the help of the consulting firm McKinsey & Company to increase revenue. Founded by nuns in the 1850s, Providence states its mission is to be "steadfast in serving all, especially those who are poor and vulnerable." In 2021, Providence's spending on charity care was less than 1 percent of its expenses, yet its revenue exceeded $27 billion that year. Washington state attorney general Bob Ferguson has accused Providence of violating state law, in part by using debt collectors to pursue more than 55,000 patient accounts, patients who, under state and federal law, were entitled to free care under Medicaid. [48] After the exposé and lawsuit, Providence agreed to refund any payments made. In another flagrant example, University of Virginia Health, part of the public university of the same name founded by Thomas Jefferson in 1819, over a six-year period ending in 2018 filed 36,000 lawsuits against patients for amounts ranging from $13 to $1 million.[49]

In order to succeed in this cutthroat business environment even Ascension, the Catholic tax-exempt nonprofit giant that runs more than 140 hospitals, recently partnered with the private equity firm TowerBrook Capital Partners. The partnership's first investment was in R1 RCM, a debt collection and billing company accused of "illegally trying to collect money from patients, including while they were still in the emergency room."[50] In the last fifty years, healthcare charities have gone from taking care of the indigent to taking their homes. When the financial health of the organization is more important than the health of patients, the concept of charity becomes laughable.

Perhaps the purest distillation of profit over people's health was the largest IPO of 2020, Royalty Pharma, a company that invests in the rights to future drug sales. But this "pharmaceutical" company doesn't actually develop any drugs, it only buys stakes in third-party medicines, jacking up prices to get their cut of the profits.[51, 52] But the height of absurdity may be Philip Morris, the tobacco giant responsible for millions of premature deaths that still sells its cigarettes in more than 180 countries, investing billions in its new healthcare company, Vectura Fertin Pharma, hoping to leverage their expertise in "inhalation technology."[53] We now have venture capitalists and corporations who don't actually do anything to improve health, and even worsen it, making obscene profits on healthcare, and "charities" who merge with these profiteers to survive, all while many Americans can't afford decent healthcare.

With profit as the goal of healthcare corporations and venture capitalists, the industry has moved past its 1973 charge of reducing costs, to harming patients in the service of profit. I don't believe this was an intended goal of the HMO act, but over the past fifty years we've seen a steady progression in that direction. From healthcare's humble not-for-profit beginnings, as discussed in earlier chapters, CEOs of healthcare corporations now commonly earn seven-figure salaries. Today, you don't even have to work in healthcare to profit from it, you just have to be a wealthy investor. PE and VC investments in healthcare make up almost 30 percent of *all* venture capital—derisively known as "vulture capital"—funding in our country, and totals $23 billion.[54] From 1990 to 2015, "healthcare has led all sectors in total returns to shareholders" according to McKinsey, exceeding even the famously lucrative IT sector.[55] Studies show that these PE firms buy up medical and dental practices and facilities, especially mental health facilities, creating local monopolies and jacking up prices. The profits however are all for investors and are not shared with doctors or other workers.[56, 57] A 2024 study shows just how voracious PE has been in buying up specialty physician practices, with PE ownership increasing from 816 practices in 119 metropolitan areas in 2012, to 5,779 in 307 metropolitan areas in 2021. PE also tries to sew up monopolies in regions, with single PE firms exceeding 30 percent ownership in over a third of the metropolitan areas examined, and in many it was over 50 percent.[58] And these local monopolies have had direct consequences for patient care, not for the better.

Even more outrageous, by making mental healthcare so difficult to obtain, and therefore so profitable, mental healthcare companies and facilities have become the darling of rich investors, investors interested in making money, not improving health. PE investment in mental health is soaring and in 2016 accounted for 60 percent of all sales in behavioral healthcare.[59] PE investment—sometimes referred to as "pirate equity"—focuses on outsized returns over short time horizons (generally five to seven years) and thus plays an aggressive role in the governance of their portfolio companies and charges higher management fees than traditional mutual funds. This means that healthcare companies they acquire are "on the clock" from day one to improve financial results to make the company attractive to a new buyer. To achieve the steep and fast returns these private-equity-run healthcare companies are after, they are heavily leveraged with debt. This makes them vulnerable to downturns in the economy, interest rate increases, and stressors like the COVID pandemic and clinician shortages. The leading credit rating agency Moody's released its December 2020 Investors Service Report which called 90 percent of PE-owned healthcare companies "under financial stress" and 88 percent of healthcare companies that they rated B3 negative (high risk) or below were PE-owned.[60] It looks like we're headed for a subprime mortgage-like meltdown of these companies. The question is: Will we bail them out or rebuild a more sustainable future?

The big losers, of course, are the patients, their families, and the American taxpayer. In other words, us. The *Wall Street Journal* quoted one critic who points out, "What's good for shareholders is bad for patients,"[61] and a 2020 Bloomberg article entitled "How Private Equity is Ruining American Healthcare" quoted one dermatologist working for a PE-owned healthcare chain as saying, "You can't serve two masters. You can't serve patients and investors."[62] A 2021 study showed that PE investment in nursing homes both worsened the quality of care and increased costs,[63] and a 2022 study found that when PE firms acquired physician specialty practices the average price charged per appointment went up $71 (20.2 percent), with $48 of this being out of pocket for the patient.[64] Among hospitals, those acquired by private equity have more adverse events, such as in-hospital falls and hospital-acquired infections,[65] and that overall costs rise and quality falls when healthcare providers are acquired by PE.[66] More than one-half of physicians' practices that are acquired by PE firms are re-sold within three years, and of these, 98 percent are sold to another PE firm.[67] It's hard to imagine any commitment to long-term patient care in this slash and dump model.

Perhaps most disturbing, a 2022 report by the Private Equity Stakeholder Project found, "Private equity firms are increasingly investing in behavioral services for children and adolescents." Moreover, "Cost-cutting tactics at private-equity-owned youth behavioral companies, such as cutting staff, relying on unlicensed staff, and failing to maintain facilities, can lead to abuse, neglect, and unsafe living conditions for youth." Just one example they cite is the PE company Bain Capital, which acquired an outfit called CRC Health Group (a company that runs youth treatment programs) and its subsidiary, Aspen Education Group, that catered to the "troubled teen" industry (TTI). Under Bain the companies almost doubled their revenue, and paid Bain $22.6 million in fees. Bain sold CRC in 2015 for almost $1.2 billion, double its purchase price. While Bain and its investors made out like bandits, the teens did not fare so well. An investigation by Oregon's Department of Human Services found that students were subjected to abusive treatment, including sleep deprivation, strenuous work projects, and sexualized role-play. Multiple lawsuits were settled out of court and regulatory actions shut many of their facilities, but not before their exorbitant profits were harvested.[68]

With such huge profits at stake, healthcare companies are not about to accept restrictions or oversight without a fight. And fight they do, with huge budgets for lobbying and political donations. As we learned at the beginning of this chapter, the healthcare industry spends more on lobbying than *any* other sector of our economy. They are not shy about political donations either. Pharmaceutical companies and their lobbying groups gave roughly $1.6 million to lawmakers during the first six months of 2021 in an effort to block legislation that would allow Medicare to negotiate drug prices.[69] As we just saw, healthcare is the largest and most lucrative investment category for the financial industry, which is far and away the largest source of campaign contributions to federal candidates and parties.[70] Thus, the healthcare industry wields an outsized influence on politics and policy in this country, and is a major force fighting change. The industry spends a lot on messaging the public too. For example, the pharmaceutical industry alone spent more than $5.5 billion on advertising in the first half of 2022 alone.[71] Thus, any efforts at challenging the healthcare industry's profits and influence meet considerable political headwinds, as occurred with California's AB 1400.

So many profit from our system, and continue to devise new ways to extract wealth from the suffering of others, that attempts to prioritize health and well-being under our current model will always be a game of whack-a-mole. It's a fundamental principle of business to "charge what the market will bear," which is how we ended up with $600 EpiPens, the relatively cheap to produce injectors that can save the life of a child having an allergic reaction. As Martin Shkreli, the CEO of Turing Pharmaceuticals, said after boosting the price of the fifty-year-old medication Daraprim 5,000 percent overnight: "No one wants to say it, no one's proud of it, . . . But this is a capitalist society, a capitalist system and capitalist rules." In fact, as Nirmal Mulye, founder and president of Nostrum Pharmaceuticals, explained after raising the price of the seventy-year-old antibiotic nitrofurantoin more than four-fold, he had a "moral requirement to sell the product at the highest price." [72] Big Pharma and the Sakler family, who made billions pushing opiates, are just successful capitalists, their profits bolstered by effective pricing and marketing—legitimate business tools. Entrepreneurs like Elizabeth Holmes, cofounder and CEO of Theranos, the now-defunct medical testing company that misrepresented the technology it sold, Martin Shkreli, and the Saklers only faced prosecution when their business practices became noteworthy. In 2021, Holmes was found guilty of defrauding investors [73] and Shkreli was ordered to repay the $64.8 million in profits he gained by violating antitrust laws. But while these settlements forced re-compensation to investors, in neither case was harm to patients addressed. Laughably, if it weren't so tragic, in that same year, "A jury . . . found that an opioid manufacturer [Teva] and distributor contributed to the deadly opioid crisis in New York, inundating the state with prescription painkillers that led to thousands of deaths. . . ." The company was found guilty of perpetuating a "public nuisance." [74]

Why is this, one may wonder, when there exists a legal precedent for handling irresponsible corporate officers? The Responsible Corporate Officer Doctrine, also known as the Park Doctrine (1975), which has legal roots going back to 1943, imposes criminal liability upon responsible corporate officers for violating FDCA (Food Drug and Cosmetic Act) rules. In other words, corporate officers can be held legally liable for "prohibited acts." The aim of the doctrine is specifically to protect patients from the harms of an unsafe or fraudulent medical marketplace by targeting the executives who run the companies that make revenues on these products while violating federal law. Yet the US Department of Justice (DOJ), which handles these prosecutions, uses the doctrine extremely rarely, on average only about once every two years. A 2022 JAMA Internal Medicine study concluded that "the government has not exercised the full scope of its authority to prosecute corporate officials responsible for the illegal behavior of the drug and device companies they run."[75]

Why our government looks the other way is an important question, and no doubt relates to the fact that the healthcare industry is the single largest source of lobbying funds given to elected officials of any industry in the country. Remember that the opiate crisis was FDA and DEA sanctioned; the Saklers operated in accordance with our system's incentives. They just overreached, so they paid a voluntary fine and filed for bankruptcy. Lamentably, focusing on these few individuals and companies who were caught actually bolsters the bona fides of the system, allowing it to say that cheaters are indeed brought to justice. Those who profit are happy to throw a few scapegoats under the bus if it means they can continue to treat people like commodities, especially if the scapegoats are particularly unsympathetic, like "Pharma bro" Martin Shkreli, or worse, a woman who dares to act like a man and perpetrated clear deceptions, like Elizabeth Holmes. These individuals who made headlines did only minimal damage. They were spare change in the $4 trillion corporate and venture capital boondoggle that we call healthcare.

Dramatic as these stories are, what is hurting us far more is the everyday damage done by the economic model, a zero-sum paradigm where more for you means less for me, and vice versa, where getting care means taking somebody else's slot. It turns ordinary people, not just the healthcare industry, into merchants of death. Scarcity is fundamental to capitalism, as Shkreli well knew, since it drives up demand and prices. But supply and demand economics does not distinguish between what might be wanted, like a new iPhone, and what is needed, like a new kidney. Economic forces enrich some, while causing pain and death to others. Were the shareholders of the COVID vaccine makers discussed in the last section evil, were they closet Shkrelis? I doubt it. They were just regular people wanting to protect and grow their investment. Yet in voting to refuse to share vaccine technology, votes that protected their economic interests, they were sentencing thousands—perhaps hundreds of thousands—of people to death in poorer countries, and maybe even others in their own community.

The American model of medical care allows the average American to remain smugly indifferent in the face of homelessness, incarceration, and death. People just don't connect the dots, they just don't realize that the profits made by the investment fund generating the money to pay for their child's fancy college were made by the fund closing the hospital that might save their child's life when she inadvertently overdoses at a dorm party. And allowing our system to throw mental healthcare under the bus is hopelessly foolish. Its appetite for profit does not stop at squeezing out the mentally ill; care shortages are appearing throughout medicine. Wait times to get in to see all physicians increased 24 percent from 2004 to 2022, and if you've tried to get care in the last year or two I'm sure you'll agree that the situation has only worsened. [76] Treating health like a business lets us believe and act like illness and death, and most especially mental illness, only affects others, and will never touch us. Nothing could be further from the truth.

CHAPTER EIGHT

Reform 101: How We Can Fix Our Healthcare Mess

*"Wealth is the slave of a wise
man, the master of a fool."*
—Seneca, c. 50 C.E.

LET'S JOIN THE DEVELOPED WORLD
MODELS FROM OTHER COUNTRIES

Let's back up and look at American healthcare in general. A few years ago a good friend of mine developed renal cell carcinoma (cancer of the kidneys). Fortunately, this cancer is relatively treatable if caught early, and recurs in only a minority of cases. His tumor was removed and medically it seemed that he had dodged a bullet. He felt fortunate in knowing he had good insurance and that health insurers are not permitted to cancel policies just because the insured gets sick. But soon his premiums began going up, and up, and up, until they became prohibitive. His insurer did not allow him to switch plans, saying he was not eligible. True, his health insurance was not cancelled, but he was effectively forced out by his insurer; they did not want someone with his potential medical and economic liability to be their responsibility. He did not dodge the financial bullet. No other affluent country in the world allows this to happen.

Our healthcare system has not always been such a malfunctioning outlier. In 1973 Americans spent an average of $2,746 (inflation adjusted to 2020 dollars) yearly on their healthcare, which made up 7.3 percent of the GDP. These figures were in the same ballpark as those of other developed nations for what many considered the best medical system in the world. Then we brought in corporations to manage our healthcare. We even helped finance these companies with federal money. Now, a half century later, US healthcare costs have increased by five-fold to $12,535 per person, and consume 19.7 percent of our GDP.[1] Healthcare costs now contribute to two out of three citizens' bankruptcies, and overdose deaths have increased seven-fold.[2] Our life expectancy has fallen behind other comparable countries such that we now live, on average, five years less than our foreign neighbors. The HMO act and the financial takeover that it encouraged took an archaic and flawed model, abandoned by all other developed nations, and put it on steroids.

The US is the only developed nation that lacks a national healthcare system to cover at least the basic healthcare needs of its citizens. It alone allows companies and investors to determine who will get care, how much that care will cost, and who won't get care at all. By erecting barriers to caring for those who might drain their profits, like my friend, these companies effectively decide who will live and who will die. Our profit-driven healthcare experiment simply has not worked, except to enrich some. As we've seen, at a fundamental level, the dynamics of a free market don't fit healthcare. Pretending health and its care is a free market not needing oversight has only encouraged corporate and investor opportunism.

Over the past seventy-five years, all other countries with stable economies and political systems on the planet decided that the lives and health of their citizens were worth caring for. One outlier is Germany, which with typical Germanic efficiency instituted national health insurance under Otto Von Bismarck over a century ago. Despite the complaints we hear, usually spread by those who profit from our healthcare system, the reality is that citizens in countries with national healthcare systems all say they are more satisfied than citizens in the US.[3] Their care is delivered at a fraction of the cost of our care. A 2022 Commonwealth Fund study found that only one-quarter of US women of reproductive age gave a high rating our healthcare system, as compared to 58 to 84 percent in other countries,[4] and in 2023 Gallup found that only 35 percent of Americans had a positive view of our healthcare system, while 49 percent viewed it negatively.[5] According to a 2019 Gallup poll, 70 percent feel US healthcare has major problems or is in a state of crisis.[6] In 2023 Gallup found that a majority of Americans rated the US healthcare system as fair or poor,[7] and a clear majority feel the government is responsible for ensuring all have health insurance.[8] A steadily increasing majority (63 percent) of Americans favor a government-run single-payer healthcare model for the country.[9] In a 2020 *Washington Post* essay, Wendell Potter described how in his role as a health insurance executive he systematically "misled people to protect profits," functioning as a self-described "corporate propagandist." He strived to make foreign healthcare systems look "just as bad as ours." Looking back, he now says, "I live with that horror, and my role in it, every day."[10]

The US actually came close to adopting national healthcare after World War II under President Harry S. Truman. Like many Americans, Truman believed that healthcare is a human right. His plan was ultimately shot down, in large part due to the AMA assault on it as "Communist." In fact, it was the AMA that coined the attack term "socialized medicine" that is still widely (and inaccurately) employed to fight universal healthcare.[11] President Bill Clinton made an attempt at national healthcare in 1993, a core pledge of his presidential campaign. His plan fell victim to the devastating "Harry and Louise" television ads which depicted a couple of middle-aged Americans fretting over the bureaucratic complexities of healthcare reform, and urged watchers to call their congressional representatives. The campaign was primarily funded by the Health Insurance Association of America (HIAA), but also the AMA and others. It should be noted that many physicians, myself included, did not agree with the AMA's stance, and only around 12 percent of physicians in this country are paying members of the AMA.[12] In 2017, a poll found that 56 percent of physicians supported (42 percent of them "strongly") single-payer healthcare. I suspect these numbers have increased in the past five years.[13]

SUCCESSFUL MODELS AND WORKING WITH WHAT WE ALREADY HAVE

"Universal healthcare," "single-payer," "socialized medicine," "Medicare for all": what do these terms all mean? They seem to be used interchangeably in recent public discourse, but they mean very different things. What they all do share, however, is that they are alternatives to our current healthcare mess. Whatever people think they mean, polls show that for a large majority of Americans they mean an alternative preferable to our current system. To those profiting from our current policies, they are anathema, a threat to their existence.

There are really only four basic models of healthcare management in current use, and many countries use hybrids, including the US. For those interested in taking a deeper dive into healthcare systems around the world, I heartily recommend the journalist T. R. Reid's surprisingly entertaining and informative book *The Healing of America: A Global Quest for Better and Cheaper Healthcare*.[14]

The first model Reid describes is the good old out-of-pocket, fee-for-service model (FFS) we Americans are so familiar with. In this model, doctors or other clinicians charge a person receiving care according to what service is rendered. Until modern times this was how most of the world operated. After World War II other developed countries decided unregulated FFS was too chaotic, too inefficient, and fundamentally unjust. They concluded healthcare was a right of its citizens and organized themselves to provide it. In contrast, the US, especially in the '60s and '70s as discussed in Chapter One, doubled down on the FFS model and invited for-profit insurers and other corporations to step in and broker healthcare transactions, taking their cut in the process. This made an inefficient model worse, effectively sidestepping the long accepted checks and balances of medical ethics and encouraging unfettered profiteering.

These profiteers in our current system call it a "free market," but it is neither free nor a market. We don't comparison-shop when we're having a heart attack or when our child is being carted off in an ambulance. We don't get to choose which doctors or hospitals are contracted with our health insurance, and if we do get any choice about health insurance we are limited to a very few rigid, nonnegotiable plans. Those wanting care and those providing that care (doctors and other clinicians) have little choice in who they will work with, and no choice in what the payment arrangement will be—these are determined by insurers and healthcare systems in secret negotiations, with no input from those directly involved in the transaction. We all know the drill: multiple bills, add-on costs, deductibles, copays, prior authorization requirements, surprise billing, out-of-network fees, denial of claims, etc., etc. Basically, these are the means healthcare systems use to increase their charges, and the techniques insurers use to evade paying those charges. It's a $4 trillion battlefield with patients caught in the middle, without a shield or weapon. If you think about it, insurance is really just about moving money around. It should be the least important part of our healthcare system, yet it drives it.

The second model described by Reid is the Beveridge model, named after William Beveridge, the social reformer who designed Britain's

National Health Service (NHS) that was implemented in 1948. Under this system, healthcare is provided and financed by the government through tax payments, just like the fire department, the police, or the public library. Many, but not all, hospitals and clinics are owned by the government; some doctors are government employees, but there are also private doctors who collect their fees from the government. In Britain, you never get a doctor bill; the government, as the sole payer, controls what doctors can do and what they can charge. This is what many mean when they refer to "socialized medicine." But Britain is a decidedly capitalist country. Other countries using this model or variations on it include Spain, most of Scandinavia, and New Zealand, all highly democratic and none are politically communist or socialist. If you are an eligible US veteran, you have the British "socialized medicine" healthcare system, since the US government, through the Department of Veterans Affairs, hires your doctors and nurses, runs your hospitals and clinics, and pays for your medications.

The third model is the Bismarck model, which uses an insurance system called "sickness funds," which are usually financed jointly by employers and employees through payroll deduction. Unlike the US insurance industry, Bismarck-type health insurance plans have to cover everybody, and they don't make a profit. Countries using this model include Germany, France, Belgium, the Netherlands, Switzerland, and Japan. They offer universal coverage using private insurance plans—with government exercising regulatory control over insurance coverage and pricing. However, both doctors and hospitals tend to be private. Japan, for example, has more private hospitals than the US. Although this is a multi-payer model—Germany has about 240 different funds—tight regulation gives the government control over costs. It's really not that different than what we have in the US, except the insurance is nonprofit and prices are carefully controlled by the government.

The fourth model Reid outlines is the National Health Insurance (NHI) model, familiar to us as the Canadian model. This is what is usually meant by the term "single-payer." It is a government-run insurance program that everyone pays into, that uses private-sector providers. Since there's no need for marketing, and no financial motive to deny claims, these universal insurance programs tend to be cheaper and much simpler administratively than in America. The single-payer model has considerable market power to negotiate for lower prices, which is why so many Americans go north to buy their medications. NHI countries rely on private-sector doctors, hospitals, and labs, but pay for their services through the government insurance plan. If you are retired and over sixty-five in the US, you are already probably on a Canadian-style NHI plan, Medicare. And it works—75 percent of Medicare users rate themselves as satisfied or very satisfied with their coverage.[15]

As well as Medicare works, it too is under threat of being dismantled. Currently around half of all Medicare recipients enroll in private supplemental Medicare Advantage (MA) plans,[16, 17] and the numbers are growing for these highly profitable and highly promoted policies. These "advantage" plans lure people, especially those who are healthier and utilize less healthcare services, by claiming to offer expanded benefits.[18] But a 2022 report by the Office of the Inspector General of Health and Human Services found that these private MA plans showed "widespread and persistent problems related to inappropriate denials of services and payment." They concluded that about 18 percent of payments, an estimated 1.5 million payments, were denied despite meeting Medicare coverage rules.[19] And according to federal audits, eight of the ten biggest Medicare Advantage insurers—representing more than two-thirds of the market—have submitted inflated bills.[20] Worse, evidence is accumulating that patients may do worse under these programs. For example, a 2024 JAMA study found people needing home health services had worse outcomes if they were covered under MA plans as compared to those under traditional Medicare.[21] In 2023, Congress began investigating abuses of the MA industry, and their inappropriate denials of care,[22] and now many hospitals and healthcare groups are dropping their contracts with MA plans, leaving enrollees scrambling for care elsewhere.[23]

Sean Cavanaugh, the top Medicare official at the Centers for Medicare & Medicaid Services (CMS) during the Obama administration, points out that these "advantage" plans make money by squeezing clinicians with poor reimbursement, and limiting patients' choice of clinician and care that they are entitled to under Medicare, all while upcoding to overcharge the Medicare program. The nonprofit physicians group Physicians for a National Health Program estimates that these MA plans are overcharging taxpayers between $88 and $140 billion a year.[24] Of course, MA plans are particularly problematic for those needing mental healthcare. Medicare Advantage plans have been found to have extremely sparse networks for psychiatric care, even worse than those of standard insurers, making mental healthcare virtually unobtainable.[25] Increasingly, general medical groups and hospitals are refusing to accept Medicare Advantage programs, leaving elderly patients unable to access any care.[26,27] "We've literally created a nonproductive industry where there are businesses that collect diagnoses on MA solely for the purpose of getting paid—not to improve care that these folks receive, but to improve the payments that the plans receive." It is, as Cavanaugh puts it, a healthcare industry that offers "no benefit to society."[28]

We have to ask ourselves: are we outraged at our "socialized" fire departments, roads and highways, and water systems? Yet in the healthcare debate social initiatives that clearly benefit all are attacked as un-American, and plans that benefit insurance companies and harm patients flourish. Can we envision fire departments which require confirmation of a fire insurance policy (that they are specifically contracted with) and completed and approved prior authorization forms before they will even consider putting out the fire burning our home? Over my years as a doctor, and as a patient, I've seen a constant rotisserie of scams, evasions, contracts, rule bending, and obfuscation as health insurers avoid paying for care, pharmaceutical companies charge the most they can get away with, and healthcare systems compete for healthy and wealthy clients who need little care but will pay a king's ransom when they do need it, all while doing everything they can to avoid the poor, and the truly sick, especially the mentally ill. It's just too hard to monitor the panoply of scams and tricks our system encourages. Would a single-payer system constrain patients in some ways? Yes, but the advantages afforded for them and the rest of society make it the best answer, and totally worth it. In the following sections I'll talk about how we can take steps toward a single-payer system and what we can do now, regardless of progress on that front.

MAKING A COMMITMENT THAT BASIC MEDICAL CARE IS A RIGHT

To begin, we need to reframe the debate; after all, our lives depend on it. Wasting time debating nonsense buzzwords like socialized medicine and cartoonish "Harry and Louise" ad campaigns has kept us mired in division, intentionally. We need to talk instead about offering at least basic healthcare for all Americans, and how this not only will benefit us all in terms of health—it will also save us money. We have clear examples of solutions that work, and Rube Goldberg models (like ours) that don't. The models that work are what we need to be implementing. And these can be implemented in steps.

In the early 1990s, three countries embarked on efforts to overhaul their healthcare systems: Switzerland, Taiwan, and the US. In all three countries, payment for medical care was dominated by health insurance plans tied to employment, and significant numbers of people were left with no coverage at all. Still, the other two decidedly capitalist countries successfully implemented national healthcare plans in 1994, the year President Clinton's effort went down in flames. Switzerland decided to follow the German Bismarck model, Taiwan the Canadian model. How have the three countries fared since? Looking at the 2018

Bloomberg study of healthcare efficiency cited in Chapter One, Taiwan ranked ninth and Switzerland fourteenth out of fifty-six. We tied for fifty-fourth—next-to-last place. [29] Healthcare costs in Switzerland were greater than the US in 1994, but dropped to 12.2 percent of GDP by 2016. [30] Taiwan's costs in 2017 were 6.4 percent of GDP. Ours have gone from 13.3 percent in 1994 to 19.7 percent in 2020.

Expenditures Per Person

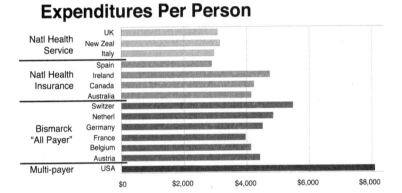

Health care expenditures per person in developed countries.

These statistics do not include other costs of caring for those with a serious mental illness, like emergency or police services. What about the crime, homelessness, and incarceration that results when people with mental illness are excluded from care? Why should companies and venture capitalists profit from the illness and misfortune of others?

If we want to undo our mess, **the first commitment we must make is that everyone in our society deserves healthcare** as is done in all other developed countries. This includes the elderly, the very young, the unemployed, the poor, all races and ethnicities, and the mentally ill. Denying someone needed healthcare for economic reasons is no more morally acceptable than for any other reason. **Excluding some from healthcare is not only primitive and cruel, it divides our community and makes our world a less pleasant place to live.** And, as we've seen, it costs more in the long run. Treating people before they are seriously ill saves in overall healthcare costs. That savings is even greater with mental illness when you include lost productivity and criminal justice costs. Tying health insurance to employment in our country means we may have to change healthcare systems when we change employment. This often means changing our primary care doctor, and any specialists we might need, adding needless complexity, and hampering job mobility lest one fall between the healthcare cracks.

The second commitment to make is that profiteers, that is to say for-profit corporations and investors, have no place guiding healthcare decisions. Healthcare should be based on need, with all in the healthcare system having fiduciary responsibility to the patient, not profits. That is not to say that people and companies cannot make a decent living by serving healthcare needs, but they cannot be the ones dictating costs and allocating resources, nor can they allocate resources to serve investment goals rather than health goals. Some will be unhappy with these changes, but we have to stop looking the other way and allowing some to kill for profit. Treating medical care as a nonprofit endeavor worked for 2,000 years and continues to work well in other countries. We all will benefit when our healthcare system once again prioritizes healthy members of society over healthy profits.

With a commitment to healthcare for all and removing profiteering, the next step becomes easy and logical. **We must choose among the three models of healthcare other than the fee-for-service**—the Beveridge model, the Bismarck model, or the NHI model—or we can use a hybrid of the four, as do many countries, without the illogical and absurd business competition of our current system. In fact, unless we model ourselves on Bulgaria, it would be hard to find a system that works as poorly as ours. As we've noted, the US already uses all four models, but only partially and in opposition to each other, each competing to minimize the care they will cover. These competing factions set up cumbersome and expensive barriers to block ill people from falling under their responsibility. Although we could grow our Beveridge model, like the VA, I think that would be difficult and would require major infrastructure changes. A transition of this magnitude was an easier path for Great Britain immediately after WWII, when their entire country needed to be rebuilt, and their healthcare needs were massive owing to the war. To set up a system like Germany's would likewise be problematic. Mandating the many insurance companies' fees and benefits that this system requires would be met with fierce resistance (as Bill Clinton and Barack Obama discovered), and insurance companies would no doubt continue with their cat and mouse games to evade constraints on profit.

The easiest and most logical way to move forward is to expand one of the other systems, like Medicare and Medicaid, which we already have in place and are already centralized, and follow the highly successful NHI, or Canadian model. A 2023 YouGov poll found that 84 percent of Americans who receive Medicare and 78 percent of those who receive Medicaid had positive views of their programs.[31] Contrast this with a 2023 Gallup poll that found that less than half of Americans rate American healthcare as good or excellent.[32] The results in terms of health gains of universal care after age 65 in the US (Medicare) are clear, as the figure below shows.

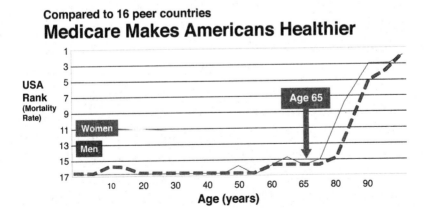

Medicare makes Americans Healthier.

The transition to this model worked out superbly for Taiwan, and it could for us. Medicare and Medicaid could simply be merged and slowly expanded. Medicaid could raise the income levels it serves and Medicare could progressively take on children and those under 65. A gradual transition would give our massive healthcare industry time to adapt. Many currently in administrative roles who are trained healthcare professionals could return to clinical care roles. Removing profiteering from healthcare could be a benefit to healthcare workers, who could once again feel like their profession is a calling, an honor, not some get-rich scheme or a sentence to an understaffed work camp. Medicaid expansion enacted during the pandemic raised the minimum income to qualify and allowed many to achieve coverage successfully. [33] There is no reason we shouldn't continue to revise the income limits up, and the age of Medicare down. And what of those "rugged individuals" who aren't willing to give up what they have now? There is no reason why we cannot have a hybrid system, as we do now. Most European countries allow private services to flourish alongside the public system. In Canada, two-thirds of people carry private insurance to cover services not covered by their NHI, like vision and dental, outpatient prescriptions. Some may choose to buy supplemental plans (as many on Medicare do today), but these should be not-for-profit like the rest of Medicare, and monitored closely as in other countries, and over time choose whether or not they want to join the rest of us.

It would not be difficult to treat science and medicine as public property—infrastructure just like streets and fire departments. Scientific discoveries, especially those made with government funding, should be published and open for use by all. After all, the public pays for them. It's time to stop blocking the knowledge and technology that can improve and save lives, letting some profit while others die.

Some ask how we would pay for universal healthcare. The answer is, as we have seen, that we are already paying for it, to the tune of $4 trillion dollars a year. This is twice as much as other countries pay for their far better universal healthcare. Physicians for a National

Health Program, a physician organization with more than 20,000 members that advocates for a single-payer healthcare system, points out,

> Administrative costs consume 31 percent of US health spending, versus 16.7 percent in Canada. The US could save enough on administrative expenses (nearly $400 billion annually) with a single payer to cover all the uninsured . . . Taxes already pay for over 60 percent of US health spending, when tax subsidies to private insurance and the benefit costs of public employees are factored in. Americans pay the highest healthcare taxes in the world. The bottom line is that we currently pay *more* than we would under national health insurance, but don't get it.[34]

The cost of our inefficient healthcare system drains our society in so many ways, from our shortened lifespan and increased maternal and infant deaths (and the extra care they require), to administrative costs, increased disability, and incarceration. The list goes on. In many US cities, up to one-fifth of law enforcement staff time is devoted to responding to people with mental illness rather than chasing real criminals.[35] It's estimated that we spend about $80 billion a year on incarcerations, around half of which is for those with mental illness. And that doesn't include social costs.[36] In 2021 alone, Portland Fire and Rescue reported 4,300 homeless-related fires, and in Los Angeles the number was over 9,000 according to the LA Fire Department.[37] Even our auto industry is affected. It is estimated that paying healthcare benefits for its workers adds $1,500 to the price of every Ford and General Motors vehicle produced.[38,39] This is more than the price of the steel used in making the vehicle, putting these American companies at a competitive disadvantage with foreign manufacturers. We are paying for our current system in so many, many ways we don't even notice. If you think about it, much of our healthcare, and most mental healthcare under our for-profit model, is double jeopardy.

We pay for our care many times over: in taxes, to the insurer in the form of premiums, and again to our clinician, the pharmacy, the laboratory, etc., for the services that our insurer won't cover. Businesses paid an average of $13,360 per employee for healthcare premiums in 2021, with employees kicking in another $3,331.[40] Add in another $1,500 that both pay into Medicare currently[41] and we're over $18,000 in cost per person. That could buy us a great national healthcare system, one without the need or incentive to kick some people out, one that includes everyone.

Although people are leery about change, Americans are fed up with our current system. In a 2023 survey, the majority of insured adults (58 percent) reported they had experienced a problem using their health insurance in the past twelve months—such as denied claims, provider network problems, and pre-authorization problems.[42]

The good news is that we have made significant progress toward universal healthcare coverage. Prior to the passage of the Affordable Care Act (ACA) in 2010, 17.8 percent of nonelderly Americans were without health insurance. By 2021, that number had decreased to 10.2 percent. There is broad consensus in our country about the need for universal health coverage.[43,44,45] A 2020 KFF poll showed that over two-thirds of Americans favor a government-run "public option" healthcare plan, which would allow us the flexibility to choose.[46] Similarly, a 2020 Pew Research Center poll found that 63 percent of Americans believe that the government has the responsibility to provide health coverage for all if a mix of government and private programs were allowed, and this number is increasing. Only 6 percent felt that the government should not be responsible for healthcare.[47] Tweaks to our current system only further entrench a fundamentally flawed model. For example, while the ACA increased the number of people with insurance coverage, it exacerbated other problems, like further locking other people into bad jobs for fear of losing their employer-covered insurance. This would not happen with truly universal coverage.[48]

It's time we reframe the debate to talk about results rather than theory, policy, and politics, and look at our situation honestly. We've already decided to spend the money, we just need to spend it better. Let's focus on lives, measures of health, and dollars. The evidence is irrefutable. Vitriol against higher taxes and "socialized medicine" obscures the larger truth that universal healthcare will keep us healthier *and* cost less overall. Arguing about terms and taxes is just a shell game by those profiting from our current corrupt system. They don't want to give it up. We can no longer ignore the fact that by turning healthcare over to private contractors, our government has abdicated responsibility to protect us from predatory businesses in our most vulnerable arena.

HOW WE CAN MOVE FORWARD ACKNOWLEDGING THE TRUE COSTS OF NOT INVESTING IN MENTAL HEALTHCARE

One Sunday in February of 2022, I sat reading the *New York Times* while eating breakfast. On the front page was the story of how Martial Simon, a homeless man known for his incoherent rants, shoved Michelle Alyssa Go to her death in front of a subway car. For years Mr. Simon had been in "revolving door" treatment. The story told how he had been hospitalized twenty times, but never received consistent care. Minutes later, I picked up my local paper the *San Francisco Chronicle.* On its front page, an article entitled "The disastrous results of S.F.'s program to house homeless in hotels" described the failure of a 2019 law designed to assist the then 4,000 (now estimated to be 8,000) unhoused people in San Francisco who struggle with addiction and mental illness. The law changed rules so that the most ill, disruptive, and dangerous individuals could be forced into court-ordered treatment. Three years on, two (!) individuals had been treated under the program, and none stayed in the program.[49] San Francisco implemented a bold plan in 2017 to cut in half its chronically homeless population over the subsequent five years. Rather than decrease, the population has grown.[50]

Laws are meaningless if we have neither the facilities nor the will to implement them.

We can't expect the homeless mentally ill to utilize housing without treatment, or to access regular treatment without stable housing. As a 2020 study found, 86 percent of people experiencing chronic homelessness were able to achieve housing when enrolled in a permanent supportive housing program, as opposed to only 36 percent who were not.[51] The two must go hand-in-hand, combined with strong social and vocational support. Some SMI simply may not have the insight, judgment, or rationality to accept treatment without monitoring and guidance, at least initially. In the first seven months of 2022, fourteen out of 1,071 patients at the Psychiatric Emergency Services department of San Francisco General Hospital, the city's only such unit, were admitted between eleven and twenty times. One came more than twenty times. Five individuals alone over the past five years had at least 1,781 ambulance transports. The price tag paid by taxpayers? $4 million. And these patients are getting worthless, ineffective care.[52] A 2024 study found that the homeless, once admitted, stay in the hospital 25 percent longer because of difficulty in sending them out to a safe environment, with current hospitalization costs running about $3,000/day.[53] In contrast, another 2024 study of the "Housing First" program in Denver, that prioritizes permanent housing of the mentally ill, found that participants attended more office-based psychiatric visits, were more accepting of medication, and had fewer emergency department visits than the control group.[54] A 2024 study estimates that mental illness costs the US economy $282 billion annually, the equivalent of an average economic recession. But in the case of mental illness, it's a recession that occurs every year without fail.[55]

My patients and I run up against this lack of adequate resources all the time. A patient of mine recently had an exacerbation of his symptoms; he hadn't slept in days, and his delusions of being in extreme danger at the hands of a vast criminal conspiracy terrified him. He and his family desperately wanted him hospitalized. He, through family, even had excellent insurance coverage. However, when he showed up at the hospital he was denied admission. Staff said that he did not "meet criteria" for hospitalization. Translated, this means he did not meet criteria for a "5150" or involuntary hospitalization. He was not suicidal or homicidal, and his family could house and feed him. Psychiatric hospital beds were in such short supply that the hospital staff couldn't waste a precious hospital bed (they run at full capacity virtually all the time) on someone who did not legally require hospitalization. I'm sure they worried that his insurance might refuse to pay for his care since he didn't meet "criteria," leaving them stuck for the cost. If he had threatened violence or mayhem he would have been admitted. Criminal behavior would get him help, not his need for care. Yet by providing such care we might prevent tragedies like Ms. Go's murder.

Most of us would feel a lot more comfortable living with those with mental illness in our midst if we felt that our government and healthcare system provided adequate and appropriate support and treatment for them. As the policy analyst Steven Eide points out: "Most people don't want to live next to a homeless shelter that cares for mentally ill people because they don't trust the government and shelter providers to run such facilities in a way that would keep neighborhood conditions stable. Who can blame them?"[56] As long as we fail to provide the mentally ill with needed and timely care, the cycle will continue. We pay dearly for the lack of mental health treatment through increased costs in physical care to the indigent, petty crime, incarceration, and the criminal justice system, as well as a lower quality of life in our communities, not to mention the death and disability of those who could be helped.

DON'T DISCRIMINATE BY WHICH ORGAN IS ILL

Why should access to healthcare be dependent on which organ is affected? We don't separate reimbursement plans by whether they focus on the kidneys or lungs. Our brains, like any other organ, can falter and fail. And my years working in the hospital have taught me that illness is never entirely physical or mental. Failing to treat mental disorders on par with physical disorders costs us all, in money and heartache, and has health consequences for everyone.

Our treatments of many chronic physical illnesses like autoimmune disorders, diabetes, Parkinsons disease, and hypertension are palliative and no more curative than treatments of mental illness. Most cancers elude cure and treatments might offer some extension of life, but at a terrible cost in terms of side effects—including the risk of inducing another malignancy. Yet we don't question the importance or value of those interventions. Where are the anti-oncology, anti-cardiology, anti-endocrinology movements? Surgeons, once reviled for taking care of the ugly underbelly of medicine, are now esteemed, earning two to three times what psychiatrists and primary care doctors earn. Could this prejudice be reversed for psychiatrists who, like surgeons in the past, show the perseverance and heroism to take care of society's outcasts?

Even non-psychiatrists who try to treat their patients' mental illness along with their physical maladies experience frustrating hurdles. Kaiser Health News (KHN) describes the experience of a family medicine doctor who spent thirty minutes asking questions about his patient's exercise and sleep habits, counseling him on breathing exercises and writing a prescription for attention-deficit/hyperactivity disorder medication. At the end of the visit, he submitted a claim to the patient's insurance using one code for obesity, one for rosacea—a common skin condition—one for anxiety, and one for ADHD. Several weeks later, the insurer sent him a letter saying it wouldn't pay for the visit. "The services billed are for the treatment of a behavioral health condition," the letter said, and under the patient's health plan, those benefits are covered by a separate company.[57] The time he would have to spend submitting additional claims would simply not be worth the meager reimbursement. Another family physician told KHN that he stopped using psychiatric diagnosis codes in claims altogether. If he sees a patient with depression, he codes it as fatigue. Anxiety he codes as cardiac palpitations. This was the only way to get paid, he said.

We Americans behave as if we'll never become ill, or at least as if illness is so far off we don't need to worry about it now. We have crafted a healthcare system that reflects these beliefs. This is doubly true of mental illness; few of us worry that we'll develop schizophrenia and end up on the streets. But mental illness, at least in minor form, is quite common, occurring in around one in five US adults.[58] More than other sorts of illness, mental illness affects other family members, friends, and the community. It is hard to comprehend, deeply disturbing, and shameful to the person and also those associated with them. In our effort to cast it out, deny its specter of shame, we end up unintentionally playing into the hands of insurance companies eager to deny mental health coverage and erect a maze of treatment hurdles and restrictions.

I've heard insurers express concern that wider availability of mental healthcare will cause more people to seek treatment just to feel better, to improve their lives. But healthcare should help people feel better. Cancer, which is seen as a serious illness can kill, but so can strep throat, which may be seen as more minor. Should we treat one and not the other? Should we not treat sadness, or anxiety? They too can kill. Psychotherapy can work wonders; why should it be cut out of healthcare and available only to the very wealthy?

Though people don't generally admit it, as the Kaiser study cited in Chapter Two showed, 60–90 percent of primary care medical appointments are prompted by stress or psychological problems rather than medical illness.[59] However, people worry—and rightfully so—that if they admit to emotional concerns their physical concerns will be dismissed by a healthcare world in which mental health issues are viewed with suspicion—or dismissed out-of-hand. So they hide what is truly bothering them lest they get dismissed as a whiner, or "crock," or any one of many disparaging terms that our medical system and society use for those with emotional concerns, those who don't fit our "rugged individual" paradigm.

The fear, and reality, is that once someone admits to emotional problems, their physical ones may be disregarded. Seeing mental health as separate from physical health just serves to promote stigma and its exclusion from healthcare. In my many years of doing consultation-liaison work in the hospital and medical-surgical clinics, I found patients facing medical and surgical treatment were happy and even relieved to talk with me as a psychiatrist. Once we made a personal connection they were not hesitant to reveal their struggles, their anxieties and apprehension. However, asking them to go and see someone over in the (entirely separate) mental health building, where they could be identified or view themselves as a psychiatric patient was a non-starter. The separation of healthcare into mental and physical realms simply doesn't work. The "separate but equal" strategy we have been using to achieve parity is succeeding about as well as it did to combat the unequal treatment received by people of color in the last century.

The public's skewed perception of mental health treatment, still rooted in suspicion and fear, like the fear of mental illness itself, is a major barrier to be overcome. Treatments of our brain, the seat of our soul, are judged harshly and by different standards. As anthropologist Roy Grinker points out, "safe brain-based treatments like electroconvulsive therapy (ECT) continue to be met with fear and secretiveness, if not hostility."[60] Yet, ECT successfully treats severe depression in 65-80 percent of cases,[61] and a 2022 Canadian study showed that among people hospitalized for depression those who got ECT had an almost 50 percent reduction in suicide over the next year.[62] Contrast this with people in the hospital who undergo cardiac defibrillation: only 6.5 percent survive to be discharged.[63] We cheer when the handsome TV hero delivers a powerful electric shock to a patient's heart. Yet we recoil in horror when seeing the same done to the brain, especially when grossly misportrayed in movies like *Requiem for a Dream* and *One Flew Over the Cuckoo's Nest*. ECT is viewed as a form of punishment or torture, yet in actuality it is up to *ten times* more successful than in-hospital cardiac defibrillation.

We could take steps now to remedy discriminatory treatment for the mentally ill. We don't have to wait for a new healthcare system. Existing parity laws could actually be enforced by our government, backed up by more than a slap on the wrist. If insurers had to pay more in fines than for care, they'd pay for care. That's simply a good business decision. And with proper treatment available, homelessness and incarceration would decrease, and the fear and prejudice against mental illness could diminish.

ADEQUATE FUNDING AND RESOURCES FOR EFFECTIVE, INDIVIDUAL TREATMENTS

I vividly recall the heart-wrenching story that a patient of mine told of how he ended up in the hospital. Troy suffered from schizophrenia and had been living on the streets. He had taken his last $10 to a convenience store to buy something to eat. When the clerk short-changed him, he began to protest. Troy turned to the other customers in line for support, but they just looked away, annoyed by the delay he was causing. The clerk said nothing, but reached for the phone. Troy knew what was at the end of the phone call: a trip to jail and loss of his few possessions, and perhaps a beating—or worse. Hungry and penniless he walked to the hospital. He may have been crazy but he was not stupid. As a society we spent thousands of dollars a day on his inpatient care, only to have him return to the streets without adequate follow-up, all over a $10 bill. What this man really needed was comprehensive and supportive treatment, a path back into the society he felt scorned by.

As we look at the sheer magnitude of our homelessness and mass incarceration challenges, it's easy to conclude that the SMI are untreatable. Yet studies show that our treatments of mental illness—*when properly administered*—are just as effective as for most chronic physical ones. [64] The problem is that we don't adequately implement these treatments. We won't pay for them or set up the structures and resources to deliver them. Quality care as rendered in other countries demonstrates that proper treatment works, and saves money. I know that what even my most ill patients want is acceptance, a place to feel that they matter and are safe to be themselves. This basic need means that all too often the SMI fall prey to criminals who want only their money either by inducing them to use drugs or robbing them, or in the case of women, using them for sex. All too often they acquiesce out of fear, or a wish to be accepted and cared for in at least some way. We can and should do better. As Mahatma Gandhi famously said, "The true measure of any society can be found in how it treats its most vulnerable."

Lack of cooperation with treatment, often based on impaired judgment and insight, which are core features of serious mental illness, can be a major hurdle to treatment. But we don't refuse to treat uncooperative children, the unconscious, or the demented who, like the SMI, need lifesaving care but do not have the intellectual capacity to appreciate their situation or options. Not cooperating with care because of a lack of understanding, insight, and judgment is very different than refusing care due to thoughtful, deeply held beliefs. The predicament of the SMI is particularly fraught because psychiatric treatments are rarely curative, except ECT, and not without side effects. But thoughtful, caring programs do work, and the use of peer counselors, those who have struggled with their own mental health issues, can boost treatment acceptance greatly. The problem is that insurance companies do not pay for quality mental healthcare, and as a result the resources to deliver that care have dwindled.

In the 1980s a nurse colleague and I ran a clinic that administered long-acting (every two to four weeks) injectable antipsychotic medication to SMI patients. Getting people to come in for their shots every few weeks was always hit or miss. Then we added on a weekly group meeting, with cookies and beverages, where people could sit and talk with each other, and ask us questions. Not only did everyone show up for their medication—they showed up *every* week, early, even on weeks they weren't scheduled for medication. Close friendships grew, and a sense of community and concern for the well-being of others in the group. A pill or shot may have lessened their symptoms, but they were a lot more interested in finding a place where they felt valued and welcome, with people who understood their struggles, and where they were appreciated for their understanding of the struggles of others. I think that our interest helped, but the care and interest of their peers was perhaps most important. There is safety and comfort in community, which is undoubtedly why so many of the homeless, even very paranoid individuals, band together in encampments.

However, many insurers won't pay for more than one healthcare intervention per day, such as receiving both medication and a group meeting on the same day, not to mention cookies and beverages. So this group, which was held at a VA with refreshments paid for out of our pockets, wouldn't be possible in most care settings. None of these people had vehicles, and most walked to the hospital. Yet in ninety minutes, two clinicians met the medication, general health support and referral, supportive therapy, and socialization needs of a dozen serious mentally ill individuals, the sort of people who used to be institutionalized. Over many years, not a single one of these people required hospitalization. Preventive care, support, an ongoing relationship with one's healthcare team, and, importantly, a feeling of community, go a long way toward maintaining mental health.

Other countries use community-based assisted care models, where the community embraces rather than shuns the mentally ill, and these programs work. Ironically, the most famous and most successful of these was inspired by the US's original CMHC model. The Italian psychiatrist Franco Basaglia spent six months in the US in 1969 and imported the CMHC model to Trieste, Italy, in 1971. Trieste has since been recognized by the WHO as a model, the world standard for community psychiatry. Its guiding principles include "the shift from a condition of inmates to one of citizens . . . the restitution to community . . . (and) the reconstruction of an income and a social role. . . ."[65] Once needing 1,200 psychiatric hospital beds for its 232,395 inhabitants, Trieste now needs only six general hospital beds and thirty overnight community center beds. Trieste provides supportive housing, twenty-four-hour community centers and crisis response as well as home care, social clubs, and paid jobs.[66] Also, they recognize that housing is a health issue. Without safe shelter, good physical and mental health is impossible. Housing helps foster another vital component, the sense of belonging to the community. There are efforts now to re-import the Trieste model to the US.[67]

The needs of the mentally ill are many and diverse. Those of someone in West Virginia addicted to prescription opiates living with their family are very different than the needs of someone with schizophrenia camping under a freeway in Los Angeles. For some, less severely affected, wider availability of psychotherapy might do the trick. Others, like the SMI, will usually need comprehensive care that includes medication, but also close monitoring, counseling, support, housing, and a path into the community with a meaningful role. Neither medication alone, nor moving someone from the streets to an unsupervised, squalid, rat- and crime-infested dilapidated hotel room, without adequate support is adequate, as San Francisco discovered when their 2019 plan to house the homeless flopped spectacularly. We have interventions that do work, especially in combination, like individual placement and support (IPS), a supported employment program that has been shown to help patients with even serious mental illness succeed in competitive employment.[68] As a 2016 review found, "abundant evidence shows that people with mental disorders who gain employment experience broad benefits, including enhanced self-esteem, community integration, social support, and quality of life . . . Many countries now recognize that employment is an effective mental health treatment."[69] The basic problem is that cheap, simplistic, piecemeal, cookie-cutter interventions pushed by our current healthcare system are not working.

The use of peer counselors, who themselves have mental illness, has been extremely successful and often renders forced treatment unnecessary. Many with SMI are suspicious, and often have experienced

REFORM 101: HOW WE CAN FIX OUR HEALTHCARE MESS   199

mistreatment by society in general and the healthcare and criminal justice systems in particular. Peers who can speak from personal experience with mental illness and successful treatment can go a long way toward reestablishing trust. Some US cities have implemented peer-led crisis response teams like CAHOOTS (Crisis Assistance Helping Out On The Streets), a mobile crisis-intervention program that has been in place for thirty years in Eugene, Oregon.[70] CAHOOTS is publicly funded, and despite taking only 2 percent of the police budget, handles 20 percent of 911 calls. Out of an estimated 24,000 calls CAHOOTS responded to in 2019, they called for police backup only 311 times (1.3 percent of calls). Moreover, no staff member has ever experienced a serious injury in over 30 years. In 2017, CAHOOTS teams answered 17 percent of the Eugene Police Department's overall call volume and saved the city of Eugene an estimated $8.5 million in public safety spending.[71] Denver, Colorado, and Phoenix, Arizona, have recently imported the CAHOOTS model. In Denver the Support Team Assistance Response, or STAR, as it is called, removes police from some 911 calls, sending a mental health clinician and a paramedic instead. The implementation of STAR has resulted in a 34 percent reduction in low-level crimes.[72] These statistics don't even include money saved by avoiding lengthy ER visits and other medical care.

It's a sad fact that people with schizophrenia actually fare better in developing nations as compared to the US. A key factor is social inclusion, rather than exclusion. For example, as Indian science writer T. V. Padma wrote in *Science*: in India "the disorganized rural labour markets offer more opportunities, such as field work for people with disabilities, which helps them integrate and overcome their illness."[73] In America, this sort of approach flies in the face of our system of discreet billable medical interventions. Insurance companies don't pay for peer counselors or support in employment. How could they verify services or skills? They would balk at seeing it as healthcare, something that falls under their responsibility. These sorts of programs need to be publicly funded, with mechanisms in place to track what is and is not working for patients and the community.

American interventions in many mental illnesses, not only schizo-phrenia, bring worse outcomes than those in other countries. As described in Ethan Watters's wonderfully enlightening book *Crazy Like Us*, from depression in Japan, to PTSD in Sri Lanka, the adoption of American-style interventions overseas have yielded worse outcomes.[74] A key element missing in these interventions was community support and integration. Instead brief medication and procedure-focused treat-ment, as promoted by the US healthcare industry, were imported, with dismal results.

Also important is that other countries recognize the difference between criminal intent and illness, and whether punishment or treat-ment is indicated. I've cared for people in "conditional release" programs that require them to stay in psychiatric care as a condition for their release from prison. Most are eager patients, desperate to avoid the demons that drove them to commit the humiliating crimes that landed them in prison. If someone's behavior draws them to our attention, isn't that likely a sign they need help? Wouldn't it be better if they received care *before* they try to take their life or commit a crime? But in our country all we can offer is incarceration, not the comprehensive care they need.

The continuing surge in gun violence, and particularly mass shootings, has highlighted our inadequate mental healthcare, and brought about calls for increased funding. Indeed, much of the funding of Congress's 2022 gun safety law, passed in the aftermath of the Uvalde tragedy that year, was earmarked for mental health.[75] As the American Psychiatric Association points out, "Almost by definition, those committing gun violence other than self-defense must have some sort of mental abnor-mality. . . ."[76] While mass shooters don't necessarily have a diagnosable major mental illness, and it is difficult to predict which individual will crack and go on a rampage, we know quite well the most common demo-graphic of the type of person who becomes a mass shooter: an isolated and resentful young to middle-aged white male who feels wronged by the world. Yet somehow we forget that mass shooters are in a mental health crisis, suicidal, their act a very public cry for help. They reflect a hopelessness and desperation pervasive in our society, a symptom of the lack of societal cohesion and support, and the corrosive effect of the lack of available mental healthcare. Shouldn't we be helping *all* who need help, rather than focusing, after a tragedy, on the angry few who blow up and express their frustration in violence? Our current strategy just promotes the idea that only violence gets results, fueling further rage. And what of women, who tend to turn sadness and hopelessness inward, inflicting self-harm or selling themselves short in education, vocation, and relationships? What of the hundreds of thousands who turn to drugs for comfort? If we make mental health treatment available and integrate it into the rest of our healthcare, stigma and discrimination could fade and treatment would be more likely to be accepted.

Crucial to successful interventions for mental illness, just as for any other illness, is to approach the individual as if they need help, not as if they are a dangerous criminal in need of incarceration. In California, in 2022 Governor Gavin Newsom approved and provided $57 million in funding for SB138, CARE (Community Assistance, Recovery and Empowerment) Court, a mental health-focused arm of the civil courts in every county that would divert those with severe mental illness from the criminal justice system into care. Under the measure, family, probation officers, and community members could refer these people into treatment.[77] But other measures have failed in the California legislature, such as SB1416 that would have expanded the definition of "gravely disabled" to include people who can't look out for their own safety. This measure would have allowed the courts to appoint a conservator to make decisions for them. Its failure means that criminal acts and violence will remain the real criteria to obtain care for many. And, as we saw in Chapter One, without adequate care resources, our current system sometimes drops charges against the mentally ill who commit violent crimes and discharges them back into the community, where they re-commit violent acts.[78] This hardly makes a community want to welcome the mentally ill, and is once again giving the insurance industry a free pass on mental healthcare, at taxpayers' expense. Solutions like Care Courts could help, but only if we actually have the staff, housing, facilities, and will to treat rather than punish.[79]

Why is it a problem if someone can't live independently, or needs support at work? Does that mean they have no value? That is the fundamental fallacy in America's myth of the rugged individual. To be dependent is to be human; we all depend on other people in so many ways. As Grinker points out, "disabilities don't always produce isolation . . . disabilities can connect people in relationships of care and reciprocity."[80]

I meet with Joshua, the young man introduced in Chapter One with delusions of being a famous musician, for only a brief session every two weeks. We generally cover the same things, mainly his fantasy about his life as a music star. But this small amount of care, connection, and interest, and the steady efforts on the part of his parents have kept him taking his medications and off the street and out of the hospital for years. Instead, he's playing his keyboard safely in their home. Too many SMI, especially those who are poor and isolated, don't have this sort of safety net. Providing adequate funding for treatments that work is essential. Putting real teeth in parity laws, and enforcing them, so that we pay for mental healthcare on a scale equivalent to physical care will go a long way toward making needed treatment available, even without wholesale change to our healthcare system.

ATTRACTING MORE MENTAL HEALTH PROFESSIONALS TO THE FIELD

The shortage of mental health professionals described in Chapter Two and throughout this book continues to worsen. Years of neglect and refusal to fund mental health and substance abuse treatment has taken its toll. I get several calls a day from people wanting psychiatric care. I can't accommodate them, and my colleagues are swamped too. Even masters-level psychotherapists I know are completely overwhelmed. As we saw in Chapter Two, a 2017 study found that 60 percent of counties in this country do not have a single psychiatrist,[81] and the numbers have only declined since then.

The disincentives to enter and stay in the mental health field persist: the poor reimbursement, the crushing workload, onerous documentation requirements, restrictions on the quality and amount of care one can render, and the reality of working with extremely challenging and needy patients who may not want help—coupled with an almost complete lack of public support—dims even the most enthusiastic clinician's drive. Psychiatric training requires four years of college, four years of medical school, and four years of residency training (and up to six for child and adolescent psychiatrists). This is longer than that required of internal medicine, family practitioner, and pediatric doctors (three years). Yet, as we've seen in Chapter Two, insurers pay psychiatrists less than primary care doctors for delivering the exact same services,[82] and erect more barriers to care, like limitations on treatment duration and PARs. Added to this frustration, psychiatric care tends to be more time intensive since it delves further into the complex and sometimes murky social determinants of health. While an orthopedic surgeon might operate on someone's broken leg without knowing about that person's home environment, a difficult home environment could be the very problem bringing someone to psychiatric care. Small wonder that so many psychiatrists refuse to contract with health insurers; because of restrictions on payment they couldn't provide quality healthcare and survive financially if they did.

This shortage of available mental healthcare means, as we've seen, that people have to go elsewhere for their care, like to the non-psychiatric doctors who write over 80 percent of antidepressant prescriptions.[83] But while non-psychiatrists are generally willing to treat common depression, most are not comfortable treating more severe cases, and those with SMI are just plain out of luck.

If we do away with the artificial line drawn between the brain and the rest of the body, a distinction born of fear and ignorance, I think more people will enter the fields of mental health. Clinicians of all stripes will be unshackled from barriers preventing them from addressing psychiatric problems. We could begin undoing this now. Enforcing existing parity laws would be a start. The homeless crisis has become impossible to ignore; mental healthcare has become so inadequate and difficult to access that few of us do not personally know of someone caught in the hell of trying to get mental healthcare. That person you avoid on the sidewalk is someone's son, or daughter, or brother, or sister. Books describing the personal experience of mental illness like Mark Vonnegut's *Just Like Someone Without Mental Illness Only More So*,[84] Elyn Saks' *The Center Cannot Hold*,[85] Kaye Redfield Jamison's *An Unquiet Mind*,[86] Ellen Forney's *Marbles*,[87] and Andrew Solomon's *The Noonday Demon*,[88] to name just a few, are putting a human face on mental illness and raising awareness.

Most people are fascinated by the mind. I get asked about what it's like to be a psychiatrist all the time. In this country over 100,000 undergraduate degrees in psychology are conferred each year, roughly the same number as in engineering and biological/biomedical sciences.[89] Yet we have only the same number, a little over 100,000, practicing psychologists in our entire country.[90] In comparison, we have 1.6 million working engineers.[91] What happens to all of those eager psychology graduates? They hear of and see the long road of frustration and disincentives born of prejudice toward those who wish to treat ailments of our brain. They see that they will get paid less than *half* of their equivalently trained physical medicine colleagues such as nurse practitioners and physicians assistants. I think if people felt they could make a difference in other's mental health by offering quality comprehensive care rather than tilting, alone, against windmills, in a system that mocks and excludes their work, the field would grow dramatically.

Still, there is hope. People can be motivated by things other than money. With the plight of the mentally ill and homelessness garnering more public attention, more young doctors are stepping up to address this underserved area of medicine. Between 2011 and 2021 the number of medical school graduates entering psychiatric training has increased from 4.1 to 6.5 percent,[92] even with public animosity toward the field and pathetic reimbursement rates. I think growing public awareness of homelessness, violence, suicide, and overdose deaths has motivated some to step up to the plate. People can be motivated by things like compassion and curiosity.

WHAT CAN WE DO RIGHT NOW?

It's famously been said that Americans will always do the right thing . . . after exhausting all the alternatives. Well, I think we're there at that point. How much longer do we want to tolerate healthcare that works poorly and is bankrupting us? We know that timely, effective care, especially mental healthcare, is not only humane, it improves life for all of us, and saves us money. To move forward we can make a commitment to three basic principles:

1: Let's provide at least basic healthcare, especially mental healthcare, to all, since this would benefit us all.

2. Let's re-orient the healthcare industry, top to bottom, behind the goal of improving health, not extracting profit. Let's keep healthcare in the public domain, not hidden behind patent paywalls.

3. Let's establish equal rights for all organs. Segregating healthcare by organ makes no sense. When we think about treating mental illness, stop for a moment. How would we regard the situation if the individual was having a heart attack, or facing breast cancer?

4. To these ends there are consequential strategies we can initiate now:

- *Rather than argue parity, ban distinctions between coverage of physical and mental care.* Separate policies, benefits, and divisions between mental and physical health by insurance companies should be forbidden.
- *Decriminalize mental illness.* Lanterman–Petris–Short (LPS) laws should be rewritten such that mandated treatment rather than incarceration should be recommended for those who commit crimes where mental illness is a major factor. In line with this, first responders to mental health crises should be medical personnel, not law enforcement. Wider use of peer counselors and temporary treatment beds in community health centers can often obviate the need for hospitalization or incarceration.
- *Humane and effective mandated treatment should be expanded, especially in an outpatient setting.* We can fulfill the promise of President Kennedy and aggressively fund community mental health centers. Treatment should include supported housing and social support to keep people engaged in the community with a meaningful role.
- *Hold our elected officials to their duty to enforce existing antitrust and CPOM laws.* States forbid profit-seeking entities from controlling or interfering with a physician's ethical duties to put patient's interests first. We should enforce these laws, and not allow corporations to hide behind claims of being not-for-profit or shielded by "straw doctors" or venture capital and private equity shells.
- *Aggressively enforce the Park Doctrine in the healthcare arena.* Corporate officers of healthcare companies should, like healthcare clinicians, be responsible for acts that cause harm to others.

- *Expose conflicts of interest.* Government needs to enforce existing conflict of interest/kickback/anti-racketeering laws in the healthcare industry, particularly as they relate to Big Pharma and the insurance industry. Physicians are forbidden from investing in profit-generating enterprises that they control; this prohibition should include all healthcare clinicians from nurses, to therapists, to chiropractors.
- *Ban lobbying by entities doing business in healthcare.* The healthcare industry spends more money lobbying than any other business in this country. Every dollar spent on lobbying is a dollar taken away from patient care, and is key to why corporate practice of medicine laws, the Park Doctrine, and kickbacks in healthcare are ignored.
- *Repeal the Institution for Mental Diseases (IMD) exclusion rule.* This misguided anachronism from the days of deinstitutionalization needlessly blocks poor Medicaid recipients' access to mental healthcare.
- *Repeal the Bayh–Dole act.* Discoveries with the potential to improve health and save lives belong in the public domain so all can benefit. This boondoggle allows private companies to reap profits from discoveries made with taxpayers' dollars, and exclude many from lifesaving care.

Figure Credits

Page 4: Adapted from Physicians for a National Health Program, Adam Gaffney, with permission. Data from the Canadian Institute for Health Information and the National Center for Health Statistics (CDC) and U.S. Department of Commerce.

Page 10, top: Adapted from Physicians for a National Health Program, Adam Gaffney, with permission. Data from OECD (Organization for Economic Co-operation and Development): https://stats.oecd.org/Index.aspx?DataSetCode=SHA#, accessed 9/29/2023

Page 10, bottom: Adapted from Physicians for a National Health Program, Adam Gaffney, with permission. Data from OECD (Organization for Economic Co-operation and Development): https://stats.oecd.org/Index.aspx?DataSetCode=SHA#, accessed 9/29/2023.

Page 28: Data from: Mental Illness Policy Org. https://mentalillnesspolicy.org/wp-content/uploads/Chap6NEWHospitalizedvsIncarcerated1960-2014-300x202.jpg; HUD Exchange. "PIT Estimates of Homelessness in the U.S." https://www.hudexchange.info/resource/4832/2015-ahar-part-1-pit-estimates-of-homelessness/; Ornstein, Norm and Leifman, Steve. "Locking People Up is no Way to Treat Mental Illness: If We Stopped Using Prisons to Warehouse Psychiatric Patients, We Could Heal People and Save Tax Dollars." *The Atlantic*, May 30, 2022. https://www.theatlantic.com/ideas/archive/2022/05/mental-illness-treatment-funding-incarceration/643115/.

Page 67: Adapted from Drs. Steffie Woolhandler and David Himmelstein. Data from the Bureau of Labor Statistics, National Center for Health Statistics. Original available at https://www.citizen.org/article/updated-powerpoint-presentations-on-health-policy-issues-relevant-to-health-care-reform-and-a-national-single-payer-health-system/.

Page 68: Himmelstein, David, David U., Terry Campbell, and Steffie Woolhandler. "Health Care Administrative Costs in the United States and Canada, 2017." *Annals of Internal Medicine* 172, no. 2 (January 7, 2020): 134. https://doi.org/10.7326/m19-2818. (Updated).

Page 183: Adapted from Physicians for a National Health Program, Ed Weisbart.

Page 185: From *U.S. Health in International Perspective*. National Academies Press eBooks, 2013. https://doi.org/10.17226/13497.

Notes

Introduction: Bedlam by the Bay

1   Powers, Ron. *No One Cares About Crazy People: My Family and the Heartbreak of Mental Illness in America*. New York: Hachette, 2018.

2   Centers for Disease Control and Prevention. "Provisional Suicide Deaths in the United States, 2022." Accessed January 18, 2024. https://www.cdc.gov/media/releases/2023/s0810-US-Suicide-Deaths-2022.html.

3   NCHS: A Blog of the National Center for Health Statistics. "Provisional Data Shows U.S. Drug Overdose Deaths Top 100,000 in 2022." May 18, 2023. https://blogs.cdc.gov/nchs/2023/05/18/7365/.

4   Centers for Disease Control and Prevention. "Deaths from Excessive Alcohol Use in the United States." Accessed January 18, 2024. https://www.cdc.gov/alcohol/features/excessive-alcohol-deaths.html.

5   Centers for Disease Control and Prevention. Morbidity and Mortality Weekly Report. "COVID-19 Mortality Update - United States, 2022." May 5, 2023. https://www.cdc.gov/mmwr/volumes/72/wr/mm7218a4.htm.

6   McPhillips, Deidre. "Youth, Young Adults Are Dying From Suicide and Homicide at Highest Rates in Decades, CDC Report Says." CNN, June 15, 2023. https://www.cnn.com/2023/06/15/health/youth-suicide-homicide/index.html.

7   Centers for Disease Control and Prevention. "Suicide and Homicide Death Rates Among Youth and Young Adults Aged 10–24: United States, 2001–2021." June 15, 2023. https://stacks.cdc.gov/view/cdc/128423.

8   Centers for Disease Control and Prevention. Vital Statistics Rapid Release. "Provisional Estimates of Suicide by Demographic Characteristics: United States, 2022." November 2023. https://www.cdc.gov/nchs/data/vsrr/vsrr034.pdf.

9   "FBI Says US Murders Dropped in 2022, but Theft Rose." Reuters, October 16, 2023. https://www.reuters.com/world/us/fbi-says-us -murders-dropped-2022-theft-rose-2023-10-16/.

10   Barry, Rebecca, Jennifer J. Anderson, Lan Mai Tran, Anees Bahji, Gina Dimitropoulos, S. Monty Ghosh, Julia Kirkham, et al. "Prevalence of Mental Health Disorders Among Individuals Experiencing Homelessness." *JAMA Psychiatry*, April 17, 2024. https://doi.org /10.1001/jamapsychiatry.2024.0426.

11   Walker, Elizabeth Reisinger, Robin E. McGee, and Benjamin G. Druss. "Mortality in Mental Disorders and Global Disease Burden Implications: A Systematic Review and Meta-analysis." *JAMA Psychiatry* 72, no. 4 (Apr 2015): 334-341.

12   Leucht, Stefan, Sandra Hierl, Werner Kissling, Markus Dold, and John M. Davis. "Putting the Efficacy of Psychiatric and General Medicine Medication into Perspective: Review of Meta-Analyses." *British Journal of Psychiatry* 200, no. 2 (2012): 97-106.

13   Montori, Victor. *Why We Revolt, a Patient Revolution for Careful and Kind Care.* Saint Paul: The Patient Revolution, 2017.

14   Witters, Dan. "U.S. Depression Rates Reach New Highs." Gallup, May 17, 2023. https://news.gallup.com/poll/505745/depression-rates -reach-new-highs.aspx.

15   Substance Abuse and Mental Health Services Administration. "2022 National Survey on Drug Use and Health (NSDUH) Releases." Accessed January 18, 2024. https://www.samhsa.gov/data /release/2022-national-survey-drug-use-and-health-nsduh-releases.

16   McPhillips, Deidre. "More than 1 in 6 US Adults and Adolescents had a Substance Use Disorder in 2022, Federal Survey Finds." CNN, November 13, 2023. https://us.cnn.com/2023/11/13/health/substance -use-disorder-mental-health-survey/index.html.

17   McPhillips, Deidre. "90% of US Adults Say the United States is Experiencing a Mental Health Crisis, CNN/KFF Poll Finds." CNN, October 5, 2022. https://us.cnn.com/2022/10/05/health/cnn-kff-mental -health-poll-wellness/index.html.

18   IPSOS. "Mental Health Replaces COVID as the Top Health Concern among Americans." September 26, 2022. https://www.ipsos.com/en-us /news-polls/mental-health-top-healthcare-concern-us-global-survey.

19   Iscoe, Adam. "The System That Failed Jordan Neely." *The New Yorker*, May 10, 2023. https://www.newyorker.com/magazine/2023/05/22 /the-system-that-failed-jordan-neely.

Chapter One: A Little History: How and Why We Made This Mess

1   Appelbaum, Binyamin. *The Economists' Hour: False Prophets, Free Markets, and the Fracture of Society.* New York: Little, Brown and Company, 2019.

2   Ehrenreich, Barbara, and John Ehrenreich. "The Medical-Industrial Complex." *New York Review of Books* (December 17, 1970).

3   Relman, Arnold. "The new medical-industrial complex." *New England Journal of Medicine* 303, no. 17 (Oct 23, 1980): 963–70. doi: 10.1056 /NEJM198010233031703.

4   Centers for Medicare & Medicaid Services. "National Health Expenditure." Accessed January 18, 2024. https://www.cms.gov/files/zip/nhe-tables.zip

5   "Fit as Fiddles: Regulation May Hurt Other Financial Firms, but Health Insurers Thrive on It." *The Economist*, December 5, 2015. http://www .economist.com/news/finance-and-economics/21679475-regulation-may -hurt-other-financial-firms-health-insurers-thrive-it-fit.

6   Myshko, Denise. "UnitedHealth Group's Revenue Grew Almost 15% in 2023." *Managed Healthcare Executive*, January 12, 2024. https://www .managedhealthcareexecutive.com/view/unitedhealth-group-s-revenue -grew-almost-15-in-2023.

7   Muoio, Dave. "Kaiser Permanente Reports $4.1B Profit, Exceeds $100B Operating Revenues in 2023." Fierce Healthcare, February 12, 2024. https://www.fiercehealthcare.com/providers/kaiser-permanente-reports -41b-profit-exceeds-100b-operating-revenues-2023.

8   Jennings, Katie. "Venture Funding for Mental Health Startups Hits Record High as Anxiety and Depression Skyrocket." *Forbes*, June 7, 2021. https://www.forbes.com/sites/katiejennings/2021/06/07/venture -funding-for-mental-health-startups-hits-record-high-as-anxiety -depression-skyrocket.

9   Brenan, Megan. "Record High in U.S. Put off Medical Care Due to Cost in 2022." *Gallup*, January 17, 2023. https://news.gallup.com/poll/468053 /record-high-put-off-medical-care-due-cost-2022.aspx.

10   "The High Cost of Health: Analyzing America's Healthcare Affordability Crisis." *Payzen*, April 2024. Accessed May 1, 2024. https ://payzen.com/wp-content/uploads/2024/04/PayZen-Healthcare -Affordability_Whitepaper_v5.pdf.

11   Marken, Stephanie. "Few Americans Know How Much Their Healthcare Costs." Gallup, January 31, 2024. https://news.gallup.com /poll/609434/few-americans-know-healthcare-costs.aspx.

12   "How Rich Hospitals Profit From Patients in Car Accidents." *New York Times*, February 1, 2021. https://www.nytimes.com/2021/02/01 /upshot/rich-hospitals-profit-poor.html?referringSource=article Share.

13   "Some California Hospitals Refused COVID-19 Transfers for Financial Reasons, State Emails Show." *Wall Street Journal*, updated October 19, 2020. https://www.wsj.com/articles/some-california-hospitals-refused -covid-19-transfers-for-financial-reasons-state-emails-show -11603108814.

14   Mahar, Maggie. *Money-Driven Medicine: The Real Reason Healthcare Costs So Much*. New York: HarperCollins, 2006.

15   Crowley, Ryan, Omar Atiq, and David Hilden. "Financial Profit in Medicine: A Position Paper From the American College of Physicians."

Annals of Internal Medicine 174, no. 10 (Oct 2021): 1447–9. doi:10.7326 /M21-1178.

16   Rosenthal, Elisabeth. *An American Sickness: How Healthcare Became Big Business and How You Can Take It Back.* New York: Penguin Press, 2017.

17   "Prescription Drug Prices in the United States Are 2.56 Times Those in Other Countries." RAND Corporation, January 28, 2021. https://www .rand.org/news/press/2021/01/28.html.

18   Dunleavy, Kevin. "TEVA Ponies up $410M to Settle with Investors Who Said Company Hid Price-Fixing Scheme." Fierce Pharma, January 19, 2022. https://www.fiercepharma.com/pharma/teva-ponies -up-420-million-to-settle-investors-who-alleged-company-hid-price -fixing-scheme.

19   Campaign for Sustainable Rx Pricing. "Dose of Reality: Breaking Down the Big Pharma Dollar, Part III." Accessed January 19, 2024. https ://www.csrxp.org/dose-of-reality-breaking-down-the-big-pharma -dollar-part-iii/.

20   "Biosimilar Drugs Promise to Slash Health-Care Costs in Rich Countries: The World's Top-Selling Drug Now Faces Biosimilars That Are 80% Cheaper." *The Economist*, November 10, 2018.

21   Statista. "Average Price of Humira by Country." Accessed January 19, 2024. https://www.statista.com/statistics/312014/average-price-of -humira-by-country/.

22   Silverman, Ed. "Net Prices for Medicines Fell Considerably in 2023's Last Quarter, Mostly Thanks to Humira Biosimilars." *STAT*, April 1, 2024. https://www.statnews.com/pharmalot/2024/04/01/medicines -prices-humira-biosimilar-novo-abbvie-lilly-mounjaro-diabetes -obesity-hiv/.

23   Rosenthal, Elisabeth. *An American Sickness: How Healthcare Became Big Business and How You Can Take It Back.* New York: Penguin Press, 2017, 59.

24   Abelson, Reed. "Hospitals Must Now Post Prices. But It May Take a Brain Surgeon to Decipher Them." *New York Times*, December 4, 2019. https://www.nytimes.com/2019/12/04/health/hospitals-trump-prices -transparency.html.

25   Mathews, Anna, Tom McGinty, and Melanie Evans. "How Much Does a C-Section Cost at One Hospital? Anywhere from $6,241 to $60,584." *Wall Street Journal*, February 11, 2021. https://www.wsj.com/articles /how-much-does-a-c-section-cost-at-one-hospital-anywhere-from-6 -241-to-60-584-11613051137.

26   Evans, Melanie, Anna Mathews, and Tom McGinty. "Hospitals Often Charge Uninsured People the Highest Prices, New Data Show." *Wall Street Journal*, July 16, 2021. https://www.wsj.com/articles /hospitals-often-charge-uninsured-people-the-highest-prices-new-data -show-11625584448.

27   Kliff, Sarah, and Josh Katz. "Hospital Prices: A Hidden System Revealed." *New York Times*, August 22, 2021. https://www.nytimes.com/interactive/2021/08/22/upshot/hospital-prices.html.

28   Jiang, John Xuefeng, Daniel Polsky, Jeff Littlejohn, et al. "Factors Associated with Compliance to the Hospital Price Transparency Final Rule: A National Landscape Study." *Journal of General Internal Medicine* 37, no. 14 (Nov 2022): 3577–84. doi:10.1007/s11606-021-07237-y.

29   "Capitalist Death Panels: If Corporate Vultures Get Their Way, We'll Be Dead." *The Intercept*, March 25, 2020. https://theintercept.com/2020/03/25/capitalist-death-panels-if-corporate-vultures-get-their-way-well-be-dead/.

30   Muoio, Dave. "HCA Healthcare Accused of Pushing Patients toward End-of-Life Care to Boost Performance Metrics." *Fierce Healthcare*, June 21, 2023. https://www.fiercehealthcare.com/providers/hca-health care-accused-pushing-patients-toward-end-life-care-financial-gain.

31   Starr, Paul. *Remedy and Reaction: The Peculiar American Struggle over Healthcare Reform*. New Haven: Yale University Press, 2011.

32   World Health Organization. "Global Burden of Disease: 2004 Update." Updated March 2, 2004. https://www.who.int/publications/i/item/9789241563710.

33   The Commonwealth Fund. "Mirror, Mirror 2021: Reflecting Poorly." August 4, 2021. https://www.commonwealthfund.org/publications/fund-reports/2021/aug/mirror-mirror-2021-reflecting-poorly.

34   Miller, Lee and Wei Lu. "These are the Economies with the Most (and Least) Efficient Healthcare." Bloomberg Quint, September 20, 2018. https://www.bloombergquint.com/global-economics/u-s-near-bottom-of-health-index-hong-kong-and-singapore-at-top.

35   Rabin, Roni. "In Rural America, Pregnancy and Childbirth Are Often Shrouded in Secrecy." *New York Times*, updated June 20, 2023. https://www.nytimes.com/2023/02/26/health/rural-hospitals-pregnancy-childbirth.html.

36   Centers for Disease Control and Prevention. "Maternal Mortality and Morbidity Data." Accessed January 19, 2024. https://www.cdc.gov/reproductivehealth/maternal-mortality/erase-mm/data-mmrc.html.

37   Wisner, Katherine L., Caitlin Murphy, Megan M. Thomas. "Prioritizing Maternal Mental Health in Addressing Morbidity and Mortality." *JAMA Psychiatry* (Feb 21, 2024). doi:10.1001/jamapsychiatry.2023.5648.

38   National Institute on Drug Abuse. "Overdose Death Rates." Accessed January 19, 2024. https://www.drugabuse.gov/drug-topics/trends-statistics/overdose-death-rates.

39   Frank, Jerome D. *Persuasion and Healing*. Baltimore: The Johns Hopkins Press, 1961.

40   Porter, Roy. *Madness: A Brief History*. Oxford: Oxford University Press, 2002.

41   Centers for Disease Control and Prevention. "Hansen's Disease (Leprosy)."
       Accessed April 29, 2024. https://www.cdc.gov/leprosy/index.html.

42   Porter, Roy. *Madness: A Brief History*. Oxford: Oxford University Press,
       2002.

43   Phillips, M. "Forgotten Soldiers" *Wall Street Journal*, December 11, 2023.
       https://www.wsj.com/articles/SB10001424052702303997604579238383
       527930824.

44   Valenstein, Elliot S. *Great and Desperate Cures: The Rise and Decline of
       Psychosurgery and Other Radical Treatments for Mental Illness*. New York:
       Basic Books, 1986.

45   Healy, David. *The Creation of Psychopharmacology*. Cambridge: Harvard
       University Press, 2002.

46   Harrington, Anne. *Mind Fixers: Psychiatry's Troubled Search for the Biology
       of Mental Illness*. New York: Norton, 2019.

47   Grinker, Roy. *Nobody's Normal: How Culture Created the Stigma of Mental
       Illness*. New York: WW Norton, 2021.

48   Kuhn, Roland. "The treatment of depressive states with G 22355
       (imipramine hydrochloride)." *American Journal of Psychiatry* 115, no. 5
       (Nov 1958): 459–64. doi:10.1176/ajp.115.5.459. PMID: 13583250.

49   Torrey, E. Fuller. *American Psychosis: How the Federal Government
       Destroyed the Mental Illness Treatment System*. Oxford: Oxford University
       Press, 2013.

50   Rosenberg, Kenneth. *Bedlam: An Intimate Journey into America's Mental
       Health Crisis*. Garden City: Avery, 2019.

51   Isaac, Rael Jean, and Virginia C. Armat. *Madness in the Streets: How
       Psychiatry and the Law Abandoned the Mentally Ill*. New York: The Free
       Press, 1990.

52   Deutsch, Albert. *The Shame of the States*. New York: Harcourt Brace &
       Co, 1948.

53   The Federal Register. "Annual Determination of Average Cost of
       Incarceration Fee." September 1, 2021. https://www.federalregister.gov
       /documents/2021/09/01/2021-18800/annual-determination-of-average
       -cost-of-incarceration-fee-coif.

54   Vera. "The Price of Jails: Measuring the Taxpayer Cost of Local
       Incarceration." May 2015. https://www.vera.org/publications
       /the-price-of-jails-measuring-the-taxpayer-cost-of-local-incarceration.

55   Rosenhan, David. "On Being Sane in Insane Places." *Science* 179,
       no. 4070 (1973): 250–8. doi:10.1126/science.179.4070.250.

56   Cahalan, Susan. *The Great Pretender*. New York: Grand Central
       Publishing, 2019.

57   Scull, Andrew. "How a Fraudulent Experiment Set Psychiatry Back
       Decades." *The Spectator*, January 2020. https://www.spectator.co.uk
       /article/how-a-fraudulent-experiment-set-psychiatry-back-decades.

58   Toms, J. "Mind the Gap: MIND, the Mental Hygiene Movement and
       the Trapdoor in Measurements of Intellect." *Journal of Intellectual*

Disability Research 54, no. suppl 1 (2010): 16–27. doi:10.1111/j.1365 -2788.2009.01234.x.

59 Szasz, Thomas. *The Myth of Mental Illness.* New York: Dell Publishing, 1961.

60 Laing, Ronald David. *Politics of Experience.* New York: Pantheon, 1967.

61 Lieberman, Jeffrey, and Ogi Ogas. *Shrinks: The Untold Story of Psychiatry.* New York: Little, Brown and Company, 201

62 Holden, Constance. "Giving Mental Illness Its Research Due." *Science* 232, no. 4754 (1986): 1084–5. doi: 10.1126/science.3704637.

63 The American Presidency Project. "Special Message to the Congress on Mental Illness and Mental Retardation." President Kennedy, February 5, 1963. Accessed January 19, 2024. https://www.presidency.ucsb.edu /documents/special-message-the-congress-mental-illness-and-mental -retardation.

64 Isaac, Rael Jean, and Virginia C. Armat. *Madness in the Streets: How Psychiatry and the Law Abandoned the Mentally Ill.* New York: The Free Press, 1990.

65 Valenstein, Elliot. *Blaming the Brain: The Truth about Drugs and Mental Health.* New York: The Free Press, 1988.

66 "Deaths from Cold Soar as Homeless Increase." *New York Times,* December 25, 1988.

67 Haghighat, Leila, Satvik Ramakrishna, James W. Salazar, Jean Feng, Joey Chiang, Ellen Moffatt, and Zian H. Tseng. "Homelessness and Incidence and Causes of Sudden Death." *JAMA Internal Medicine* 183, no. 12 (December 1, 2023): 1306. doi:10.1001/jamainternmed .2023.5475.

68 Isaac, Rael Jean, and Virginia C. Armat. *Madness in the Streets: How Psychiatry and the Law Abandoned the Mentally Ill.* New York: The Free Press, 1990.

69 Sacks, Oliver, "The Lost Virtues of the Asylum." *The New York Review of Books.* September 24, 2009. https://www.nybooks.com/articles/2009 /09/24/the-lost-virtues-of-the-asylum.

70 "The Solution to America's Mental Health Crisis Already Exists." *New York Times,* October 4, 2022. https://www.nytimes.com/2022/10/04 /opinion/us-mental-health-community-centers.html.

71 Isaac, Rael Jean, and Virginia C. Armat. *Madness in the Streets: How Psychiatry and the Law Abandoned the Mentally Ill.* New York: The Free Press, 1990.

72 NAMI. "Medicaid IMD Exclusion." Accessed December 12, 2023. https://www.nami.org/advocacy/policy-priorities/improving-Health /Medicaid-IMD-Exclusion.

73 SAMHSA. "Homeless Programs and Resources." Accessed December 12, 2023. https://www.samhsa.gov/homelessness-programs-resources.

74 Barry, Rebecca, Jennifer J. Anderson, Lan Mai Tran, Anees Bahji, Gina Dimitropoulos, S. Monty Ghosh, Julia Kirkham, et al. "Prevalence of Mental Health Disorders Among Individuals Experiencing Homelessness."

JAMA Psychiatry, April 17, 2024. https://doi.org/10.1001/jamapsychiatry .2024.0426.

75   "Understanding: California Statewide Study of People Experiencing Homelessness." Benioff Homelessness and Housing Initiative, University of California, San Francisco. https://homelessness.ucsf.edu/sites/default /files/2023-06/CASPEH_Report_62023.pdf.

76   Hjorthøj, Carsten, Anne Stürup, John McGrath, and Merete Nordentoft. "Years of Potential Life Lost and Life Expectancy in Schizophrenia: A Systematic Review and Meta-Analysis." *Lancet* 4, no. 4 (2017): 295-301. doi:10.1016/S2215-0366(17)30078-0.

77   Bureau of Justice Statistics. "Mental Health Problems of Prison and Jail Inmates." September 6, 2006. Accessed January 20, 2024. https://bjs.ojp .gov/press-release/mental-health-problems-prison-and-jail-inmates.

78   Rosenberg, Kenneth. *Bedlam: An Intimate Journey into America's Mental Health Crisis*. Garden City: Avery, 2019.

79   Powers, Ron. *No One Cares About Crazy People*. New York: Hachette, 2017.

80   Isaac, Rael Jean, and Virginia C. Armat. *Madness in the Streets: How Psychiatry and the Law Abandoned the Mentally Ill*. New York: The Free Press, 1990.

81   Dewees, E. "Legislation for the mentally ill" [letter to the editor]. *Los Angeles Times*, December 5, 1987.

82   Reingle Gonzalez, Jennifer M., and Nadine M. Connell. "Mental Health of Prisoners: Identifying Barriers to Mental Health Treatment and Medication Continuity." *American Journal of Public Health* 104, no. 12 (2014): 2328–33. doi:10.2105/AJPH.2014.302043.

83   Curran Jill, Brendan Saloner, Tyler Winkelman, and G. Caleb Alexander. "Estimated Use of Prescription Medications Among Individuals Incarcerated in Jails and State Prisons in the US." *JAMA Health Forum* 4, no. 4 (2023): e230482. doi:10.1001/jamahealth forum.2023.0482.

84   Limon, Elvia, and Jason Sanchez. "Today's Headlines: The Mentally Ill Languish in California Jails Without Trial or Treatment." *Los Angeles Times*, September 14, 2022. https://www.latimes.com/world-nation /newsletter/2022-09-14/. mentally-ill-california-jails-without-treatment-trials-todays-headlines.

85   Mental Illness Policy Org. "Quick Guide to Most Important Ways Federal Government Can Help the Most Seriously Mentally Ill." Accessed January 20, 2024. https://mentalillnesspolicy.org /federalmentalillnesslegislation/guide2fedlegislation.html.

86   USA Facts. "How Much do States Spend on Prisons?" Accessed January 20, 2024. https://usafacts.org/articles/how-much-do-states-spend-on-prisons/.

87   Houghton, Katheryn. "When Mental Illness Leads to Dropped Charges, Patients Often Go without Stabilizing Care." KFF Health News, August 15, 2022. https://khn.org/news/article/mental-illness -dropped-charges-competency-care/.

88   Rosenberg, Kenneth. *Bedlam: An Intimate Journey into America's Mental Health Crisis.* Garden City: Avery, 2019.

89   Treatment Advocacy Center. "Overlooked in the Undercounted: The Role of Mental Illness in Fatal Law Enforcement Encounters." January 3, 2024. https://www.treatmentadvocacycenter.org/reports_publications /overlooked-in-the-undercounted-the-role-of-mental-illness-in-fatal -law-enforcement-encounters/.

Chapter Two: The Impact on Patients and Families

1   Witters, Dan. "U.S. Depression Rates Reach New Highs." Gallup, September 14, 2023. https://news.gallup.com/poll/505745/depression -rates-reach-new-highs.aspx.

2   "2022 National Survey on Drug Use and Health (NSDUH) Releases." SAMHSA. Accessed January 20, 2024. https://www.samhsa.gov/data /release/2022-national-survey-drug-use-and-health-nsduh-releases.

3   Athey, Alison, Beau Kilmer, and Julie Cerel. "An Overlooked Emergency: More Than One in Eight US Adults Have Had Their Lives Disrupted by Drug Overdose Deaths." *American Journal of Public Health* 114, no. 3 (March 1, 2024): 276–79. doi:10.2105/ajph.2023.307550.

4   Jaffe, Don. "Shortage of Psychiatric Hospital Beds for Mentally Ill (Summary TAC Report): Mental Illness Policy Org." Mental Illness Policy Org, January 23, 2019. https://mentalillnesspolicy.org/imd /shortage-hospital-beds.html.

5   New American Economy. "New Study Shows 60 Percent of U.S. Counties Without a Single Psychiatrist: One-Third of All Psychiatrists Nationwide Trained Abroad." October 23, 2017. https://www.new americaneconomy.org/press-release/new-study-shows-60-percent-of -u-s-counties-without-a-single-psychiatrist/

6   Bommersbach, Tanner J., Alastair J. McKean, Mark Olfson, and Taeho Greg Rhee. "National Trends in Mental Health-Related Emergency Department Visits among Youth, 2011-2020." *JAMA* 329, no. 17 (May 2, 2023): 1469. doi:10.1001/jama.2023.4809.

7   Hoffmann, Jennifer A., Megan Attridge, Michael S. Carroll, Norma-Jean Simon, Andrew F. Beck, and Elizabeth R. Alpern. "Association of Youth Suicides and County-Level Mental Health Professional Shortage Areas in the US." *JAMA Pediatrics* 177, no. 1 (January 1, 2023): 71. doi:10.1001/jamapediatrics.2022.4419.

8   Arakelyan, Mary, Seneca D Freyleue, Divya Avula, Jennifer McLaren, A. James O'Malley, and JoAnna K Leyenaar. "Pediatric Mental Health Hospitalizations at Acute Care Hospitals in the US, 2009-2019." *JAMA* 329, no. 12 (March 28, 2023): 1000. doi:10.1001/jama.2023.1992.

9   Ahn-Horst, Rosa Y., and Florence T. Bourgeois. "Mental Health-Related Outpatient Visits Among Adolescents and Young Adults, 2006–2019." *JAMA Network Open* 7, no. 3 (March 7, 2024): e241468. doi:10.1001/jamanetworkopen.2024.1468.

10   Loo, Theoren, Myra Altman, Dena M Bravata, and Christopher
        Whaley. "Medical Spending Among US Households With Children
        With a Mental Health Condition Between 2017 and 2021." *JAMA
        Network Open* 7, no. 3 (March 11, 2024): e241860. doi:10.1001
        /jamanetworkopen.2024.1860.

11   Cafferty, Rachel, Jacqueline Grupp-Phelan, and Bruno J. Anthony.
        "Children and Adolescents with Suicidal Ideation and the Emergency
        Department." *JAMA*, December 28, 2023. doi:10.1001/jama.2023
        .26291.

12   Richtel, Matt, and Annie Flanagan. "Hundreds of Suicidal Teens Sleep
        in Emergency Rooms. Every Night." *New York Times*, May 9, 2022.
        https://www.nytimes.com/2022/05/08/health/emergency-rooms-teen
        -mental-health.html.

13   Green, Cori M., Jane Meschan Foy, and Marian F. Earls. "Achieving the
        Pediatric Mental Health Competencies." *Pediatrics* 144, no. 5 (October 21,
        2019): e20192758. doi:10.1542/peds.2019-2758.

14   Miron, Oren, Kun-Hsing Yu, Rachel Wilf-Miron, and Isaac S. Kohane.
        "Suicide Rates among Adolescents and Young Adults in the United
        States, 2000–2017." *JAMA* 321, no. 23 (June 18, 2019): 2362. doi:10.1001
        /jama.2019.5054.

15   Carlo, Andrew D., Brian S. Barnett, and Richard G. Frank. "Behavioral
        Health Parity Efforts in the US." *JAMA* 324, no. 5 (August 4, 2020):
        447. doi:10.1001/jama.2020.3505.

16   SAMHSA. "2018 NSDUH Annual National Report." August 2019.
        Accessed January 20, 2024. https://www.samhsa.gov/data/report/2018
        -nsduh-annual-national-report.

17   Law, Tara. "Why Overdose Deaths Skyrocketed after Opioid
        Prescriptions Dropped." *TIME*, September 19, 2022. https://time.com
        /6214811/overdose-deaths-opioid-prescriptions/.

18   "KFF Tracking Poll July 2023: Substance Use Crisis and Accessing
        Treatment." KFF, August 15, 2023. https://www.kff.org/other/poll-finding
        /kff-tracking-poll-july-2023-substance-use-crisis-and-accessing-treatment/.

19   Associated Press. "Over Half of Car Crash Victims Had Drugs or
        Alcohol in Their Systems, a Study Says." NPR, December 13, 2022.
        https://www.npr.org/2022/12/13/1142598789/drivers-crashes-drugs
        -alcohol-nhtsa-study.

20   Turban, Jack. "Ghost Networks of Psychiatrists Make Money for
        Insurance Companies but Hinder Patients' Access to Care." *STAT*,
        July 25, 2023. https://www.statnews.com/2019/06/17/ghost
        -networks-psychiatrists-hinder-patient-care/.

21   Malowney, Monica, Sarah Keltz, Daniel Fischer, and J. Wesley Boyd.
        "Availability of Outpatient Care from Psychiatrists: A Simulated-Patient
        Study in Three U.S. Cities." *Psychiatric Services* 66, no. 1 (January 1,
        2015): 94–96. doi:10.1176/appi.ps.201400051.

22   Cama, Shireen, Monica Malowney, Anna Jo Bodurtha Smith,
        Margaret Spottswood, Elisa Cheng, Louis Ostrowsky, Jose Rengifo,

and J. Wesley Boyd. "Availability of Outpatient Mental Healthcare by Pediatricians and Child Psychiatrists in Five U.S. Cities." *International Journal of Health Services* 47, no. 4 (May 5, 2017): 621–35. doi:10.1177/0020731417707492.

23   Bishop, Tara F., Matthew J. Press, Salomeh Keyhani, and Harold Alan Pincus. "Acceptance of Insurance by Psychiatrists and the Implications for Access to Mental Healthcare." *JAMA Psychiatry* 71, no. 2 (February 1, 2014): 176. doi:10.1001/jamapsychiatry.2013.2862.

24   Cummings, Janet R. "Rates of Psychiatrists' Participation in Health Insurance Networks." *JAMA* 313, no. 2 (January 13, 2015): 190. doi:10.1001/jama.2014.12472.

25   Parker-Pope, Tara, Christina Caron, and Mónica Cordero Sancho. "Why Therapists Are Worried about America's Growing Mental Health Crisis." *New York Times*, September 6, 2023. https://www.nytimes.com/interactive/2021/12/16/well/mental-health-crisis-america-covid.html.

26   Benjenk, Ivy, and Jie Chen. "Trends in Self-Payment for Outpatient Psychiatrist Visits." *JAMA Psychiatry* 77, no. 12 (December 1, 2020): 1305. doi:10.1001/jamapsychiatry.2020.2072.

27   Lopes, Lunna, Alex Montero, Marley Presiado, and Liz Hamel. "Americans' Challenges With Healthcare Costs." KFF, March 1, 2024. https://www.kff.org/health-costs/issue-brief/americans-challenges-with-health-care-costs/.

28   Levey, Noam N. "100 Million People in America Are Saddled with Healthcare Debt - KFF Health News." KFF Health News, January 10, 2023. https://khn.org/news/article/diagnosis-debt-investigation-100-million-americans-hidden-medical-debt/.

29   "Healthcare Debt in the U.S.: The Broad Consequences of Medical and Dental Bills." KFF, June 7, 2023. https://www.kff.org/health-costs/report/kff-health-care-debt-survey/.

30   "KFF Health Tracking Poll—March 2022: Economic Concerns and Health Policy, the ACA, and Views of Long-Term Care Facilities." KFF, March 31, 2022. https://www.kff.org/health-costs/poll-finding/kff-health-tracking-poll-march-2022/.

31   Kluender, Raymond, Neale Mahoney, Francis Wong, and Wesley Yin. "Medical Debt in the US, 2009-2020." *JAMA* 326, no. 3 (July 20, 2021): 250. doi:10.1001/jama.2021.8694.

32   Himmelstein, D. U., Lawless, R. M., Thorne, D., Foohey, P., & Woolhandler, S. (2019). "Medical bankruptcy: still common despite the Affordable Care Act." *American Journal of Public Health*, 109(3), 431–433. https://doi.org/10.2105/ajph.2018.304901.

33   Rosenthal, Elisabeth. "GoFundMe Has Become a Healthcare Utility." KFF Health News, February 23, 2024. https://kffhealthnews.org/news/article/gofundme-health-care-funding-hospitals-surprise-bills/.

34   Hussein, Fatima. "Regulators Try to Stop Unlawful Nursing Home Debt Collection." AP News, September 8, 2022. https://apnews.com/article

/health-nursing-homes-government-and-politics-cd4fa9b5b61c4fa83
a6338449651531c.

35   Han, Xuesong, Xin Hu, Zhiyuan Zheng, Kewei Sylvia Shi, and K.
     Robin Yabroff. "Associations of Medical Debt With Health Status,
     Premature Death, and Mortality in the US." *JAMA Network Open* 7,
     no. 3 (March 4, 2024): e2354766. doi:10.1001/jamanetworkopen
     .2023.54766.

36   Pfeffer, Jeffrey, Dan Witters, Sangeeta Agrawal, and James K. Harter.
     "Magnitude and Effects of 'Sludge' in Benefits Administration: How
     Health Insurance Hassles Burden Workers and Cost Employers."
     Academy of Management Discoveries (July 31, 2020). doi:10.5465
     /amd.2020.0063.

37   Kyle, Michael Anne, and Austin B. Frakt. "Patient Administrative
     Burden in the US Healthcare System." *Health Services Research* 56, no. 5
     (September 8, 2021): 755–65. doi:10.1111/1475-6773.13861.

38   Ungar, Laura. "5 Days in Psychiatric Care Led to $21,000 Hospital Bill."
     ABC News, October 31, 2019. https://abcnews.go.com/Health/days
     -psychiatric-care-led-21k-hospital-bill/story?id=66662495.

39   Stensland, Michael D., Peter Watson, and Kyle L. Grazier. "An
     Examination of Costs, Charges, and Payments for Inpatient Psychiatric
     Treatment in Community Hospitals." *Psychiatric Services* 63, no. 7
     (July 1, 2012): 666–71. doi:10.1176/appi.ps.201100402.

40   Venter, Cara. "Donations Tie Drug Firms and Nonprofits." Mind
     Freedom International (MFI), July 16, 2021. https://mindfreedom.org
     /campaign/media/mf/inquirer-on-drug-firms.

41   Perlberg, Heather. "The Doctor Will See You Once You Sign This
     Binding Arbitration Agreement." Bloomberg, December 28, 2020.
     https://www.bloomberg.com/news/features/2020-12-28/the-doctor
     -will-see-you-once-you-sign-this-binding-arbitration-agreement.

42   Mariner, Wendy. "Standards of Care and Standard Form Contracts:
     Distinguishing Patient Rights and Consumer Rights in Managed Care."
     Journal of Contemporary Health Law Policy 15, no. 1 (1998): 1-55. https
     ://scholarship.law.edu/jchlp/vol15/iss1/3/.

43   Lagomasino, Isabel T., Susan Stockdale, and Jeanne Miranda. "Racial-
     Ethnic Composition of Provider Practices and Disparities in Treatment
     of Depression and Anxiety, 2003–2007." *Psychiatric Services* 62, no. 9
     (September 1, 2011): 1019–25. doi:10.1176/ps.62.9.pss6209_1019.

44   Statista. "Number of Homeless People in the U.S., by Race 2022,"
     June 2, 2023. https://www.statista.com/statistics/555855/number-of
     -homeless-people-in-the-us-by-race/.

45   Bor, Jacob, Atheendar Venkataramani, David R. Williams, and
     Alexander C. Tsai. "Police Killings and Their Spillover Effects on the
     Mental Health of Black Americans: A Population-Based, Quasi-
     Experimental Study." *The Lancet* 392, no. 10144 (July 1, 2018): 302–10.
     doi:10.1016/s0140-6736(18)31130-9.

46   Evans, Melanie. "Hospitals Give Tech Giants Access to Detailed
        Medical Records." *Wall Street Journal*, January 20, 2020. https://www
        .wsj.com/articles/hospitals-give-tech-giants-access-to-detailed-medical
        -records-11579516200.

47   Millenson, Michael L. "It's Time to Open up Healthcare's Secret
        Analytics." *STAT*, July 25, 2023. https://www.statnews.com/2021/12/06
        /its-time-to-open-up-health-cares-secret-analytics/.

48   De La Merced, Michael J. "AthenaHealth's $17 Billion Takeover Is the
        Latest Private Equity Megadeal." *New York Times*, November 22, 2021.
        https://www.nytimes.com/2021/11/22/business/athenahealth-hellman
        -friedman-bain-capital.html.

49   Ross, Casey. "How a Decades-Old Database Became a Hugely Profitable
        Dossier on the Health of 270 Million Americans." *STAT*, July 25, 2023. https
        ://www.statnews.com/2022/02/01/ibm-watson-health-marketscan-data/.

50   Ross, Casey. "How a Complex Web of Businesses Turned Private Health
        Records from GE into a Lucrative Portrait of Patients," *STAT*, July 31,
        2023, https://www.statnews.com/2022/05/23/hipaa-patient-ge-data
        -privacy-profit/.

51   Yoo, Ji Su. "Risks to Patient Privacy: A Re-Identification of Patients in
        Maine and Vermont Statewide Hospital Data." Technology Science, n.d.
        Accessed June 3, 2024. https://techscience.org/a/2018100901/.

52   Ross, Casey. "Internal Documents Show Privacy Lapses at a Data
        Powerhouse That Holds Health Records and Consumer Information on
        Millions of Americans." *STAT*, July 25, 2023. https://www.statnews.com
        /2022/07/28/health-data-privacy-iqvia-experian/.

53   EHRIntelligence. "Athenahealth Fined $18.25M for Illegal EHR
        Kickback Scheme." EHRIntelligence, January 29, 2021. https://ehr
        intelligence.com/news/athenahealth-fined-18.25m-for-illegal-ehr
        -kickback-scheme.

54   McCoy, Thomas H., and Roy H. Perlis. "Temporal Trends and
        Characteristics of Reportable Health Data Breaches, 2010-2017." *JAMA*
        320, no. 12 (September 25, 2018): 1282. doi:10.1001/jama.2018.9222.

55   Broderick, Tim. "Healthcare Data Breaches Hit New Highs in 2023."
        Modern Healthcare, January 28, 2024. https://www.modernhealthcare
        .com/cybersecurity/healthcare-data-breaches-2023-anthem-lbm.

56   McCoy, Matthew S., Ari B Friedman, and Allison K. Hoffman.
        "The Scope and Legal Implications of Tracking Technologies on
        Hospital Websites." *JAMA* 330, no. 3 (July 18, 2023): 217. doi:10.1001
        /jama.2023.8546.

57   Todd Feathers, Simon Fondrie-Teitler, Angie Waller, and Surya Mattu.
        "Facebook Is Receiving Sensitive Medical Information from Hospital
        Websites." *STAT*, July 25, 2023. https://www.statnews.com/2022/06/16
        /facebook-meta-pixel-hospitals-data/.

58   Niforatos, Joshua D., Alexander R. Zheutlin, and Jeremy B. Sussman.
        "Prevalence of Third-Party Data Tracking by US Hospital Websites."

JAMA Network Open 4, no. 9 (September 22, 2021): e2126121.
doi:10.1001/jamanetworkopen.2021.26121.

59   Palmer, Katie, Todd Feathers, and Simon Fondrie-Teitler. "'Out of Control':
Dozens of Telehealth Startups Sent Sensitive Health Information to Big
Tech Companies." *STAT*, December 13, 2022. https://www.statnews
.com/2022/12/13/telehealth-facebook-google-tracking-health-data.

60   Jackson, Brian R. "Why HIPAA Isn't Enough to Protect Your Health
Data." KevinMD.com, April 27, 2023. https://www.kevinmd.com
/2023/04/why-hipaa-isnt-enough-to-protect-your-health-data.html.

61   Wilkerson, John. "Senators Probe Telehealth Companies for Tracking
and Monetizing Sensitive Health Data." *STAT*, February 7, 2023.
https://www.statnews.com/2023/02/07/telehealth-privacy-cerebral
-workit-monument-data-congress.

Chapter Three: Restricting Care

1   Grumbach, Kevin, Dennis Osmond, Karen Vranizan, Deborah Jaffe,
and Andrew B. Bindman. "Primary Care Physicians' Experience of
Financial Incentives in Managed-Care Systems." *The New England
Journal of Medicine* 339, no. 21 (November 19, 1998): 1516–21.
doi:10.1056/nejm199811193392106.

2   Kelly, Ryan Charles, Richard Holt, Lane Desborough, Shideh
Majidi, Marissa Town, Diana Naranjo, Laurel H. Messer, Katharine
Barnard-Kelly, Jeannette Soderberg, and Katharine Barnard-Kelly.
"The Psychosocial Burdens of Living with Diabetes." *Diabetic Medicine*
(October 12, 2023). doi:10.1111/dme.15219.

3   Fierce Healthcare. "Here Are the 20 Highest Paid Specialties in 2022 as
Average Physician Pay Drops 2.4%: Doximity." March 23, 2023. https
://www.fiercehealthcare.com/providers/here-are-20-highest-paid
-specialties-2022-average-physician-pay-drops-24-doximity.

4   Smith, Erik Bruce. "Ending Physician Noncompete Agreements—Time
for a National Solution." *JAMA Health Forum* 2, no. 12 (December 3,
2021): e214018. doi:10.1001/jamahealthforum.2021.4018.

5   Mark, Julian. "FTC Bans Contracts That Keep Workers From Jumping
to Rival Employers." *Washington Post*, April 24, 2024. https://www
.washingtonpost.com/business/2024/04/23/ftc-noncompete-agreements/.

6   Bannow, Tara. "FTC's Noncompete Ban Would Force Sweeping Changes
in Health Care, if It Survives Legal Battle." *STAT*, April 23, 2024. https
://www.statnews.com/2024/04/23/ftc-vote-ban-noncompete-agreements/.

7   Mahar, Maggie. *Money Driven Medicine: The Real Reason Healthcare Costs
So Much.* New York: HarperCollins, 2006.

8   Carey, Benedict. "Drug Rehabilitation or Revolving Door?" *New York
Times*, December 22, 2008. https://www.nytimes.com/2008/12/23
/health/23reha.html.

9   "What Doctors Wish Patients Knew about Prior Authorization."
American Medical Association, September 11, 2023. https://www.ama

-assn.org/practice-management/prior-authorization/what-doctors
-wish-patients-knew-about-prior-authorization.

10   "2017 AMA Prior Authorization Physician Survey." *American Medical Association*. Accessed January 21, 2024. https://www.ama-assn.org/sites /ama-assn.org/files/corp/media-browser/public/arc/prior-auth-2017.pdf.

11   "2022 AMA Prior Authorization (PA) Physician Survey." *American Medical Association*. Accessed January 21, 2024. https://mailview.bulletin healthcare.com/mailview.aspx?m=2022021101ama&r=8047939 -ea82&l=04b-cf6&t=c.

12   "Rosendale Takes Aim at Drug-Benefit Managers." *KRTV NEWS Great Falls*, June 20, 2018. https://www.krtv.com/news/2018/06/20 /rosendale-takes-aim-at-drug-benefit-managers/.

13   Hamilton, David. "Express Scripts Fine Settles PBM Mess—for Now." *CBS News*, May 28, 2008. https://www.cbsnews.com/news/express -scripts-fine-settles-pbm-mess-for-now/.

14   State of California, Department of Consumer Affairs. "Designating all or Portions of the Decision, In the matter of the Citation Against: ESI Mail Pharmacy, Inc. dba Express Scripts." Accessed January 20, 2024. https ://www.pharmacy.ca.gov/enforcement/precedential/no_2019_01.pdf.

15   Silverman, Ed. "FTC Will Investigate Pharmacy Benefit Managers and Their Role in Prescription Drug Costs." *STAT*, June 8, 2022. https://www .statnews.com/pharmalot/2022/06/08/ftc-pbm-medicines-cvs-probe/.

16   Mattingly, T. Joseph, Kenechukwu Ben-Umeh, Ge Bai, and Gerard F. Anderson. "Pharmacy Benefit Manager Pricing and Spread Pricing for High-Utilization Generic Drugs." *JAMA Health Forum* 4, no. 10 (October 20, 2023): e233660. doi:10.1001/jamahealthforum.2023.3660.

17   McAuliff, Michael. "PBM Bills Drove Lobbying Spending in 2023." *Modern Healthcare*. Accessed January 21, 2024. https://www.modern healthcare.com/politics-policy/lobbying-spending-pbm-reform -phrma-aha.

18   Aboulenein, Ahmed. "US Pharmacy Benefit Lobbying Group Ramps Up Spending as Lawmakers Close In." Reuters, January 25, 2024. https ://www.reuters.com/business/healthcare-pharmaceuticals/us-pharmacy -benefit-lobby-group-ramps-up-spending-lawmakers-close-2024-01-25/.

19   "RE: Support for Reforming Pharmacy Benefits Managers." Letter from the National Association of Attorneys General. February 20, 2024. https://www.naag.org/wp-content/uploads/2024/02/PBM-Letter -_NAAG-Letterhead-Final.pdf.

20   Silverman, Ed. "FTC Says Pharmacy Benefit Managers Are Stonewalling Requests for Information." *STAT*, February 27, 2024. https://www.statnews.com/pharmalot/2024/02/27/ftc-pbm-medicine -drugs-prices-rebates-pharmacies-cvs-cigna-unitedhealth-antitrust/.

21   Cohrs, Rachel, and John Wilkerson. "Congress Punts on PBM Reform Efforts." *STAT*, February 26, 2024. https://www.statnews.com/2024/02/26 /congress-punts-on-pbm-reform-efforts/.

22   "Frustrated Pharmacists Are Opting out of the Insurance System, Saving
      Some Customers Hundreds of Dollars." *NBC News*, August 19, 2022.
      https://www.nbcnews.com/health/health-care/frustrated-pharmacists-are
      -opting-insurance-system-saving-customers-hu-rcna36706.

23   Empinado, Hyacinth. "Watch: This Small-Town Pharmacy May Be a
      Model for More Affordable Drugs." *STAT*, July 31, 2023. http
      s://www.statnews.com/2022/11/21/this-small-town-pharmacy-may
      -be-a-model-for-more-affordable-drugs/.

24   Haque, Waqas, Satheesh Chencheri, Beth A Virnig, Anne Blaes,
      Christopher M. Booth, Stacie B. Dusetzina, and Arjun Gupta. "Price
      Comparison of Human and Veterinary Formulations of Common
      Medications." *JAMA Internal Medicine* 182, no. 11 (November 1, 2022):
      1216. doi:10.1001/jamainternmed.2022.3938.

25   "Digital Healthcare Platform Ordered to Pay Civil Penalties and Take
      Corrective Action for Unauthorized Disclosure of Personal Health
      Information." U.S. Department of Justice, Office of Public Affairs,
      February 22, 2023. https://www.justice.gov/opa/pr/digital-healthcare
      -platform-ordered-pay-civil-penalties-and-take-corrective-action.

26   Ravindranath, Mohana. "GoodRx Leaked Sensitive Health
      Information to Facebook and Google, FTC Alleges." *STAT*,
      February 1, 2023. https://www.statnews.com/2023/02/01/goodrx-ftc
      -health-data-leak/.

27   Frakt, Austin. "The Astonishingly High Administrative Costs of U.S.
      Healthcare." *New York Times*, July 18, 2018. https://www.nytimes.com
      /2018/07/16/upshot/costs-health-care-us.html.

28   Shrank, William H., Teresa L. Rogstad, and Natasha Parekh. "Waste in
      the US Healthcare System." *JAMA* 322, no. 15 (October 15, 2019): 1501.
      doi:10.1001/jama.2019.13978.

29   Woolhandler, Steffie, Terry Campbell, and David U. Himmelstein.
      "Costs of Healthcare Administration in the United States and Canada."
      The New England Journal of Medicine 349, no. 8 (August 21, 2003):
      768–75. doi:10.1056/nejmsa022033.

30   Chernew, Michael E., and Harrison Mintz. "Administrative Expenses
      in the US Healthcare System." *JAMA* 326, no. 17 (November 2, 2021):
      1679. doi:10.1001/jama.2021.17318.

31   Kocher, Robert. "The Downside of Healthcare Job Growth." *Harvard
      Business Review*, December 20, 2014. https://hbr.org/2013/09/the
      -downside-of-health-care-job-growth.

32   Bernard, Rebekah, MD. "Who Do Patients Really Need: Physicians
      or Administrators?" MedicalEconomics, November 12, 2020.
      https://www.medicaleconomics.com/view/who-do-patients-really
      -need-physicians-or-administrators.

33   Sahni, Nikhil R. Brandon Carrus, and David M. Cutler. "Administrative
      Simplification and the Potential for Saving a Quarter-Trillion Dollars in

Healthcare." *JAMA* 326, no. 17 (November 2, 2021): 1677. doi:10.1001 /jama.2021.17315.

34   Rosenthal, Elisabeth. "Medicine's Top Earners Are Not the M.D.s." *New York Times*, May 18, 2014. https://www.nytimes.com/2014/05/18 /sunday-review/doctors-salaries-are-not-the-big-cost.htm.

35   Herman, Bob. "HCA Healthcare, Cigna Chiefs Top the Lists of Best-Paid CEOs among Providers, Insurers." *STAT*, June 6, 2023. https://www.statnews.com/2022/07/18/hca-cigna-best-paid-ceos -providers-health-insurance/.

36   Herman, Bob, J. Emory Parker, Adam Feuerstein, Lizzy Lawrence, and Mohana Ravindranath. "Healthcare CEOs Hauled in $4 Billion Last Year as Inflation Pinched Workers, Analysis Shows." *STAT*, October 3, 2023. https://www.statnews.com/2023/08/17/health-ceo-salaries-compensation/.

37   Himmelstein, David U., Terry Campbell, and Steffie Woolhandler. "Healthcare Administrative Costs in the United States and Canada, 2017." *Annals of Internal Medicine* 172, no. 2 (January 7, 2020): 134. doi:10.7326/m19-2818.

38   Gondi, Suhas, Sanjay Kishore, and Jim McWilliams. "Professional Backgrounds of Board Members at Top-Ranked US Hospitals." *Journal of General Internal Medicine* 38, no. 10 (February 8, 2023): 2428–30. doi:10.1007/s11606-023-08056-z.

39   "Nonprofit Hospital CEO Compensation: How Much Is Enough?" *Health Affairs Forefront*, February 10, 2022. doi:10.1377/forefront .20220208.925255.

40   Gold, Jenny. "Kaiser Mental Health Patients Struggle for Timely Treatment." *Los Angeles Times*, December 16, 2019. https://www.latimes .com/business/story/2019-12-16/kaiser-mental-health-treatment.

41   Egelko, Bo. "Kaiser to Spend $150M to Improve Mental Healthcare Services under Settlement Agreement." *San Francisco Chronicle*, October 13, 2023. https://www.sfchronicle.com/politics/article/kaiser -agrees-spend-150m-improve-mental-health-18423174.php.

42   Downing, N. Lance, David W. Bates, and Christopher A. Longhurst. "Physician Burnout in the Electronic Health Record Era: Are We Ignoring the Real Cause?" *Annals of Internal Medicine* 169.1 (2018): 50–51.

43   Gaffney, Adam, Stephanie Woolhandler, Christopher Cai, David H. Bor, Jessica Himmelstein, Danny McCormick, and David U. Himmelstein. "Medical Documentation Burden among US Office-Based Physicians in 2019." *JAMA Internal Medicine* 182, no. 5 (May 1, 2022): 564. doi:10.1001/jamainternmed.2022.0372.

44   Marx, Rani. "Me and My Electronic Health Record." *Journal of Patient Experience* 8 (January 1, 2021). doi:10.1177/23743735211038778.

45   "Electronic Health Records Vendor to Pay Largest Criminal Fine in Vermont History and a Total of $145 Million to Resolve Criminal and Civil Investigations." United States Attorney's Office, District of Vermont,

April 8, 2020. https://www.justice.gov/usao-vt/pr/electronic-health
-records-vendor-pay-largest-criminal-fine-vermont-history-and-total-145.

46   Court, Emma. "Health-Records Company Pushed Opioids to Doctors
        in Secret Deal With Drugmaker." Bloomberg, January 29, 2020. https
        ://www.bloomberg.com/news/articles/2020-01-29/health-records
        -company-pushed-opioids-to-doctors-in-secret-deal.

47   Chua, Kao-Ping, Marc C. Thorne, Sophia Ng, Mary J. Donahue, and
        Chad M. Brummett. "Association between Default Number of Opioid
        Doses in Electronic Health Record Systems and Opioid Prescribing
        to Adolescents and Young Adults Undergoing Tonsillectomy." *JAMA
        Network Open* 5, no. 6 (June 30, 2022): e2219701. doi:10.1001
        /jamanetworkopen.2022.19701.

Chapter Four: The Impact of Language

1   Lakoff, George. "Don't Think of an Elephant! Know Your Values and
        Frame the Debate." Chelsea Green: Chelsea Green Publishing, 2014.

2   Rogers, Carl. *Client-Centered Therapy*. Boston: Houghton-Mifflin, 1951.

3   Merriam-Webster. "Patient." https://www.merriam-webster.com
        /dictionary/patient.

4   Beasley, John W., Richard G. Roberts, and Allan H. Goroll. "Promoting
        Trust and Morale by Changing How the Word Provider Is Used." *JAMA*
        325, no. 23 (June 15, 2021): 2343. doi:10.1001/jama.2021.6046.

5   Mangione, Salvatore, Brian F. Mandell, and Stephen G. Post. "The
        Language Game: We Are Physicians, Not Providers." *American Journal
        of Medicine* 134, no. 12 (Dec. 2021):1444–6. doi: 10.1016/j.amjmed.2021
        .06.031.

6   Arendt, Hannah. *Eichman in Jerusalem: A Report on the Banality of Evil*.
        New York: Viking Press, 1963.

7   Shevell, Michael. "What Do We Call 'Them'?: The 'Patient' versus
        'Client' Dichotomy." *Developmental Medicine & Child Neurology* 51, no. 10
        (September 7, 2009): 770–72. doi:10.1111/j.1469-8749.2009.03304.x.

8   Mariner, Wendy. "Standards of Care and Standard Form Contracts:
        Distinguishing Patient Rights and Consumer Rights in Managed Care."
        Journal of Contemporary Health Law and Policy 15, no. 1 (Fall 1998): 1-55.

9   Annas, George J. "A National Bill of Patients' Rights." *The New England
        Journal of Medicine* 338, no. 10 (March 5, 1998): 695–700. doi:10.1056
        /nejm199803053381020.

10   Annas, George J., Leonard H. Glantz, and Wendy K. Mariner. "The
        Right of Privacy Protects the Doctor-Patient Relationship." *JAMA* 263,
        no. 6 (February 9, 1990): 858. doi:10.1001/jama.1990.03440060104041.

11   U.S. Supreme Court Amici Curiae re: Dobbs v. Jackson Women's Health
        Organization, et al. https://www.acog.org/-/media/project/acog/acogorg
        /files/advocacy/amicus-briefs/2021/20210920-dobbs-v-jwho-amicus
        -brief.pdf.

12   Borowitz, Andy. "Women Declare Themselves Corporations to Force
       Supreme Court to Grant Them Rights as People." *The New Yorker*, June 27,
       2022. https://www.newyorker.com/humor/borowitz-report/women
       -declare-themselves-corporations-to-force-supreme-court-to-grant-them
       -rights-as-people.

13   Appelbaum, Binyamin. *The Economists' Hour: False Prophets, Free Markets,
       and the Fracture of Society.* New York: Little, Brown and Company, 2019.

14   Sandel, Michael. *The Tyranny of Merit: What's Become of the Common
       Good?* New York: Farrar, Straus and Giroux, 2020.

15   Boiler, John. "Five Reasons You Should Quit Using the Word 'Client.'"
       AdAge. http://adage.com/article/guest-columnists/reasons-quit-word
       -client/239375/, January 29, 2013.

16   Tomes, Nancy. *Remaking the American Patient: How Madison Avenue and
       Modern Medicine Turned Patients into Consumers.* Chapel Hill: University
       of North Carolina Press, 2016.

17   "Create a Personal Online Physician Brand That Works." American
       Medical Association, May 21, 2018. https://www.ama-assn.org
       /delivering-care/patient-support-advocacy/create-personal-online
       -physician-brand-works.

18   Sydell, Laura. "Fake Patient Reviews Are Making It Increasingly
       Hard to Seek Medical Help on Google, Yelp and Other Directory
       Sites." *Washington Post*, June 5, 2021. https://www.washingtonpost
       .com/business/2021/06/04/fake-medical-reviews-google-zocdoc
       -trustpilot/.

19   Bloche, M. Gregg, MD. *The Hippocratic Myth: Why Doctors Are Under
       Pressure to Ration Care, Practice Politics, and Compromise Their Promise to
       Heal.* St. Martin's Press, 2011.

20   American Psychological Association. "APA Resolution for the
       Use of the Term *Patient* in American Psychological Association
       Policies, Rules, and Publications Activities When Referring to the
       Health-Related and Scientific Activities of Health Service Psychologists
       and Scientists in Health-Related Services and Settings." August 2018.
       Accessed January 22, 2024. https://www.apa.org/about/policy
       /resolution-term-patient.pdf.

21   Jensen, David. "Unlawful and/or Unethical Dual Relationship? A Word
       to the Wise." CAMFT, November 17, 2017. https://www.camft.org
       /Resources/Legal-Articles/Chronological-Article-List/unlawful
       -unlawful-andor-unethical-dual-relationshipandor-unethical-dual
       -relationship.

22   Miller, Alice. *Drama of the Gifted Child: The Search for the True Self.* New
       York: Basic Books, 1997.

23   Farkas, Barry. "The Language of Medicine." *New York Times*, April 6,
       2015. http://www.nytimes.com/2015/04/06/opinion/the-language-of
       -medicine.html.

Chapter Five: Business Models and the Practice of Psychiatry

1   Cummings, Nicholas, and Gary VandenBos. "The Twenty Years Kaiser-Permanente Experience with Psychotherapy and Medical Utilization: Implications for National Health Policy and National Health Insurance." *Health policy quarterly* 1, no. 2 (1981): 159–75. https://pubmed.ncbi.nlm.nih.gov/10252343.

2   Zhu, Jane M., Stephanie Renfro, Kelsey Watson, Ashmira Deshmukh, and K. John McConnell. "Medicaid Reimbursement for Psychiatric Services: Comparisons across States and with Medicare." *Health Affairs* 42, no. 4 (April 1, 2023): 556–65. doi:10.1377/hlthaff.2022.00805.

3   Xu, Wendy, Chi Song, Yiting Li, and Sheldon M. Retchin. "Cost-Sharing Disparities for Out-of-Network Care for Adults with Behavioral Health Conditions." *JAMA Network Open* 2, no. 11 (November 6, 2019): e1914554. doi:10.1001/jamanetworkopen.2019.14554.

4   Davenport, Stoddard, Travis Gray, Stephen Melek. "Addiction and Mental Health vs. Physical Health: Widening Disparities in Network Use and Provider Reimbursement." *Milliman*, November 20, 2019. https://www.milliman.com/en/insight/addiction-and-mental-health-vs-physical-health-widening-disparities-in-network-use-and-p.

5   Consumer Health Ratings. "Doctors' Charges, Physician Prices, Average Cost, Anesthesia." Accessed January 22, 2024. https://consumerhealthratings.com/healthcare_category/doctors-charges-physician-prices-average-cost-anesthesia/.

6   Abelson, Reed. "Mental Health Treatment Denied to Customers by Giant Insurer's Policies, Judge Rules." *New York Times*, March 5, 2019. https://www.nytimes.com/2019/03/05/health/unitedhealth-mental-health-parity.html.

7   Reuters. "UnitedHealth Settles Charges It Denied Mental Health, Substance Abuse Coverage." *US News & World Report*, August 12, 2021. https://www.usnews.com/news/top-news/articles/2021-08-12/unitedhealth-settles-charges-it-denied-mental-health-substance-abuse-coverage.

8   Davenport, Stoddard, Travis Gray, Stephen Melek. "How Do Individuals with Behavioral Health Conditions Contribute to Physical and Total Healthcare Spending?" *Milliman*, August 13, 2020. https://www.milliman.com/en/insight/How-do-individuals-with-behavioral-health-conditions-contribute-to-physical.

9   Hassanein, Nada. "Insurers Often Shortchange Mental Healthcare Coverage, despite a Federal Law." *USA TODAY*, October 16, 2023. https://www.usatoday.com/story/news/nation/2023/10/15/insurers-shortchange-mental-health-care-coverage-despite-federal-law/71174634007/.

10   Rosenberg, Kenneth Paul. *Bedlam: An Intimate Journey into America's Mental Health Crisis.* New York: Avery (Random House), 2019.

11   Hansard, Sara. "Insurers Falling Down on Mental Health Parity, Agencies Say." Bloomberg Law, January 25, 2022. https://news.bloomberg

law.com/employee-benefits/insurers-falling-down-on-mental-health
-coverage-agencies-say.

12   Asimov, Nanette. "Kaiser Made $8 billion in Profits Last Year. So
      Why are Patients Struggling to get Mental Healthcare?" *San Francisco
      Chronicle*, September 29, 2022. https://www.sfchronicle.com/bayarea
      /article/Who-is-going-to-hold-Kaiser-accountable-17474027.php.

13   Stecker, Tiffany. "California Plans Deny Mental Health Claims Despite
      New Law (1)." Bloomberg Law, December 21, 2022. https://news
      .bloomberglaw.com/health-law-and-business/california-plans-deny
      -mental-health-claims-despite-new-law.

14   Sinsky, Christine A., Lacey Colligan, Ling Li, Mirela Prgomet, Sam
      Reynolds, Lindsey E. Goeders, Johanna I. Westbrook, Michael Tutty,
      and George T. Blike. "Allocation of Physician Time in Ambulatory
      Practice: A Time and Motion Study in 4 Specialties." *Annals of
      Internal Medicine* 165, no. 11 (September 6, 2016): 753. doi:10.7326
      /m16-0961.

15   Mark, Tami L., William Joseph Olesiuk, Mir M. Ali, Laura J. Sherman,
      Ryan Mutter, and Judith L. Teich. "Differential Reimbursement of
      Psychiatric Services by Psychiatrists and Other Medical Providers."
      Psychiatric Services 69, no. 3 (March 1, 2018): 281–85. doi:10.1176/appi
      .ps.201700271.

16   Michaud, Catherine, Matthew T. McKenna, Stephen Begg, Niels
      Tomijima, Meghna Majmudar, Maria T. Bulzacchelli, Shahul H.
      Ebrahim, et al. "The Burden of Disease and Injury in the United
      States 1996." *Population Health Metrics* 4, no. 1 (October 18, 2006).
      doi:10.1186/1478-7954-4-11.

17   Centers for Disease Control and Prevention. "Provisional Suicide Deaths
      in the United States, 2022" (CDC Newsroom Press Release). Accessed
      January 19, 2024. https://www.cdc.gov/media/releases/2023/s0810-US
      -Suicide-Deaths-2022.html.

18   Centers for Disease Control and Prevention. "Provisional Data Shows
      U.S. Drug Overdose Deaths Top 100,000 in 2022." May 18, 2023.
      https://blogs.cdc.gov/nchs/2023/05/18/7365/.

19   Centers for Disease Control and Prevention. "Deaths from Excessive
      Alcohol Use in the United States." November 15, 2022. https://www.cdc
      .gov/alcohol/features/excessive-alcohol-deaths.html.

20   Ahmad, Farida B., Jodi A. Cisewski, Jiaquan Xu and Robert N.
      Anderson, and the Centers for Disease Control and Prevention.
      "COVID-19 Mortality Update — United States, 2022." *Morbidity and
      Mortality Weekly Report* 72, no. 18 (May 5, 2023): 493–6. doi:10.15585
      /mmwr.mm7218a4.

21   Figueroa, Jose, Jessica Phelan, John Orav, Vikram Patel, Ashish Jha.
      "Association of Mental Health Disorders With Healthcare Spending
      in the Medicare Population." *JAMA Network Open* 3, no. 3 (2020):
      e201210. doi:10.1001/jamanetworkopen.2020.1210.

22   "How Do Individuals with Behavioral Health Conditions Contribute to
      Physical and Total Healthcare Spending?" *Milliman*, August 13, 2020.
      https://www.milliman.com/en/insight/How-do-individuals-with
      -behavioral-health-conditions-contribute-to-physical.

23   Fairley, Michael, Keith Humphreys, Vilija R. Joyce, Mark Bounthavong,
      Jodie A. Trafton, Ann Combs, Elizabeth M. Oliva, et al. "Cost-
      Effectiveness of Treatments for Opioid Use Disorder." *JAMA Psychiatry*
      78, no. 7 (July 1, 2021): 767. doi:10.1001/jamapsychiatry.2021.0247.

24   Frank, Philipp, G. David Batty, Jaana Pentti, Markus Jokela, Lydia
      Poole, Jenni Ervasti, Jussi Vahtera, Glyn Lewis, Andrew Steptoe,
      and Mika Kivimäki. "Association between Depression and Physical
      Conditions Requiring Hospitalization." *JAMA Psychiatry* 80, no. 7 (July 1,
      2023): 690. doi:10.1001/jamapsychiatry.2023.07.

25   Momen, Natalie C., Oleguer Plana-Ripoll, Esben Agerbo, Maria
      Klitgaard Christensen, Kim Moesgaard Iburg, Thomas Munk
      Laursen, Preben Bo Mortensen, et al. "Mortality Associated with
      Mental Disorders and Comorbid General Medical Conditions."
      JAMA Psychiatry 79, no. 5 (May 1, 2022): 444. doi:10.1001/jama
      psychiatry.2022.0347.

26   Frank, Philipp, G. David Batty, Jaana Pentti, Markus Jokela, Lydia
      Poole, Jenni Ervasti, Jussi Vahtera, Glyn Lewis, Andrew Steptoe,
      and Mika Kivimäki. "Association between Depression and Physical
      Conditions Requiring Hospitalization." *JAMA Psychiatry* 80, no. 7 (July 1,
      2023): 690. doi:10.1001/jamapsychiatry.2023.0777.

27   Richmond-Rakerd, Leah S., Stephanie D'Souza, Barry Milne,
      Avshalom Caspi, and Terrie E. Moffitt. "Longitudinal Associations
      of Mental Disorders with Physical Diseases and Mortality among 2.3
      Million New Zealand Citizens." *JAMA Network Open* 4, no. 1 (January 13,
      2021): e2033448. doi:10.1001/jamanetworkopen.2020.33448.

28   Taylor, Heather L., Nir Menachemi, Amy Gilbert, J. L. Chaudhary, and
      Justin Blackburn. "Economic Burden Associated with Untreated Mental
      Illness in Indiana." *JAMA Health Forum* 4, no. 10 (October 13, 2023):
      e233535. doi:10.1001/jamahealthforum.2023.3535.

29   Zhang, Zefeng, Sandra Jackson, Cathleen Gillespie, Robert Merritt, and
      Quanhe Yang. "Depressive Symptoms and Mortality among US Adults."
      JAMA Network Open 6, no. 10 (October 9, 2023): e2337011. doi:10.1001
      /jamanetworkopen.2023.37011.

30   Carmin, Cheryl N., Raymond L. Ownby, Cynthia A. Fontanella,
      Danielle L. Steelesmith, and Philip F. Binkley. "Impact of Mental
      Health Treatment on Outcomes in Patients With Heart Failure and
      Ischemic Heart Disease." *Journal of the American Heart Association*,
      March 20, 2024. doi:10.1161/jaha.123.031117.

31   Park, Chan Soon, Eue Keun Choi, Kyungdo Han, Hyo-Jeong Ahn,
      Soonil Kwon, Hyun Jung Lee, Seil Oh, and Gregory Y.H. Lip.
      "Increased Cardiovascular Events in Young Patients with Mental

Disorders: A Nationwide Cohort Study." *European Journal of Preventive Cardiology*, April 28, 2023. doi:10.1093/eurjpc/zwad102.

32   Ceban, Felicia, Danica Nogo, Isabelle P. Carvalho, Yena Lee, Flora Nasri, Jiaqi Xiong, Leanna M.W. Lui, et al. "Association between Mood Disorders and Risk of COVID-19 Infection, Hospitalization, and Death." *JAMA Psychiatry* 78, no. 10 (October 1, 2021): 1079. doi:10.1001/jamapsychiatry.2021.1818.

33   Nemani, Katlyn, Chenxiang Li, Mark Olfson, Esther Blessing, Narges Razavian, Chen Ji, Eva Petkova, and Donald C. Goff. "Association of Psychiatric Disorders with Mortality among Patients with COVID-19." *JAMA Psychiatry* 78, no. 4 (April 1, 2021): 380. doi:10.1001/jama psychiatry.2020.4442.

34   Wang, Siwen, Luwei Quan, Jorge E. Chavarro, Natalie Slopen, Laura D. Kubzansky, Karestan C. Koenen, Jae Hee Kang, Marc G. Weisskopf, Westyn Branch-Elliman, and Andrea L. Roberts. "Associations of Depression, Anxiety, Worry, Perceived Stress, and Loneliness Prior to Infection with Risk of Post-COVID-19 Conditions." *JAMA Psychiatry* 79, no. 11 (November 1, 2022): 1081. doi:10.1001/jamapsychiatry.2022.2640.

35   Johns Hopkins Bloomberg School of Public Health. "Prescriptions for Antidepressants Increasing among Individuals with No Psychiatric Diagnosis." July 7, 2021. https://www.jhsph.edu/news/news-releases /2011/mojtabai-antidepressant-prescriptions.html.

36   Goldhill, Olivia. "How a Depression Test Devised by a Zoloft Marketer Became a Crutch for a Failing Mental Health System." *STAT*, July 31, 2023. https://www.statnews.com/2023/02/21/depression-test-phq9 -zoloft-pfizer-mental-health/.

37   Brueck, Hilary. "The 9-Question Survey Many Doctors Use to Diagnose Depression Was Actually Created by an Antidepressant Manufacturer." *Business Insider*, February 23, 2023. https://www.insider.com/big -pharma-developed-the-widely-used-depression-screening-test-2023-2.

38   Brauser, Deborah. "Brief Scale Linked to Antidepressant Overprescribing." *Medscape*, August 16, 2017. https://www.medscape .com/viewarticle/831505?form=fpf.

39   Tadmon, Daniel, and Mark Olfson. "Trends in Outpatient Psychotherapy Provision by U.S. Psychiatrists: 1996–2016." *American Journal of Psychiatry* 179, no. 2 (February 1, 2022): 110–21. doi:10.1176 /appi.ajp.2021.21040338.

40   Fournier, Jay C., Robert J. DeRubeis, Steven D. Hollon, Sona Dimidjian, Jay D. Amsterdam, Richard C. Shelton, and Jan Fawcett. "Antidepressant Drug Effects and Depression Severity." *JAMA* 303, no. 1 (January 6, 2010): 47. doi:10.1001/jama.2009.1943.

41   Mintz, David. "Combining Drug Therapy and Psychotherapy for Depression." *Psychiatric Times*, November 16, 2020. https://www .psychiatrictimes.com/view/combining-drug-therapy-and-psychotherapy -depression.

42   Jennings, Katie. "Venture Funding for Mental Health Startups Hits
        Record High as Anxiety, Depression Skyrocket." *Forbes*, June 7, 2021.
        https://www.forbes.com/sites/katiejennings/2021/06/07/venture
        -funding-for-mental-health-startups-hits-record-high-as-anxiety
        -depression-skyrocket/?sh=500838fd1116.

43   Becker, Sam. "Mental Health Emerges as the Fastest-Growing
        Marketplace for Startups, and it's not Even Close." *Fast Company*,
        March 24, 2023. https://www.fastcompany.com/90871198/mental
        -health-startups-fast-growing-marketplace-a16z-list.

44   Facher, Lev. "Venture Capital Is Investing Little in New Treatment for
        Addiction, Report Finds." *STAT*, February 1, 2023. https://www
        .statnews.com/2023/02/02/investment-addiction-cures-low-report/.

45   Galagali, Tarun, and Leonard Schlesinger. "The Blind Spots of
        Blitzscaling in Mental Health Tech." *STAT*, July 31, 2023. https://www
        .statnews.com/2021/12/28/mental-health-tech-blitzscaling-blind-spots/.

46   Goldberg, Simon B., Sin U. Lam, Otto Simonsson, John Torous, and
        Shufang Sun. "Mobile Phone-Based Interventions for Mental Health:
        A Systematic Meta-Review of 14 Meta-Analyses of Randomized
        Controlled Trials." *PLOS Digital Health* 1, no. 1 (January 18, 2022):
        e0000002. doi:10.1371/journal.pdig.0000002.

47   Bae Hayoung, Hyemin Shin, Han-Gil Ji, Jun Soo Kwon, Hyungsook Kim,
        Ji-Won Hur. "App-Based Interventions for Moderate to Severe Depression:
        A Systematic Review and Meta-Analysis." *JAMA Network Open* 6, no. 11
        (2023): e2344120. doi:10.1001/jamanetworkopen.2023.44120.

48   Fischer, Molly. "The Therapy-App Fantasy." *The Cut*, March 29, 2021.
        https://www.thecut.com/amp/article/mental-health-therapy-apps.html.

49   "Dramatic Growth in Mental-Health Apps Has Created a Risky
        Industry." *The Economist*, December 9, 2021. https://www.economist.com
        /business/2021/12/11/dramatic-growth-in-mental-health-apps-has
        -created-a-risky-industry.

50   Aguilar, Mario. "Talkspace's Leadership Exodus Leaves behind Pressing
        Questions—and a Pile of Cash." *STAT*, July 31, 2023. https://www
        .statnews.com/2021/11/22/talkspace-hirschhorn-frank-stock/.

51   "The Digital Mental Health Market Is Booming. Here's Why Some
        Experts Are Concerned." Fierce Healthcare, April 21, 2021. https
        ://www.fiercehealthcare.com/tech/digital-mental-health-market
        -booming-here-s-why-some-experts-are-concerned.

52   Mosendz, Polly, and Caleb Melby. "Cerebral App Over-Prescribed
        ADHD Meds, Ex-Employees Say." Bloomberg, March 12, 2022.
        https://www.bloomberg.com/news/features/2022-03-11/cerebral
        -app-over-prescribed-adhd-meds-ex-employees-say.

53   "Special Fraud Alert: OIG Alerts Practitioners to Exercise Caution
        When Entering Into Arrangements with Purported Telemedicine
        Companies." Department of Health and Human Services, Office of the

Inspector General. July 20, 2022. https://oig.hhs.gov/documents /root/1045/sfa-telefraud.pdf.

54   Jackson, Brian. "Why HIPAA Isn't Enough to Protect Your Health Data." *KevinMD.com*, April 5, 2023. https://www.kevinmd .com/2023/04/why-hipaa-isnt-enough-to-protect-your-health-data.html.

55   Robbins, Alexandra. "The Problem with Satisfied Patients." *The Atlantic*, April 17, 2015. https://www.theatlantic.com/health/archive/2015/04 /the-problem-with-satisfied-patients/390684/.

56   Jerant, Anthony F., Alicia Agnoli, and Peter Franks. "Satisfaction with Healthcare Among Prescription Opioid Recipients." *Journal of the American Board of Family Medicine* 33, no. 1 (January 1, 2020): 34–41. doi:10.3122/jabfm.2020.01.190090.

57   Fenton, Joshua J., Anthony F. Jerant, Klea D. Bertakis, and Peter Franks. "The Cost of Satisfaction." *Archives of Internal Medicine* 172, no. 5 (March 12, 2012): 405. doi:10.1001/archinternmed.2011.1662.

58   Saifee, Danish H., Zhiqiang Zheng, Indranil R. Bardhan, and Atanu Lahiri. "Are Online Reviews of Physicians Reliable Indicators of Clinical Outcomes? A Focus on Chronic Disease Management." *Information Systems Research* 31, no. 4 (December 1, 2020): 1282–300. doi:10.1287 /isre.2020.0945.

59   Sydell, Laura. "Fake Patient Reviews Are Making It Increasingly Hard to Seek Medical Help on Google, Yelp and Other Directory Sites." *Washington Post*, June 5, 2021. https://www.washingtonpost.com /business/2021/06/04/fake-medical-reviews-google-zocdoc-trustpilot/.

60   Thompson, Stuart. "Fake Reviews Are Rampant Online. Can a Crackdown End Them?" *New York Times,* November 13, 2023. https ://www.nytimes.com/2023/11/13/technology/fake-reviews-crackdown.html.

61   Lembke, Anna. "Why Doctors Prescribe Opioids to Known Opioid Abusers." *The New England Journal of Medicine* 367, no. 17 (October 25, 2012): 1580–81. doi:10.1056/nejmp1208498.

62   Stone, Judy. "Why the U. of Minnesota Research Scandal Threatens Us All." *Forbes*, May 27, 2015. https://www.forbes.com/sites/judy stone/2015/05/27/why-the-umn-research-scandal-threatens-us-all/.

63   Buchkowsky, Susan S., and Peter J. Jewesson. "Industry Sponsorship and Authorship of Clinical Trials over 20 Years." *Annals of Pharmacotherapy* 38, no. 4 (April 1, 2004): 579–85. doi:10.1345/aph.1d267.

64   Angell, Marcia. *The Truth About the Drug Companies: How They Deceive Us and What To Do About It.* New York: Random House, 2004.

65   Heres, Stephan, John M. Davis, Katja Maino, Elisabeth Jetzinger, Werner Kissling, and Stefan Leucht. "Why Olanzapine Beats Risperidone, Risperidone Beats Quetiapine, and Quetiapine Beats Olanzapine: An Exploratory Analysis of Head-to-Head Comparison Studies of Second-Generation Antipsychotics." *American Journal of Psychiatry* 163, no. 2 (February 1, 2006): 185–94. doi:10.1176/appi.ajp.163.2.185.

66   Piller, Charles. "FDA and NIH Let Clinical Trial Sponsors Keep
        Results Secret and Break the Law." *Science*, January 13, 2020. https
        ://www.sciencemag.org/news/2020/01/fda-and-nih-let-clinical-trial
        -sponsors-keep-results-secret-and-break-law.

67   Silverman, Ed. "MD Anderson Hit with Ethics Complaint over
        Failure to Disclose Clinical Trial Results." *STAT*, July 25, 2023. https
        ://www.statnews.com/pharmalot/2021/10/14/anderson-cancer
        -clinical-trial-transparency-iqwig/.

68   Kevles, Daniel. "Unreasonable Terms." *New York Review of Books*
        (Oct 5, 2023).

69   Steenhuysen, Julie. "Moderna COVID-19 Vaccine Patent Dispute
        Headed to Court, U.S. NIH Head Says." Reuters, November 10, 2021.
        https://www.reuters.com/business/healthcare-pharmaceuticals/moderna
        -covid-19-vaccine-patent-dispute-headed-court-us-nih-head-says
        -2021-11-10/.

70   "2020 Shkreli Awards - Lown Institute." Lown Institute, April 15, 2021.
        https://lowninstitute.org/projects/shkreli-awards/2020-shkreli-awards/.

71   Lerner, Sharon. "Merck Sells Federally Financed Covid Pill to U.S. for
        40 Times What It Costs to Make." *The Intercept*, October 5, 2021.
        https://theintercept.com/2021/10/05/covid-pill-drug-pricing-merck
        -ridgeback/.

72   Ledley, Fred, Ekaterina Cleary, and Mathew Jackson. "US Tax Dollars
        Funded Every New Pharmaceutical in the Last Decade." Institute for
        New Economic Thinking, September 2, 2020. https://www.inet
        economics.org/perspectives/blog/us-tax-dollars-funded-every-new
        -pharmaceutical-in-the-last-decade.

73   Rome, Benjamin N., Alexander C. Egilman, and Aaron S. Kesselheim.
        "Trends in Prescription Drug Launch Prices, 2008-2021." *JAMA* 327,
        no. 21 (June 7, 2022): 2145. doi:10.1001/jama.2022.5542.

74   Bloomfield, Doni, Bryan S. Walsh, and Aaron S. Kesselheim.
        "Extending Drug Monopolies by Patenting Safe Drug Use." *JAMA
        Internal Medicine* 182, no. 3 (March 1, 2022): 245. doi:10.1001
        /jamainternmed.2021.7954.

75   Acharya, Swathi, Venkatesh Srinivasa, S. Kotresh, Sharanappa
        Mulimani, Anithraj Bhat, and Manohar A. Bhat. "A Comparative
        Study on Efficacy and Safety Profile of Risperidone and Iloperidone in
        Patients of Schizophrenia: Randomized Controlled Study." *International
        Journal of Basic and Clinical Pharmacology*, January 1, 2016: 1062–67.
        doi:10.18203/2319-2003.ijbcp20161569.

76   Silverman, Ed. "FTC Challenges Several Big Drugmakers over Inaccurate
        or Improper Patent Listings." *STAT*, November 7, 2023. https://www
        .statnews.com/pharmalot/2023/11/07/ftc-patents-fda-abbvie-astrazeneca
        -gsk-teva-mylan-epipen-asthma-inhaler-monpoly-generics/.

77   Silverman, Ed. "New Congressional Bill Would Thwart Patent Thickets
        in Order to Speed Generic Drugs to Market." *STAT*, January 12, 2024.

https://www.statnews.com/pharmalot/2024/01/12/medicines-patents
-generics-biosimilars/.

78   Armstrong, David. "Doctor didn't Disclose Glaxo Payments, Senator
        Says. *Wall Street Journal*, October 4, 2008. https://www.wsj.com/articles
        /SB122304669813202429.

79   Harris, Gardiner. "Drug Maker Told Studies Would Aid It, Papers Say."
        New York Times, March 20, 2009. https://www.nytimes.com/2009/03/20
        /us/20psych.html.

80   "Prescription Data Mining: A Transparent (-Ly Absurd) Defense by
        Verispan." *The Carlat Psychiatry Blog*, September 17, 2007. http://carlat
        psychiatry.blogspot.com/2007/09/prescription-data-mining-transparent
        -ly.html.

81   Sullivan, Thomas. "ACCME: 2008 Annual Report Shows Significant
        Drop in CME Income and Commercial Support." *Policy and Medicine,*
        July 19, 2009. https://www.policymed.com/2009/07/accme-2008
        -annual-report-shows-significant-drop-in-cme-income-and-commercial
        -support.html.

82   Fugh-Berman, Adriane. "Industry-Funded Medical Education Is Always
        Promotion—an Essay by Adriane Fugh-Berman." *The BMJ*, June 4,
        2021, n1273. doi:10.1136/bmj.n1273.

83   Lowes, Shelley Wood and Robert. "Psychiatrists Dominate 'Doctor-
        Dollars' Database Listing Big Pharma Payments." *Medscape*, July 25,
        2020. https://www.medscape.com/viewarticle/731028#vp_1.

84   Brauser, Deborah. "Psychiatrists Top List of Big Pharma Payments
        Again." *Medscape*, December 30, 2013. https://www.medscape.com
        /viewarticle/780835.

85   Sayed, Ahmed, Joseph Ross, John Mandrola, Lisa Lehmann, and
        Andrew Foy. "Industry Payments to US Physicians by Specialty and
        Product Type." *JAMA*. Published online March 28, 2024. doi:10.1001
        /jama.2024.1989.

86   Zhang, Audrey D., and Timothy S. Anderson. "Comparison of Industry
        Payments to Physicians and Advanced Practice Clinicians." *JAMA* 328,
        no. 24 (December 27, 2022): 2452. doi:10.1001/jama.2022.20794.

87   Davis, Lauren, Alexa T. Diianni, Sydney R. Drumheller, Noha Elansary,
        Gianna D'Ambrozio, Farahdeba Herrawi, Brian J. Piper, and Lisa
        Cosgrove. "Undisclosed Financial Conflicts of Interest in DSM-5-TR: Cross
        Sectional Analysis." *The BMJ*, January 10, 2024: e076902. doi:10.1136
        /bmj-2023-076902.

88   Scull, Andrew. *Desperate Remedies: Psychiatry's Turbulent Quest to Cure Mental
        Illness.* Cambridge: The Belknap Press of Harvard University Press, 2022.

89   Kingson, Jennifer. "The 'Psychiatrist's Bible' is Suddenly a Surprise
        Bestseller." *Axios*, June 14, 2022. https://www.axios.com/2022/06/14
        /psychiatry-dsm-mental-health-diagnosis.

90   "Drug Pricing Investigation: Industry Spending on Buybacks,
        Dividends, and Executive Compensation." Staff Report: Committee on

Oversight and Reform, U.S. House of Representatives, July 2021.
https://oversightdemocrats.house.gov/sites/democrats.oversight.house
.gov/files/COR%20Staff%20Report%20-%20Pharmaceutical%20
Industry%20Buybacks%20Dividends%20Compared%20to%20Research
.pdf.

91   Lazonick, William, and Öner Tulum. "Sick with 'Shareholder Value': US
Pharma's Financialized Business Model during the Pandemic." *Competition
& Change*, November 14, 2023. doi:10.1177/10245294231210975.

92   Bruch, Joseph Dov, Victor Roy, and Colleen M. Grogan. "The
Financialization of Health in the United States." *The New England
Journal of Medicine* 390, no. 2 (January 11, 2024): 178–82. doi:10.1056
/nejmms2308188.

93   "Special Fraud Alert: Speaker Programs." Department of Health and
Human Services. Office of Inspector General, August 23, 2022. https
://www.federalregister.gov/documents/2022/08/23/2022-18063
/publication-of-oig-special-fraud-alerts.

94   Adashi, Eli Y., and I. Glenn Cohen. "Industry-Sponsored Speaker
Programs - End of the Line?" *JAMA* 325, no. 18 (May 11, 2021): 1835.
doi:10.1001/jama.2020.26580.

95   Kim, Tae. "Goldman Sachs Asks in Biotech Research Report: 'Is Curing
Patients a Sustainable Business Model?'" CNBC, April 11, 2018. https
://www.cnbc.com/2018/04/11/goldman-asks-is-curing-patients-a
-sustainable-business-model.html.

96   Poses, Roy M., MD. "Guidelines in Whose Interest? - Pharmaceutical
Companies and the Texas Medication Algorithm Project (TMAP),"
Healthcare Renewal, December 20, 2006. https://hcrenewal.blogspot
.com/2006/12/guidelines-in-whose-interest.html.

97   Edwards, Jim. "Risperdal Payments Result in Conviction for State
Meds Official." *CBS News*, December 24, 2008. https://www.cbsnews
.com/news/risperdal-payments-result-in-conviction-for-state-meds
-official/.

98   Garber, Judith. "Overdiagnosis of Schizophrenia in Nursing Homes Is
Rampant, Especially for Black Residents." Lown Institute, October 24,
2021. https://lowninstitute.org/overdiagnosis-of-schizophrenia-in
-nursing-homes-is-rampant-especially-for-black-residents/.

99   Jaffe, Don J. *Insane Consequences: How the Mental Health Industry Fails
the Mentally Ill.* Amherst: Prometheus Books, 2017.

100   Marcus Aurelius. *The Emperor's Handbook: A New Translation of the
Meditations.* Translated by C. Scot Hicks and David V. Hicks. New
York: Scribner, 2002.

101   Valenstein, Elliot S. *Great and Desperate Cures: The Rise and Decline of
Psychosurgery and Other Radical Treatments for Mental Illness.* New York:
Basic Books, 1986.

102   Scull, Andrew. *Desperate Remedies: Psychiatry's Turbulent Quest to Cure Mental
Illness.* Cambridge: The Belknap Press of Harvard University Press, 2022.

103   Valenstein, Elliot S. *Great and Desperate Cures: The Rise and Decline of Psychosurgery and Other Radical Treatments for Mental Illness*. New York: Basic Books, 1986.

104   Yesavage, J. A., Fairchild, J. K., et al. "Effect of Repetitive Transcranial Magnetic Stimulation on Treatment-Resistant Major Depression in US Veterans: A Randomized Clinical Trial." *JAMA Psychiatry* 75, no. 9 (Sep. 1, 2018): 884–93. doi:10.1001/jamapsychiatry.2018.1483.

105   Greenberg, Gary. "What If the Placebo Effect Isn't a Trick?" *New York Times*, November 7, 2018. https://www.nytimes.com/2018/11/07/magazine/placebo-effect-medicine.html.

106   Arkowitz, Hal, and Scott O. Lilienfeld. "EMDR: Taking a Closer Look." *Scientific American*, December 5, 2018. https://www.scientificamerican.com/article/emdr-taking-a-closer-look/.

107   Singal, Jesse. *The Quick Fix: Why Fad Psychology Can't Cure Our Social Ills*. New York: Farrar, Straus, and Giroux, 2021.

108   Satel, Sally and Scott Lilienfeld. *Brainwashed: the Seductive Appeal of Mindless Neuroscience*. New York: Basic Books, 2013.

Chapter Six: Business Models and Psychotherapy

1   Keefe, Rachel. "Psychotropic Medication Usage Among Foster and Non-Foster Youth on Medicaid." Abstract, Presentation of The American Academy of Pediatrics National Conference, 2021. https://www.aap.org/en/news-room/news-releases/aap/2021/children-in-foster-care-much-more-likely-to-be-prescribed-psychotropic-medications-compared-with-non-foster-children-in-medicaid-program/.

2   "Treatment Planning and Medication Monitoring Were Lacking for Children in Foster Care Receiving Psychotropic Medication." Department of Health and Human Services, Office of the Inspector General Report, September 13, 2018. https://oig.hhs.gov/oei/reports/oei-07-15-00380.asp.

3   Llamocca, Elyse, Danielle L. Steelesmith, Donna Ruch, Jeffrey A. Bridge, and Cynthia A. Fontanella. "Association between Social Determinants of Health and Deliberate Self-Harm among Youths with Psychiatric Diagnoses." *Psychiatric Services* 74, no. 6 (June 1, 2023): 574–80. doi:10.1176/appi.ps.20220180.

4   "2022 Survey of America's Physicians, Part One of Three: Examining how the Social Drivers of Health Affect the Nation's Physicians and their Patients." *The Physicians Foundation*, February 2022. https://physiciansfoundation.org/wp-content/uploads/2022/03/SDOH-Survey-Report.pdf.

5   Grinker, Roy R. *Nobody's Normal: How Culture Created the Stigma of Mental Illness*. New York: WW Norton, 2021, 28.

6   Baxter, Lewis R. "Caudate Glucose Metabolic Rate Changes with Both Drug and Behavior Therapy for Obsessive-Compulsive Disorder."

Archives of General Psychiatry 49, no. 9 (September 1, 1992): 681. doi:10.1001/archpsyc.1992.01820090009002.

7   Grinker, Roy R. *Nobody's Normal: How Culture Created the Stigma of Mental Illness*. New York: WW Norton, 2021.

8   Jaffe, Don J. *Insane Consequences: How the Mental Health Industry Fails the Mentally Ill*. Amherst: Prometheus Books, 2017.

9   Bodkin, J. Alexander, Harrison G. Pope, Michael J. Detke, and James I. Hudson. "Is PTSD Caused by Traumatic Stress?" *Journal of Anxiety Disorders* 21, no. 2 (January 1, 2007): 176–82. doi:10.1016/j.janxdis.2006.09.004.

10   Ruffalo, Mark. "Psychotherapy as a Medical Treatment." *Psychiatric Times*, June 29, 2021. https://www.psychiatrictimes.com/view /psychotherapy-as-a-medical-treatment.

11   Leichsenring, Falk, Christiane Steinert, Sven Rabung, and John P. A. Ioannidis. "The Efficacy of Psychotherapies and Pharmacotherapies for Mental Disorders in Adults: An Umbrella Review and Meta-analytic Evaluation of Recent Meta-analyses." *World Psychiatry* 21, no. 1 (January 11, 2022): 133–45. doi:10.1002/wps.20941: Cuijpers, Pim, Clara Miguel, Mathias Harrer, et al . "Psychological Treatment of Depression: A Systematic Overview of a 'Meta-Analytic Research Domain.'" *Journal of Affective Disorders* 335 (August 1, 2023): 141–51. doi:10.1016/j.jad.2023.05.011.

12   Caldwell, Ben. "50 States of MFT Licensure: Reflections." Psychotherapy Notes, May 12, 2009. https://www.psychotherapynotes .com/50-states-of-mft-licensure-reflections/.

13   "About the Board - Board of Behavioral Sciences," California Board of Behavioral Sciences, n.d. Accessed June 3, 2024. https://www.bbs.ca.gov /about/board_info.html.

14   "Occupational Employment and Wages—May 2022." News Release, Bureau of Labor Statistics, U.S. Department of Labor. April 25, 2023. https://www.bls.gov/news.release/pdf/ocwage.pdf.

15   "Mental and Behavioral Health—African Americans." U.S. Department of Health and Human Services, Office of Minority Health. Accessed January 25, 2024. https://minorityhealth.hhs.gov/omh/browse.aspx?lvl =4&lvlid=24.

16   Remmert, Jocelyn E., Gabriella Guzman, Shahrzad Mavandadi, and D. W. Oslin. "Racial Disparities in Prescription of Antidepressants among U.S. Veterans Referred to Behavioral Healthcare." *Psychiatric Services* 73, no. 9 (September 1, 2022): 984–90. doi:10.1176/appi.ps .202100237.

17   Moreno, Sabrina. "CDC: Black Americans Most Likely to go to ER for Mental Healthcare." *Axios*, March 21, 2023. https://www.axios .com/2023/03/01/black-americans-mental-health-care.

18   Chang-Sing, Erika, Colin Smith, Jane Gagliardi, et al. "Racial and Ethnic Disparities in Patient Restraint in Emergency Departments by Police Transport Status." *Emergency Medicine, JAMA Network Open*, February 21, 2024. doi:10.1001/jamanetworkopen.2024.0098.

19   Peters J., Zachary, Loredana Santo, Danielle R. Davis, and Carol
      DeFrances. "Emergency Department Visits Related to Mental Health
      Disorders among Adults, by Race and Hispanic Ethnicity: United States,
      2018-2020." *Centers for Disease Control and Prevention: National Health
      Statistics Report* 181 (March 1, 2023). doi:10.15620/cdc:123507.

20   Barnett, Michael L., Ellen Meara, Terri Lewinson, Brian Hardy,
      Deanna Chyn, Moraa Onsando, Haiden A. Huskamp, Ateev Mehrotra,
      and Nancy E. Morden. "Racial Inequality in Receipt of Medications for
      Opioid Use Disorder." *The New England Journal of Medicine* 388, no. 19
      (May 11, 2023): 1779–89. doi:10.1056/nejmsa2212412.

21   Baumgaertner, Emily. "Medication Treatment for Addiction Is Shorter
      for Black and Hispanic Patients, Study Finds." *New York Times*,
      November 9, 2022. https://www.nytimes.com/2022/11/09/health
      /opioid-addiction-treatment-racial-disparities.html.

22   Hamp, Auntré, Karen Stamm, Luona Lin, and Peggy Christidis.
      "2015 APA Survey of Psychology Health Service Providers." *American
      Psychological Association*, 2016. https://www.apa.org/workforce
      /publications/15-health-service-providers.

23   Northey, William F. "Characteristics and Clinical Practices of Marriage
      and Family Therapists: A National Survey." *Journal of Marital and Family
      Therapy* 28, no. 4 (October 1, 2002): 487–94. doi:10.1111/j.1752-0606.2002
      .tb00373.x.

24   Peckham, Carol. "Medscape Psychiatrist Lifestyle Report 2017: Race
      and Ethnicity, Bias, and Burnout." *Medscape*, January 11, 2017. https
      ://www.medscape.com/features/slideshow/lifestyle/2017/psychiatry.

25   "New Study Shows 60 Percent of U.S. Counties without a Single
      Psychiatrist: One-Third of All Psychiatrists Nationwide Trained
      Abroad." *New American Economy*, October 23, 2017. https://www
      .newamericaneconomy.org/press-release/new-study-shows-60-percent-of
      -u-s-counties-without-a-single-psychiatrist/.

26   Cuijpers, Pim, Annemieke Van Straten, Lisanne Warmerdam, and
      Gerhard Andersson. "Psychotherapy Versus the Combination of
      Psychotherapy and Pharmacotherapy in the Treatment of Depression:
      A Meta-Analysis." *Depression and Anxiety* 26, no. 3 (March 1, 2009):
      279–88. doi:10.1002/da.20519.

27   Pampallona, Sandro, Paola Bollini, Giuseppe Tibaldi, Bruce Kupelnick,
      and Carmine Munizza. "Combined Pharmacotherapy and Psychological
      Treatment for Depression." *Archives of General Psychiatry* 61, no. 7 (July 1,
      2004): 714. doi:10.1001/archpsyc.61.7.714.

28   Driessen, Ellen, Jack Dekker, Jaap Peen, Henricus L. Van, Giuseppe
      Maina, Gianluca Rosso, Sylvia Rigardetto, et al. "The Efficacy of Adding
      Short-term Psychodynamic Psychotherapy to Antidepressants in the
      Treatment of Depression: A Systematic Review and Meta-analysis of
      Individual Participant Data." *Clinical Psychology Review* 80 (August 1,
      2020): 101886. doi:10.1016/j.cpr.2020.101886.

29   Harman, Chloë. "The Fallacy of 'alternative' Medicine." *Nature Reviews Nephrology* 5, no. 7 (July 1, 2009): 361. doi:10.1038/nrneph.2009.96.

30   Kalman, Thomas P., Victoria N. Kalman, and Roger Granet. "Do Psychopharmacologists Speak to Psychotherapists? A Survey of Practicing Clinicians." *Psychodynamic Psychiatry* 40, no. 2 (June 1, 2012): 275–85. doi:10.1521/pdps.2012.40.2.275.

31   Leichsenring, Falk, Christiane Steinert, Sven Rabung, and John P. Ioannidis. "The Efficacy of Psychotherapies and Pharmacotherapies for Mental Disorders in Adults: An Umbrella Review and Meta-analytic Evaluation of Recent Meta-analyses," *World Psychiatry* 21, no. 1 (January 11, 2022): 133–45, doi:10.1002/wps.20941.

32   Carroll, Lewis. *Alice's Adventures in Wonderland*. New York, Boston: T. Y. Crowell & Co., 1893.

33   Wikipedia contributors. "Dodo Bird Verdict." *Wikipedia*, December 5, 2023. https://en.wikipedia.org/wiki/Dodo_bird_verdict.

34   Fine, Sidney, and Esther Fine. "Four Psychoanalytic Perspectives: A Study of Differences in Interpretive Interventions." *Journal of the American Psychoanalytic Association* 38, no. 4 (December 1, 1990): 1017–41. doi:10.1177/000306519003800406.

35   Ofshe, Richard, and Ethan Watters. *Making Monsters: False Memories, Psychotherapy, and Sexual Hysteria*. New York: Scribner, 1994.

36   Lilienfeld, Scott O. "Psychological Treatments That Cause Harm." *Perspectives on Psychological Science* 2, no. 1 (March 1, 2007): 53–70. doi:10.1111/j.1745-6916.2007.00029.x.

37   Federal Trade Commission. "Lumosity to Pay $2 Million to Settle FTC Deceptive Advertising Charges for Its 'Brain Training' Program," January 15, 2016. https://www.ftc.gov/news-events/press-releases/2016/01/lumosity-pay-2-million-settle-ftc-deceptive-advertising-charges.

38   Nosek, Brian A., Tom E. Hardwicke, Hannah Moshontz, Aurélien Allard, Katherine S. Corker, Anna Dreber, Fiona Fidler, et al. "Replicability, Robustness, and Reproducibility in Psychological Science." *Annual Review of Psychology* 73, no. 1 (January 4, 2022): 719–48. doi:10.1146/annurev-psych-020821-114157.

39   Simmons, J. P., Nelson, L. D., and Simonsohn, U. "False-Positive Psychology: Undisclosed Flexibility in Data Collection and Analysis Allows Presenting Anything as Significant." *Psychological Science* 22, no. 11 (Oct 17, 2011): 1359-1366. doi:10.1177/0956797611417632.

40   "Power Prose: Simine Vazire Hopes to Fix Psychology's Credibility Crisis." *The Economist*, January 10, 2024. https://www.economist.com/science-and-technology/2024/01/10/simine-vazire-hopes-to-fix-psychologys-credibility-crisis.

41   Lewis-Kraus, Gideon. "They Studied Dishonesty, Was Their Work a Lie? Behavioral Economists Dan Ariely and Francesca Gino Became Famous for their Research Into Why We Bend the Truth. Now they've Both Been Accused of Fabricating Data." *The New Yorker*, September 30,

2023. https://www.newyorker.com/magazine/2023/10/09/they
-studied-dishonesty-was-their-work-a-lie.

42   Scheiber, Noam. "The Harvard Professor and the Bloggers." *New York Times*, October 3, 2023. https://www.nytimes.com/2023/09/30/business the-harvard-professor-and-the-bloggers.html.

43   Valenstein, Elliot S. *Great and Desperate Cures: The Rise and Decline of Psychosurgery and Other Radical Treatments for Mental Illness.* New York: Basic Books, 1986.

44   Lieberman, Jeffrey, and Ogi Ogas. *Shrinks: The Untold Story of Psychiatry.* New York: Little, Brown and Company, 2015.

45   Harrington, Anne. *Mind Fixers: Psychiatry's Troubled Search for the Biology of Mental Illness.* New York: Norton, 2019.

46   Scull, Andrew. *Desperate Remedies: Psychiatry's Turbulent Quest to Cure Mental Illness.* Cambridge: The Belknap Press of Harvard University Press, 2022.

47   "Mental Health Watch." *Quackwatch.* Accessed January 25, 2024. https://quackwatch.org/mental-health/.

48   Steele, Jennifer. "Experimental Methods." *The New Yorker*, March 9, 2020. https://www.newyorker.com/magazine/2020/03/16/letters-from -the-march-16-2020-issue.

49   Federal Trade Commission. "Lumosity to Pay $2 Million to Settle FTC Deceptive Advertising Charges for Its 'Brain Training' Program," January 15, 2016. https://www.ftc.gov/news-events/press-releases/2016 /01/lumosity-pay-2-million-settle-ftc-deceptive-advertising-charges.

50   Chivers, Tom. "Does Psychology Have a Conflict-of-Interest Problem?" *Nature* 571, no. 7763 (July 1, 2019): 20–23. doi:10.1038/d41586-019-02041-5.

51   Stoll, Marlene, Alexander Lucas Mancini, Lara Hubenschmid, Nadine Dreimüller, Jochem König, Pim Cuijpers, Jürgen Barth, and Klaus Lieb. "Discrepancies from Registered Protocols and Spin Occurred Frequently in Randomized Psychotherapy Trials—A Meta-Epidemiologic Study." *Journal of Clinical Epidemiology* 128 (December 1, 2020): 49–56. doi:10.1016/j.jclinepi.2020.08.013.

52   Driessen, Ellen, Steven D. Hollon, Claudi Bockting, Pim Cuijpers, and Erick H. Turner. "Does Publication Bias Inflate the Apparent Efficacy of Psychological Treatment for Major Depressive Disorder? A Systematic Review and Meta-Analysis of US National Institutes of Health-Funded Trials." *PLOS ONE* 10, no. 9 (September 30, 2015): e0137864. doi:10.1371 /journal.pone.0137864.

53   Jaffe, Don J. *Insane Consequences: How the Mental Health Industry Fails the Mentally Ill.* Amherst: Prometheus Books, 2017. 157-9.

54   Mattke, Soeren, Hangsheng Liu, John P. Caloyeras, et al. "Workplace Wellness Programs Study: Final Report." Rand Corporation. 2013. Accessed January 26, 2024. http://www.rand.org/content/dam/rand /pubs/research_reports/RR200/RR254/RAND_RR254.pdf.

55   Baicker, Katherine, and Zirui Song. "Workplace Wellness Programs Are Big Business. They Might Not Work." *Washington Post*, June 17,

2021. https://www.washingtonpost.com/outlook/workplace-wellness
-programs-are-big-business-they-might-not-work/2021/06
/16/07400886-cd56-11eb-8014-2f3926ca24d9_story.html.

56   Song, Zirui, and Katherine Baicker. "Health and Economic Outcomes
      up to Three Years after a Workplace Wellness Program: A Randomized
      Controlled Trial." *Health Affairs* 40, no. 6 (June 1, 2021): 951–60.
      doi:10.1377/hlthaff.2020.01808.

57   Baicker, Katherine. "Do Workplace Wellness Programs Work?"
      JAMA Health Forum 2, no. 9 (2021):e213375. doi: 10.1001/jama
      healthforum.2021.3375.

58   Barry, Ellen. "Workplace Wellness Programs Have Little Benefit,
      Study Finds." *New York Times*, January 15, 2024. https://www.nytimes
      .com/2024/01/15/health/employee-wellness-benefits.html.

59   Fleming, William J. "Employee Well-being Outcomes from Individual-
      level Mental Health Interventions: Cross-sectional Evidence from
      the United Kingdom." *Industrial Relations Journal*, January 10, 2024.
      doi:10.1111/irj.12418.

60   Purser, Ronald. *McMindfulness: How Mindfulness Became the New
      Capitalist Spirituality*. London: Repeater, 2019.

61   Raphael, Rina. "Is Modern Mindfulness a Corporate Scam? This
      Management Professor Thinks So." *Fast Company*, August 22, 2019.
      https://www.fastcompany.com/90392141/is-modern-mindfulness-a
      -corporate-scam-a-critique-of-meditation-culture.

62   Montero-Marín, Jesús, Matt Allwood, Susan Ball, Catherine Crane,
      Katherine De Wilde, Verena Hinze, Benjamin Jones, et al. "School-
      Based Mindfulness Training in Early Adolescence: What Works, for
      Whom and How in the MYRIAD Trial?" *Evidence-Based Mental Health*
      25, no. 3 (July 12, 2022): 117–24. doi:10.1136/ebmental-2022-300439.

63   Kuyken, Willem, Susan Ball, Catherine Crane, et al. "Effectiveness
      and cost-effectiveness of universal school-based mindfulness training
      compared with normal school provision in reducing risk of mental health
      problems and promoting well-being in adolescence: the MYRIAD
      cluster randomised controlled trial." *Evidence-Based Mental Health* 25,
      no. 3 (Jul 12, 2022): 99–109.

64   Saxbe, Darby. "This is not the Way to Help Depressed Teenagers." *New
      York Times*, November 18, 2023. https://www.nytimes.com/2023/11/18
      /opinion/teenagers-mental-health-treatment.html.

65   Kabat-Zinn, Jon. *Wherever You Go, There You Are: Mindfulness Meditation
      in Everyday Life*. New York: MJF Books, 2005.

66   Purser, Ronald. "The Militarization of Mindfulness" *Inquiring Mind*,
      February 11, 2023. https://www.inquiringmind.com/article/3002_17
      _purser-the-militarization-of-mindfulness/.

67   Gunter, Jen. "Worshiping the False Idols of Wellness." *New York Times*,
      August 6, 2018. https://www.nytimes.com/2018/08/01/style/wellness
      -industrial-complex.html.

68   Raphael, R. *The Gospel of Wellness: Gyms, Gurus, Goop, and the False Promise of Self-Care.* New York: Henry Holt and Co., 2022.

69   St. Aubyn, Edward. *Double Blind.* New York: Edward, Farrar, Straus and Giroux, 2021.

70   Mauss, Iris B., Maya Tamir, Craig L. Anderson, and Nicole S. Savino. "Can Seeking Happiness Make People Unhappy? Paradoxical Effects of Valuing Happiness." *Emotion* 11, no. 4 (August 1, 2011): 807–15. doi:10.1037/a0022010.

Chapter Seven: Why We Maintain This Crazy System

1   Bakan, Joel. *The Corporation: The Pathological Pursuit of Profit and Power.* New York: Free Press (Simon & Schuster), 2004.

2   "Leading Lobbying Industries U.S. 2022." *Statista*, November 3, 2023. https://www.statista.com/statistics/257364/top-lobbying-industries-in-the-us/.

3   Lerner, Sharon. "Big Pharma Attacks Efforts to Guard against Coronavirus Price Gouging." *The Intercept*, July 8, 2020. https://theintercept.com/2020/06/02/big-pharma-coronavirus-treatment-price-gouging/.

4   Diamond, Dan, and Amy Goldstein. "A Bitter Pill: Biden Suffers Familiar Defeat on Prescription Drug Prices." *Washington Post*, October 30, 2021. https://www.washingtonpost.com/health/2021/10/29/biden-medicare-drug-negotiation/.

5   Wilson, Megan. "Pharma Group Leader Says Dems Who Vote for Reconciliation Bill 'Won't Get a Free Pass.'" *Politico*, August 4, 2022. https://www.politico.com/news/2022/08/04/head-of-top-pharma-group-says-dems-who-vote-for-bill-wont-get-a-free-pass-00049898.

6   Cohrs, Rachel. "Insulin Giants Eli Lilly and Novo Nordisk Boosted Their Lobbying Spending as Democrats Eyed Pricing Reform." *STAT*, January 27, 2022. https://www.statnews.com/2022/01/25/insulin-giants-eli-lilly-and-novo-nordisk-boosted-their-lobbying-spending-as-democrats-eyed-pricing-reform/.

7   Deanna Beasley. "Prices for New US Drugs Rose 35% in 2023, More than the Previous Year." Reuters, February 24, 2024. https://www.reuters.com/business/healthcare-pharmaceuticals/prices-new-us-drugs-rose-35-2023-more-than-previous-year-2024-02-23/.

8   Brot-Goldberg, Zarek, Zack Cooper, Stuart Craig, and Lev Klarnet. "Is There Too Little Enforcement in the US Hospital Sector?" Yale, Tobin Center for Economic Policy, April 2024. https://tobin.yale.edu/sites/default/files/2024-02/Hospital_Merger_Heterogeneity_manuscript.pdf.

9   Garber, Judith. "Why Antitrust Laws Aren't Stopping Some Hospital Mergers." Lown Institute, August 19, 2022. https://lowninstitute.org/why-antitrust-laws-arent-stopping-some-hospital-mergers/.

10   Garber, Judith. "Why Antitrust Laws Aren't Stopping Some Hospital Mergers." *Lown Institute*, August 19, 2022. https://lowninstitute.org/why-antitrust-laws-arent-stopping-some-hospital-mergers/.

11   Mathews, Anna Wilde and Michaels, David. "U.S. Opens United
      Health Antitrust Probe." *Wall Street Journal*, February 27, 2024.
      https://www.wsj.com/health/healthcare/u-s-launches
      -antitrust-investigation-of-healthcare-giant-unitedhealth-ff5a00d2.

12   "Action for mental health. The final report of the Joint Commission on
      Mental Illness and Health." *Journal of Rehabilitation* 27 (1961): 27–8.

13   Zimmerman, Ken. "Mental Health Needs to Be a Top Priority
      for Philanthropy. Here's Why." *Inside Philanthropy*, July 7, 2020.
      https://www.insidephilanthropy.com/home/2020/6/28/more-than
      -ever-mental-health-needs-to-a-top-priority-for-philanthropy
      -heres-why.

14   Phillips, Rachel, Cecelia Benoit. "Exploring Stigma by Association
      Among Front-line Care Providers Serving Sex Workers." *Healthcare
      Policy* 9, no. Issue (Oct. 2013): 139–51. PMID: 24289946; PMCID:
      PMC4750147.

15   Sadler, John. *Values and Psychiatric Diagnosis.* Oxford: Oxford University
      Press, 2005, 2.

16   Scull, Andrew. *Desperate Remedies: Psychiatry's Turbulent Quest to Cure
      Mental Illness.* Cambridge: The Belknap Press of Harvard University
      Press, 2022.

17   "Rugged Individualism." Wikipedia, October 3, 2023. https://en.wiki
      pedia.org/wiki/Rugged_individualism.

18   "Rugged Individualism." *Merriam-Webster Dictionary.* Accessed January 26,
      2023. https://www.merriam-webster.com/dictionary/rugged%20
      individualism.

19   Hill, Ray. "Harry Truman Goes to the Senate, Part II." *The Knoxville
      Focus.* Accessed January 26, 2024. https://www.knoxfocus.com/archives
      /harry-truman-goes-senate-part-2/.

20   Americans Stand out on Individualism" Pew Research Center. April 19,
      2016. https://www.pewresearch.org/fact-tank/2016/04/19/5-ways
      -americans-and-europeans-are-different/ft_16-04-22_usindividualism/.

21   Adamczyk, Alicia. "More than Half of Millennials Think They'll Be
      Millionaires—Here's What the Data Suggests." CNBC, May 3, 2019.
      https://www.cnbc.com/2019/05/03/half-of-millennials-think-theyll-be
      -rich-data-says-otherwise.html.

22   "American Millennials Think They Will Be Rich: The Data Suggest
      They Probably Won't Be." *The Economist*, April 22, 2019. https://www
      .economist.com/graphic-detail/2019/04/22/american-millennials-think
      -they-will-be-rich.

23   Cohen, Roger. "The Public Imperative." *New York Times*, October 4, 2009.
      https://www.nytimes.com/2009/10/05/opinion/05iht-edcohen.html.

24   Mark, Tami, Melissa Dolan, Benjamin Allaire, et al. "Untreated
      Psychiatric and Substance Use Disorders Among Caregivers With
      Children Reported to Child Protective Services." *JAMA Health Forum* 5,
      no. 4 (April 19. 2024): e240637. doi:10.1001/jamahealthforum.2024.0637.

25   Shalin, Dmitri. "Goffman's Self-Ethnographies." Center for Democratic Culture, University of Nevada, Las Vegas. Accessed January 26, 2024. http://cdclv.unlv.edu/ega/articles/ds_eg_selfethno.html.

26   "Health Insurance Coverage of the Total Population." Kaiser Family Foundation, October 27, 2023. https://www.kff.org/other/state-indicator /total-population/.

27   Starr, Paul. *Remedy and Reaction: The Peculiar American Struggle over Healthcare Reform.* New Haven: Yale University Press, 2011.

28   "ACSI: Finance and Insurance Customer Satisfaction Slides as Cost Cutting, Fees and Premiums Pinch Customers." American Customer Satisfaction Index, November 17, 2015. https://theacsi.org/news-and-resources /press-releases/2015/11/17/press-release-finance-and-insurance-2015/.

29   Pflanzer, Lydia Ramsey. "7 Most Hated and Loved Public Services, According to Researchers." *Business Insider,* January 11, 2018. http ://www.businessinsider.com/pharmaceutical-and-health-insurance -companies-arent-popular-2015-8.

30   "Honesty/Ethics in Professions | Gallup Historical Trends." Gallup, Accessed January 25, 2024. http://www.gallup.com/poll/1654/honesty -ethics-professions.aspx.

31   "The Decision to Not Get Vaccinated, From the Perspective of the Unvaccinated." The Covid States Project, Report #63. Accessed January 25, 2024. https://www.covidstates.org/reports/the-decision-to-not-get -vaccinated-from-the-perspective-of-the-unvaccinated.

32   Aboulenein, Ahmed. "Consumer Group Says Drugmakers Abuse the U.S. Patent System to Keep Prices High." Reuters, September 16, 2022. https://www.reuters.com/business/healthcare-pharmaceuticals /consumer-group-says-drugmakers-abuse-us-patent-system-keep-prices -high-2022-09-16/.

33   "Lander Held on to Vaccine Maker Stock Months into Tenure." *Politico,* February 9, 2022. https://www.politico.com/news/2022/02/09/lander -vaccine-stock-ethics-00007100.

34   Kimball, Spencer. "The Covid Pandemic Drives Pfizer's 2022 Revenue to a Record $100 Billion." *CNBC,* February 2, 2023. https://www.cnbc .com/2023/01/31/the-covid-pandemic-drives-pfizers-2022-revenue-to-a -record-100-billion.html.

35   Josephs, Jonathan. "Investors Lose Vote to Share Covid Vaccine Know-How." BBC News, April 28, 2022. https://www.bbc.com/news/business-61262065.

36   Beleche, Trinidad, Joel Ruhter, Alison Kolbe, et al. "COVID-19 Vaccine Hesitancy: Demographic Factors, Geographic Patterns, and Changes Over Time." Issue Brief: Assistant Secretary for Planning and Evaluation, Department of Health and Human Services, May 2021. https://aspe.hhs.gov/sites/default/files/migrated_legacy_files/200816 /aspe-ib-vaccine-hesitancy.pdf.

37   Laughlin, Lynda, Augustus Anderson, Anthony Martinez, and Asiah Gayfield. "22 Million Employed in Healthcare Fight against COVID-19."

U.S. Census Bureau, April 5, 2021. https://www.census.gov/library /stories/2021/04/who-are-our-health-care-workers.html.

38   Starr, Paul. *The Social Transformation of American Medicine: The Rise of a Sovereign Profession and the Making of a Vast Industry*. New York: Basic Books, 1982.

39   Kaiser, Charles F., III, and Marvin Friedlander. "Corporate Practice of Medicine." Internal Revenue Service. Accessed January 25, 2024. https://www.irs.gov/pub/irs-tege/eotopicf00.pdf.

40   Tkacik, Maureen. "Attack of the Straw Doctors." The American Prospect, February 19, 2024. https://prospect.org/health/2024-02-19 -attack-of-the-straw-doctors/.

41   Zhu, Jane M., Hayden Rooke-Ley, and Erin C. Fuse Brown. "A Doctrine in Name Only—Strengthening Prohibitions Against the Corporate Practice of Medicine." *The New England Journal of Medicine* 389, no. 11 (September 14, 2023): 965–68. doi:10.1056/nejmp2306904.

42   Morgenson, Gretchen, and Joshua Rosner. *These are the Plunderers: How Private Equity Runs—and Wrecks—America*. New York: Simon & Schuster.

43   State v. Bailey Dental Co. 211 Iowa 781, 785 (Iowa 1931). https ://casetext.com/case/state-v-bailey-dental-co.

44   Ofri, Danielle. "Why Are Nonprofit Hospitals So Highly Profitable? These Institutions Receive Tax Exemptions for Community Benefits that Often don't Really Exist." *New York Times*, February 20, 2020. https ://www.nytimes.com/2020/02/20/opinion/nonprofit-hospitals.html.

45   Ollove, Michael. "Some Nonprofit Hospitals Aren't Earning Their Tax Breaks, Critics Say." *Stateline*, February 7, 2020. https://www .pewtrusts.org/en/research-and-analysis/blogs/stateline/2020/02/07 /some-nonprofit-hospitals-arent-earning-their-tax-breaks-critics-say.

46   "2021 Winning Hospitals: Community Benefit." Lown Institute Hospital Index. Accessed January 25, 2024. https://lownhospitalsindex .org/2021-winning-hospitals-community-benefit.

47   Mathews, Anna, Tom McGinty, and Melanie Evans. "Big Hospitals Provide Skimpy Charity Care—Despite Billions in Tax Breaks." *Wall Street Journal*, July 25, 2022. https://www.wsj.com/articles /nonprofit-hospitals-vs-for-profit-charity-care-spending-11657936777.

48   Silver-Greenberg, Jessica, and Katie Thomas. "They Were Entitled to Free Care. Hospitals Hounded Them to Pay." *New York Times*, December 15, 2022. https://www.nytimes.com/2022/09/24/business/nonprofit -hospitals-poor-patients.html.

49   Hancock, Jay, and Elizabeth Lucas. "'UVA Has Ruined Us': Health System Sues Thousands of Patients, Seizing Paychecks and Claiming Homes." KFF Health News, September 19, 2021. https://khn.org/news /uva-health-system-sues-patients-virginia-courts-garnishment-liens -bankruptcy/.

50   Cohrs, Rachel. "The Catholic Hospital System Ascension Is Running a Wall Street-Style Private Equity Fund." *STAT*, November 16, 2021.

https://www.statnews.com/2021/11/16/ascension-running-wall-street
-style-private-equity-fund/.

51   Deagon, Brian. "Royalty Pharma IPO Sets Record As Largest Public
Offering, Stock Soars." *Investors Business Daily*, June 16, 2020.
https://www.investors.com/news/technology/royalty-pharma-ipo-could
-be-largest-public-offering-so-far-this-year/.

52   Garde, Damian. "Royalty Pharma, a Drug Company That Doesn't
Develop Drugs, Shatters IPO Record." *STAT*, June 16, 2020. https
://www.statnews.com/2020/06/16/the-next-record-setting-ipo-a-drug
-company-that-doesnt-develop-drugs/.

53   Goldhill, Olivia. "Tobacco Giant Philip Morris Is Investing Billions in
Healthcare. Critics Say it's Peddling Cures for Its Own Poison,"
STAT, September 27, 2022. https://www.statnews.com/2022/09/07
/tobacco-giant-philip-morris-investing-billions-in-health-care/.

54   Bannow, Tana. "Healthcare Companies Soak Up $23 Billion in Venture
Capital Funding." *Modern Healthcare*, October 9, 2018. https://www
.modernhealthcare.com/article/20181009/NEWS/181009905/healthcare
-companies-soak-up-23-billion-in-venture-capital-funding.

55   Bischoff, Clay, Brian Fox, and David Quigley. "The Next Act in
Healthcare Private Equity." McKinsey & Company, December 1, 2016.
https://www.mckinsey.com/industries/private-equity-and-principal
-investors/our-insights/the-next-act-in-healthcare-private-equity.

56   Powers, Brian, William H. Shrank, and Amol S. Navathe. "Private
Equity and Healthcare Delivery." *JAMA* 326, no. 10 (September 14, 2021):
907. doi:10.1001/jama.2021.13197.

57   Arnsdorf, Isaac. "How Rich Investors, Not Doctors, Profit from Marking
up ER Bills." *ProPublica*, June 12, 2020. https://www.propublica.org
/article/how-rich-investors-not-doctors-profit-from-marking-up-er-bills.

58   Abdelhadi, Ola, Brent D. Fulton, Laura E. Crotty Alexander, and
Richard M. Scheffler. "Private Equity-Acquired Physician Practices and
Market Penetration Increased Substantially, 2012–21." *Health Affairs* 43,
no. 3 (March 1, 2024): 354–62. doi:10.1377/hlthaff.2023.00152.

59   Brown, Benjamin, Eloise O'Donnell, and Lawrence P. Casalino. "Private
Equity Investment in Behavioral Health Treatment Centers." *JAMA
Psychiatry* 77, no. 3 (March 1, 2020): 229. doi:10.1001/jamapsychiatry
.2019.3880.

60   "Credit Stress is Rising, Setting the Stage for more Downgrades and
Defaults." Moody's Investor Service, December 12, 2022. https://www
.documentcloud.org/documents/23452687-moodys-healthcare-stress
-report.

61   Martinez, Barbara. "In Medicaid, Private HMOs Take a Big, and
Profitable, Role." *Wall Street Journal*, November 15, 2006. http://www
.wsj.com/articles/SB116354350983023095.

62   Perlberg, Heather. "Private Equity Is Ruining Healthcare, Covid Is
Making It Worse." Bloomberg, May 20, 2020. https://www.bloomberg

.com/news/features/2020-05-20/private-equity-is-ruining-health-care
-covid-is-making-it-worse.

63   Braun, Robert, Hye-Young Jung, Lawrence P. Casalino, Zachary
Myslinski, and Mark Aaron Unruh. "Association of Private Equity
Investment in US Nursing Homes with the Quality and Cost of Care
for Long-Stay Residents." *JAMA Health Forum* 2, no. 11 (November 19,
2021): e213817. doi:10.1001/jamahealthforum.2021.3817.

64   Singh, Yashaswini, Zirui Song, Daniel Polsky, Joseph Dov Bruch, and
Jane M. Zhu. "Association of Private Equity Acquisition of Physician
Practices with Changes in Healthcare Spending and Utilization." *JAMA
Health Forum* 3, no. 9 (September 2, 2022): e222886. doi:10.1001
/jamahealthforum.2022.2886.

65   Kannan, Sneha, Joseph Dov Bruch, Zirui Song. "Changes in Hospital
Adverse Events and Patient Outcomes Associated With Private Equity
Acquisition." *JAMA* 330, no. 24 (Dec. 26, 2023): 2365–75. doi:10.1001/jama
.2023.23147. https://jamanetwork.com/journals/jama/article-abstract/2813379.

66   Goozner, Merrill. "Private Equity Takeovers Are Harming Patients."
British Medical Journal (Clinical Research Ed.), July 19, 2023, 1396.
doi:10.1136/bmj.p1396.

67   Singh, Yashaswini, M. Sugunatha Reddy, and Jane M. Zhu. "Life Cycle
of Private Equity Investments in Physician Practices: An Overview of
Private Equity Exits." *Health Affairs Scholar*, April 10, 2024. https://doi
.org/10.1093/haschl/qxae047.

68   O'Grady, Eileen. "The Kids are not Alright: How Private Equity
Profits Off of Behavioral Health Services for Vulnerable and At-Risk
Youth." Private Equity Stakeholder Project, February 2022. https
://pestakeholder.org/wp-content/uploads/2022/02/PESP_Youth_BH
_Report_2022.pdf.

69   Knight, Victoria, Rachana Pradhan, Elizabeth Lucas. "Pharma Campaign
Cash Delivered to Key Lawmakers with Surgical Precision" KFF Health
News, October 27, 2021. https://khn.org/news/article/pharma-campaign
-cash-delivered-to-key-lawmakers-with-surgical-precision/.

70   "Finance/Insurance/Real Estate Sector Summary." OpenSecrets.
Accessed January 25, 2024. https://www.opensecrets.org/industries
/indus.php?Ind=F.

71   Adams, Ben. "Pharma Ad Spending Up Just 1% This Year as the Slow
Move Away from TV into Digital Continues." Fierce Pharma, August 22,
2022. https://www.fiercepharma.com/marketing/pharma-ad-spending
-just-1-year-slow-move-away-tv-and-digital-continues.

72   Drash, Wayne. "Report: Pharma Exec Says He Had 'Moral Requirement'
To Raise Drug Price 400%." CNN, September 12, 2018. https://www
.cnn.com/2018/09/11/health/drug-price-hike-moral-requirement-bn
/index.html.

73   Ross, Casey. "Why the Conviction of Elizabeth Holmes Hinged on
Defrauding Theranos Investors, Not Patients." *STAT*, January 4, 2022.

https://www.statnews.com/2022/01/04/elizabeth-holmes-theranos-fraud
-investors/.

74 Nir, Sarah Maslin, Jan Hoffman, and Lola Fadulu. "Teva
Pharmaceuticals Found Liable in Landmark Opioid Trial." *New York
Times*, December 30, 2021. https://www.nytimes.com/2021/12/30
/nyregion/teva-opioid-trial-verdict.html.

75 Daval, C. Joseph Ross, Jerry Avorn, and Aaron S. Kesselheim. "Holding
Pharmaceutical and Medical Device Executives Accountable as
Responsible Corporate Officers." *JAMA Internal Medicine* 182, no. 11
(November 1, 2022): 1199. doi:10.1001/jamainternmed.2022.4138.

76 Kelly, Susan. "It's Taking Longer To Get a Doctor Appointment,
Survey Finds." *Healthcare Dive*, September 13, 2022. https://www.health
caredive.com/news/physician-appointment-AMN-Healthcare-wait
-times/631698/.

Chapter Eight: Reform 101: How We Can Fix Our Healthcare Mess

1 "National Health Expenditures." Center for Medicare and Medicaid
Services. Accessed January 25, 2024. https://www.cms.gov/files/zip/nhe
-tables.zip.

2 "United States Drug Overdose Death Rates and Totals over Time."
Wikipedia, January 22, 2024. https://en.wikipedia.org/wiki/United
_States_drug_overdose_death_rates_and_totals_over_time.

3 Vankar, Preeti. "Percentage of Respondents Worldwide Who Were
Satisfied with Their Country's National Health System as of 2019,
by Country." *Statista*, June 20, 2022. https://www.statista.com
/statistics/1109036/satisfaction-health-system-worldwide-by-country/.

4 "Health and Healthcare for Women of Reproductive Age: How
the United States Compares with Other High-Income Countries."
Commonwealth Fund, April 5, 2022. doi:10.26099/4pph-j894. https
://www.commonwealthfund.org/publications/issue-briefs/2022/apr
/health-and-health-care-women-reproductive-age.

5 "Healthcare System | Gallup Historical Trends." Gallup, October 9, 2023.
https://news.gallup.com/poll/4708/healthcare-system.aspx.

6 McCarthy, Justin. "Seven in 10 Maintain Negative View of U.S.
Healthcare System." Gallup, January 14, 2019. https://news.gallup.com
/poll/245873/seven-maintain-negative-view-healthcare-system.aspx.

7 Neukam, Stephen. "Less than half in New Survey Rate US Healthcare
as Excellent or Good." January 19, 2023. https://thehill.com/policy
/healthcare/3819185-fewer-than-half-in-new-survey-rate-us-health
-care-as-excellent-or-good/.

8 Brenan, Megan. "Majority in U.S. Still Say Gov't Should Ensure
Healthcare." Gallup, February 24, 2023. https://news.gallup.com
/poll/468401/majority-say-gov-ensure-healthcare.aspx.

9 Jones, Bradley. "More Americans Now Favor Single Payer Program to
Provide Health Coverage." Pew Research Center, September 29, 2020.

https://www.pewresearch.org/fact-tank/2020/09/29/increasing-share-of
-americans-favor-a-single-government-program-to-provide-health-care
-coverage/.

10   Potter, Wendell. "I Sold Americans a Lie about Canadian Medicine. Now
     we're Paying the Price." *Washington Post*, August 6, 2020. https://www
     .washingtonpost.com/outlook/2020/08/06/health-insurance-canada-lie/.

11   "The Challenge of National Healthcare." National Archives, Harry S.
     Truman Library and Museum. Accessed January 27, 2024. https://www
     .trumanlibrary.gov/education/presidential-inquiries
     /challenge-national-healthcare.

12   Campbell, Kevin, MD. "Don't Believe AMA's Hype, Membership Still
     Declining." *MedPage Today*, June 19, 2019. https://www.medpagetoday
     .com/opinion/campbells-scoop/80583.

13   Miller, Phillip. "Survey: 42% of Physicians Strongly Support Single
     Payer Healthcare, 35% Strongly Oppose." Merritt Hawkins, August 14,
     2017. https://www.merritthawkins.com///uploadedFiles/mha_single
     payer_press_release_2017(1).pdf

14   Reid, Thomas Roy. *The Healing of America: A Global Quest for Better and
     Cheaper Healthcare.* New York: Penguin Books, 2010.

15   Masterson, Les. "Seniors Love Medicare, but Are Pessimistic about Its
     Long-Term Future." *Healthcare Dive*, February 20, 2019. https://www
     .healthcaredive.com/news/seniors-love-medicare-but-are-pessimistic
     -about-its-long-term-future/548721/.

16   Ochieng, Nancy, Jeannie Fuglesten Biniek, Meredith Freed, Anthony
     Damico, and Tricia Neuman. "Medicare Advantage in 2023: Enrollment
     Update and Key Trends." *KFF*, August 9, 2023. https://www.kff.org
     /medicare/issue-brief/medicare-advantage-in-2021-enrollment
     -update-and-key-trends/.

17   Wilensky, Gail R. "The Future of Medicare Advantage." *JAMA Health
     Forum* 3, no. 5 (May 5, 2022): e221684. doi:10.1001/jamahealthforum
     .2022.1684.

18   Lieberman, Steven M., Paul Ginsburg, and Samuel Valdez. "Medicare
     Advantage Enrolls Lower-Spending People, Leading to Large
     Overpayments." University of Southern California Leonard D. Schaeffer
     Center for Health Policy & Economics, June 13, 2023. doi:10.25549
     /n153-9a66.

19   Grimm, Christi A. "Some Medicare Advantage Organization Denials of
     Prior Authorization Requests Raise Concerns About Beneficiary Access
     to Medically Necessary Care." Office of the Inspector General, U.S.
     Department of Health and Human Services, April 2022. https://oig.hhs
     .gov/oei/reports/OEI-09-18-00260.pdf.

20   Abelson, Reed, and Margot Sanger-Katz. "'The Cash Monster was
     Insatiable': How Insurers Exploited Medicare Advantage for Billions."
     New York Times, October 8, 2022. https://www.nytimes.com
     /2022/10/08/upshot/medicare-advantage-fraud-allegations.html.

21   Prusynski, Rachel A., Anthony D'Alonzo, Michael P. Johnson, et al. "Differences in Home Health Services and Outcomes Between Traditional Medicare and Medicare Advantage." *JAMA Health Forum* 5, no. 3 (2024): e235454. doi:10.1001/jamahealthforum.2023.5454.

22   King, Robert. "'It Was Stunning': Bipartisan Anger Aimed at Medicare Advantage Care Denials." *Politico*, November 24, 2023. https://www.politico.com/news/2023/11/24/medicare-advantage -plans-congress-00128353.

23   Alltucker, Ken. "Hospitals, Doctors Drop Private Medicare Plans Over Payment Disputes." *USA TODAY*, October 27, 2023. https://www .usatoday.com/story/news/health/2023/10/27/hospitals-terminate -medicare-advantage-contracts-over-payments/71301991007/.

24   Payerchin, Richard. "Physician Group Slams Insurers for Overcharging Taxpayers for Medicare Advantage." *Medical Economics*, October 10, 2023. https://www.medicaleconomics.com/view/physician-group-slams -insurers-for-overcharging-taxpayers-for-medicare-advantage.

25   Zhu, Jane M., Mark K. Meiselbach, Coleman Drake, and Daniel Polsky. "Psychiatrist Networks in Medicare Advantage Plans Are Substantially Narrower Than in Medicaid and ACA Markets." *Health Affairs* 42, no. 7 (July 1, 2023): 909–18. doi:10.1377/hlthaff.2022.01547.

26   Appleby, Julie. "Medicare Advantage Increasingly Popular with Seniors— but Not Hospitals and Doctors." KFF Health News, November 29, 2023. https://kffhealthnews.org/news/article/medicare-advantage-payment -rates-friction/.

27   Emerson, Jakob. "Hospitals are Dropping Medicare Advantage Plans Left and Right." *Becker's Hospital Review*, December 14, 2023. https ://www.beckershospitalreview.com/finance/hospitals-are-dropping -medicare-advantage-left-and-right.html.

28   Herman, Bob. "Former Top Medicare Official Says Medicare Advantage's Coding Industry Offers 'No Benefit to Society.'" *STAT*, May 18, 2022. https://www.statnews.com/2022/05/18/medicare -advantage-coding-no-benefit/.

29   Miller, Lee, and Wei Lu. "These Are the Economies with the Most (and Least) Efficient Healthcare." NDTV Profit (Bloomberg), September 20, 2018. https://www.bloombergquint.com/global-economics/u-s-near -bottom-of-health-index-hong-kong-and-singapore-at-top.

30   Tikkanen, Roosa, Robin Osborn, Elias Mossialos, Ana Djordjevic and George A. Wharton. "International Healthcare System Profiles: Switzerland." Commonwealth Fund, June 5, 2020. https://www .commonwealthfund.org/international-health-policy-center/countries /switzerland.

31   Sanders, Linley. "How Americans Evaluate Social Security, Medicare, and Six Other Entitlement Programs." *YouGov*, February 8, 2023. https://today.yougov.com/topics/politics/articles-reports/2023/02/08 /americans-evaluate-social-security-medicare-poll.

32   Saad, Lydia. "Americans Sour on U.S. Healthcare Quality." Gallup, January 19, 2023. https://news.gallup.com/poll/468176/americans-sour-healthcare-quality.aspx.

33   McConville, Shannon. "Healthcare Reform in California." Public Policy Institute of California, May 2021. https://www.ppic.org/publication/health-care-reform-in-california/.

34   *Physicians for a National Health Program*. https://pnhp.org/.

35   "Road Runners: The Role and Impact of Law Enforcement in Transporting Individuals with Mental Severe Illness." Treatment Advocacy Center. Accessed January 27, 2024. https://www.treatmentadvocacycenter.org/reports_publications/road-runners-the-role-and-impact-of-law-enforcement-in-transporting-individuals-with-severe-mental-illness/.

36   "The Economic Burden of Incarceration in the U.S (2016)." National Institute of Corrections. Accessed January 27, 2024. https://nicic.gov/weblink/economic-burden-incarceration-us-2016.

37   Verzoni, Angelo. "Invisible No More," National Fire Protection Association (NPFA), March 2, 2023. https://www.nfpa.org/news-blogs-and-articles/nfpa-journal/2023/03/03/homeless.

38   Bloomberg. "Ford Health-Care Costs Said to Top $1 Billion." *IndustryWeek*, March 12, 2019. https://www.industryweek.com/talent/article/22027289/ford-healthcare-costs-said-to-top-1-billion.

39   "Ford to Replace Health Benefits with Stipends for Most Salaried Retirees." KFF Health News, June 11, 2009. https://khn.org/morning-breakout/dr00040843/.

40   Miller, Stephen. "Health Plan Cost Increases for 2022 Return to Pre-Pandemic Levels." SHRM (Society for Human Resource Management), October 8, 2021. https://www.shrm.org/resourcesandtools/hr-topics/benefits/pages/health-plan-cost-increases-return-to-pre-pandemic-levels.aspx.

41   Frankel, Matthew. "How Much Medicare Tax Does the Average American Worker Pay?" *The Motley Fool*, June 11, 2017. https://www.fool.com/retirement/2017/06/11/how-much-medicare-tax-does-the-average-american-wo.aspx.

42   Politz, Karen, Kaye Pestaina, Alex Montero, et al. "KFF Survey of Consumer Experiences with Health Insurance." *KFF*," June 15, 2023. https://www.kff.org/mental-health/poll-finding/kff-survey-of-consumer-experiences-with-health-insurance/.

43   Galvin, Gaby. "About 7 in 10 Voters Favor a Public Health Insurance Option. Medicare for All Remains Polarizing." *Morning Consult Pro*, July 20, 2023. https://morningconsult.com/2021/03/24/medicare-for-all-public-option-polling/.

44   "Poll: 69% of Voters Support Medicare for All." *The Hill*, April 24, 2020. https://thehill.com/hilltv/what-americas-thinking/494602-poll-69-percent-of-voters-support-medicare-for-all/.

45   Sanders, Linley. "How Americans Evaluate Social Security, Medicare, and Six Other Entitlement Programs." *YouGov*, February 8, 2023.

https://today.yougov.com/topics/politics/articles-reports/2023/02/08 /americans-evaluate-social-security-medicare-poll.

46   "Public Opinion on Single-Payer, National Health Plans, and Expanding Access to Medicare Coverage." *KFF*, October 16, 2020. https://www .kff.org/slideshow/public-opinion-on-single-payer-national-health-plans -and-expanding-access-to-medicare-coverage/.

47   Jones, Bradley. "More Americans Now Favor Single Payer Health Coverage than in 2019." Pew Research Center, September 30, 2020. https://www.pewresearch.org/fact-tank/2020/09/29/increasing-share -of-americans-favor-a-single-government-program-to-provide-health -care-coverage/.

48   Baicker, Katherine, Amitabh Chandra, and Mark Shepard. "A Different Framework to Achieve Universal Coverage in the US." *JAMA Health Forum* 4, no. 2 (February 2, 2023): e230187. doi:10.1001/jamahealth forum.2023.0187.

49   Moench, Mallory. "S.F. Hoped to Mandate Treatment for up to More Than 100 Mentally Ill Homeless People. Years Later, No One is in the Program." *San Francisco Chronicle*, February 7, 2023. https://www .sfchronicle.com/bayarea/article/s-f-hoped-to-mandate-treatment-for -up-to-100-17763147.php.

50   Moench, Mallory, and Kevin Fagan. "S.F. Had a Bold Plan To Cut Chronic Homelessness in Half in 5 Years. The Numbers Only Got Worse." *San Francisco Chronicle*, September 20, 2022. https://www .sfchronicle.com/sf/article/homelessness-plan-numbers-17453102.php.

51   Raven, Maria C., Matthew J. Niedzwiecki, and Margot Kushel. "A Randomized Trial of Permanent Supportive Housing for Chronically Homeless Persons With High Use of Publicly Funded Services." *Health Services Research* 55, no. S2 (September 25, 2020): 797–806. https://doi .org/10.1111/1475-6773.13553.

52   Moench, Mallory. "5 Patients Cost $4 Million in Ambulance Rides: S.F.'s Struggling Behavioral Health System Exposed in Hearing." *San Francisco Chronicle*, July 30, 2022. https://www.sfchronicle .com/sf/article/5-patients-cost-S-F-4-million-in-ambulance -17336870.php.

53   Silver, Casey M., Arielle Thomas, Susheel Reddy, et al. "Morbidity and Length of Stay After Injury Among People Experiencing Homelessness in North America." *JAMA Network Open* 7, no. 2 (2024)::e240795. doi:10.1001/jamanetworkopen.2024.0795.

54   Hanson, Devlin, and Sarah Gillespie. "'Housing First' Increased Psychiatric Care Office Visits and Prescriptions While Reducing Emergency Visits." *Health Affairs*, January 24, 2024. doi:10.1377 /hlthaff.2023.01041.

55   Abramson, Boaz, Job Boerma, and Aleh Tsyvinski. "Macroeconomics of Mental Health," *National Bureau of Economic Research*, April 1, 2024. https://doi.org/10.3386/w32354.

56   Eide, Stephen. "In Defense of Stigma." National Affairs, Winter 2020.
      https://nationalaffairs.com/publications/detail/in-defense-of-stigma.
57   Pattani, Aneri. "Patients Seek Mental Healthcare from Their Doctor but Find
      Health Plans Standing in the Way." Kaiser Family Foundation, June 8, 2022.
      https://khn.org/news/article/primary-care-mental-health-insurance-barriers/.
58   "Mental Illness." National Institute of Mental Health (NIMH).
      Accessed January 27, 2024. https://www.nimh.nih.gov/health/statistics
      /mental-illness.shtml.
59   Cummings, Nicholas, and Gary R. Vandenbos. "The Twenty Years
      Kaiser-Permanente Experience with Psychotherapy and Medical
      Utilization: Implications for National Health Policy and National Health
      Insurance." Health Policy Quarterly 1, no. 2 (1981): 159–75. https://pub
      med.ncbi.nlm.nih.gov/10252343/.
60   Grinker, Roy. Nobody's Normal: How Culture Created the Stigma of Mental
      Illness. New York: WW Norton, 2021.
61   Husain, Mustafa M., A. John Rush, Max Fink, Rebecca G. Knapp,
      Georgios Petrides, Teresa A. Rummans, Melanie M. Biggs, et al. "Speed
      of Response and Remission in Major Depressive Disorder with Acute
      Electroconvulsive Therapy (ECT)." The Journal of Clinical Psychiatry 65,
      no. 4 (April 15, 2004): 485–91. doi:10.4088/jcp.v65n0406.
62   Kaster, Tyler S., Daniel M. Blumberger, Tara Gomes, Rinku Sutradhar,
      Duminda N. Wijeysundera, and Simone N. Vigod. "Risk of Suicide
      Death Following Electroconvulsive Therapy Treatment for Depression:
      A Propensity Score-Weighted, Retrospective Cohort Study in Canada."
      The Lancet Psychiatry 9, no. 6 (June 1, 2022): 435–46. doi:10.1016/s2215
      -0366(22)00077-3.
63   Bloom, Heather, Irfan Shukrullah, Jose Cuellar, Michael S. Lloyd,
      Samuel C. Dudley, and A. Maziar Zafari. "Long-Term Survival after
      Successful Inhospital Cardiac Arrest Resuscitation." American Heart
      Journal 153, no. 5 (May 1, 2007): 831–36. doi:10.1016/j.ahj.2007.02.011.
64   Leucht, Stefan, Sandra Hierl, Werner Kissling, Markus Dold, and John
      M. Davis. "Putting the Efficacy of Psychiatric and General Medicine
      Medication into Perspective: Review of Meta-Analyses." The British
      Journal of Psychiatry 200, no. 2 (February 1, 2012): 97–106. doi:10.1192
      /bjp.bp.111.096594.
65   Mezzina, Roberto. "Creating Mental Health Services Without Exclusion
      or Restraint, But With Open Doors: Trieste, Italy." L'information
      psychiatrique 92 (Sept 2016): 747–54. https://www.cairn.info/journal-l
      -information-psychiatrique-2016-9-page-747.htm%23.
66   Frances, Allen, MD. "Restoring Respect to People with Mental Illness."
      Psychiatric Times, November 16, 2020. https://www.psychiatrictimes.
      com/view/restoring-respect-people-mentally-illness.
67   Waters, Rob. "A New Approach to Mental Healthcare, Imported from
      Abroad." Health Affairs 39, no. 3 (March 1, 2020): 362–66. doi:10.1377
      /hlthaff.2020.00047.

68   Drake, Robert E., Deborah R. Becker, and Lisa B. Dixon. "Supported
      Employment and Psychiatric Intervention." *JAMA Psychiatry* 79,
      no. 11 (November 1, 2022): 1053. doi:10.1001/jamapsychiatry.2022
      .3007.

69   Modini, Matthew, Sadhbh Joyce, Arnstein Mykletun, Helen
      Christensen, Richard A. Bryant, Philip B. Mitchell, and Samuel B.
      Harvey. "The Mental Health Benefits of Employment: Results of a
      Systematic Meta-Review." *Australasian Psychiatry* 24, no. 4 (July 10,
      2016): 331–36. doi:10.1177/1039856215618523.

70   "Peer-Led Mobile Crisis Response: How It Works—A Greenfield
      People's Budget." Accessed January 27, 2024. https://peoplesbudget
      greenfield.com/cahoots/.

71   "What Is CAHOOTS?" *White Bird Clinic*, October 29, 2020. https
      ://whitebirdclinic.org/what-is-cahoots/.

72   Dee, Thomas S., and Jaymes Pyne. "A Community Response Approach
      to Mental Health and Substance Abuse Crises Reduced Crime." *Science
      Advances* 8, no. 23 (June 10, 2022). doi:10.1126/sciadv.abm2106.

73   Padma, Tiruponithura Venkatraman. "Developing Countries: The
      Outcomes Paradox." *Nature* 508, no. 7494 (April 1, 2014): S14–15
      . doi:10.1038/508s14a.

74   Watters, Ethan. *Crazy Like Us: The Globalization of the American Psyche.*
      New York: Free Press (Simon and Schuster), 2010.

75   Knight, Victoria. "Gun Safety 'Wrapped in a Mental Health Bill': A
      Look at Health Provisions in the New Law." *California Healthline*, July 7,
      2022. https://californiahealthline.org/news/article/gun-violence-mental
      -health-legislation-suicide/.

76   Moffic, H. Steve. "It's Disingenuous to Deny the Role of Mental
      Disturbance in Gun Violence." *Psychiatric Times*, June 14, 2022. https
      ://www.psychiatrictimes.com/view/its-disingenuous-to-deny-the-role
      -of-mental-disturbance-in-gun-violence.

77   Bollag, Sophia. "Mental Care Plan Approved: Newsom Sponsored
      Measure Would Mandate Treatment, Provide Services." *San Francisco
      Chronicle*, September 1, 2022.

78   Houghton, Katheryn. "When Mental Illness Leads to Dropped Charges,
      Patients Often Go without Stabilizing Care." KFF Health News,
      August 4, 2022. https://khn.org/news/article/mental-illness-dropped
      -charges-competency-care/.

79   Kukura, Joe. "Newsom's CARE Court Deadline Looms October 1,
      but SF Lacks the Beds and Staff to Enforce It." *SFist*, March 1, 2023.
      https://sfist.com/2023/02/28/newsoms-care-court-deadline-looms
      -october-1-but-sf-lacks-the-beds-and-staff-to-enforce-it/.

80   Grinker, Roy. *Nobody's Normal: How Culture Created the Stigma of Mental
      Illness.* New York: WW Norton, 2021.

81   "New Study Shows 60 Percent of U.S Counties Without a Single
      Psychiatrist." *New American Economy*, October 23, 2017. https://www

.newamericaneconomy.org/press-release/new-study-shows-60-percent
-of-u-s-counties-without-a-single-psychiatrist/.

82   Davenport, Stoddard, Travis Gray, and Stephen Melek. "Addiction and
        Mental Health vs. Physical Health: Widening Disparities in Network
        Use and Provider Reimbursement." *Milliman*, November 20, 2019.
        https://www.milliman.com/en/insight/addiction-and-mental-health-vs
        -physical-health-widening-disparities-in-network-use-and-p.

83   "Prescriptions for Antidepressants Increasing among Individuals with
        No Psychiatric Diagnosis." Johns Hopkins Bloomberg School of Public
        Health, August 4, 2011. https://www.jhsph.edu/news/news-releases
        /2011/mojtabai-antidepressant-prescriptions.html.

84   Vonnegut, Mark. *Just Like Someone Without Mental Illness Only More So.*
        New York: Bantam Books, 2011.

85   Saks, Elyn. *The Center Cannot Hold: My Journey Through Madness.* New
        York: Hachette Books, 2007.

86   Jamison, Kaye Redfield. *An Unquiet Mind: A Memoir Of Moods And
        Madness.* New York: Knopf, 1995.

87   Forney, Ellen. *Marbles: Mania, Depression, Michelangelo + Me.* New York:
        Gotham Books, 2012.

88   Solomon, Andrew. *The Noonday Demon: An Atlas Of Depression.* New
        York: Scribner, 2014.

89   "Fast Facts: Most Popular Majors." National Center for Education
        Statistics. Accessed January 27, 2024. https://nces.ed.gov/fastfacts
        /display.asp?id=37.

90   "How Many Psychologists Are Licensed in the United States?" *American
        Psychological Association Monitor* 45, no. 6 (June 2014). https://www.apa
        .org/monitor/2014/06/datapoint.

91   "Employment and Wages of Engineers in 2015." The Economics Daily,
        U.S. Bureau of Labor Statistics, October 17, 2016. https://www.bls.gov
        /opub/ted/2016/employment-and-wages-of-engineers-in-2015.htm

92   Moran, Mark. "Psychiatry Residency Match Numbers Climb Again
        after Unprecedented Year in Medical Education." *Psychiatric News* 56,
        no. 5 (April 21, 2021). doi:10.1176/appi.pn.2021.5.27.

Index

Drama of the Gifted Child (Miller), 88
Drug Enforcement Administration (DEA), 172
drug overdose, x, 34, 38, 94
drug rehabilitation, 62
DSM. *See Diagnostic and Statistical Manual* (DSM)
duality, 125, 127–130

E

Eagleton, Thomas, 15
The Economist (periodical), 99
The Economists' Hour (Appelbaum), 84
ECT. *See* electroconvulsive therapy (ECT)
EHR. *See* electronic health records (EHRs)
Ehrenreich, Barbara, 3
Ehrenreich, John, 3
Eichmann, Adolf, 80
Eichmann in Jerusalem (Arendt), 80
Eide, Steven, 191
Elavil, 16
electroconvulsive therapy (ECT), 15, 119, 194, 196
electronic health records (EHRs), 52, 69–72, 93
electroshock therapy, 15, 119
electrotherapy, 120
Eli Lilly, 44, 109, 148
emergency rooms (ERs)
    overdose visits, 38
    pediatric mental health visits, 35–36
    as substitutes for mental health treatment, 35–37, 133
Emory University, 108
emotional impacts, 40–44
empathy, 85, 151–152
Ennis, Bruce J., 159
Envision HealthCare, 165
Epic, 70
EpiPens, 171
ER. *See* emergency rooms (ERs)
ethical rights, xv, 60–61
ethics, 85–88, 104, 107, 111–112, 113, 164
Eugene Police Department, 199
eugenics, economically driven, 9
Experian, 52
expert consensus guidelines, 116–117

Express Scripts, 63–64
eye movement desensitization and reprocessing (EMDR), 119, 121

F

Facebook, 53, 66, 101
Fake Review Watch, 102
families
    emotional impacts on, 40–41
    financial impacts on, 41–44
    pediatric mental health crisis, 35–36
Fanapt®, 108
Farkas, Barry, 88
FDA. *See* Food and Drug Administration (FDA)
Federal Anti-Kickback Statute, 113–114
Federal Trade Commission (FTC), 53, 61, 65, 66, 101, 108, 139
fee-for-service (FFS) model, 177–178
feminism, 75–76
fentanyl, 38
Ferguson, Bob, 166
fight or flight response, 128
financial impacts, 40–44
Fischer, Molly, 99
Fisher, Carrie, 118
Food and Drug Administration (FDA), xiii, 106, 107, 108, 138, 172
Food Drug and Cosmetic Act (FDCA), 172
Forbes (periodical), 45, 69, 98
Forney, Ellen, 204
Foucault, Michel, 151
France, Anatole, 84
free market, 1–2, 5–6, 150, 178
Freeman, Walter, 14
Friedman, Milton, 2
FTC. *See* Federal Trade Commission (FTC)

G

Galagali, Tarun, 98
Gandhi, Mahatma, 196
GDP. *See* gross domestic product (GDP)
gender identity, 81, 138
German healthcare system, 176, 179, 184–185
Gilead Sciences, 115
GlaxoSmithKline (GSK), 108–109
Go, Michelle Alyssa, 189, 191

New York magazine, 99
New York Times, 6, 8, 36, 39, 62, 67, 91, 102, 155, 166, 189
Newsom, Gavin, 201
NHI. *See* National Health Insurance (NHI) model
NIH. *See* National Institutes of Health (NIH)
nitrofurantoin, 171
Nixon, Richard, 2
No One Cares About Crazy People (Powers), 29–30
noncompete agreements, 60–61
The Noonday Demon (Solomon), 204
Nostrum Pharmaceuticals, 171
Novo Nordisk, 148
nursing homes, 117, 157

O
Obama, Barack, 185
ObamaCare. *See* Patient Protection and Affordable Care Act (ACA)
object relation theory, xiii
obsessive-compulsive disorder (OCD), 128
O'Connor v. Donaldson, 30
Office of Science and Technology Policy, 161
Office of the Inspector General, 100, 126, 180
olanzapine, 109
Omnibus Budget Reconciliation Act (1981), 26
On Being Sane in Insane Places (Rosenhan), 19
One Flew Over the Cuckoo's Nest (film), x, 194
One Flew Over the Cuckoo's Nest (Kesey), ix, xii–xiv
online reviews, 101–104
online therapy, 98–101
Open Payments database, 114
opioid epidemic, 11, 37–38, 56, 72, 102, 103, 171, 172
Optum, 149
Osler, William, 126
"othering," 132, 151–152
overdose, x, 34, 38, 94

P
Padma, T. V., 199
panic attacks, 128, 159
Park Doctrine (1975), 172, 206, 207

Patient Health Questionnaire-9 (PHQ-p), 96–97
Patient Protection and Affordable Care Act (ACA), xv–xvi, 92, 113, 188
patients
  becoming a patient, 150–151
  as consumers, 50, 77
  defined, 76
  as partners in treatment, 77, 83–84
  principles of care centered on, 56
  reframing of as clients, xv, 73–80, 85–88
  rights advocacy, xv
  rights of, 44–46, 73, 81–85
PE. *See* private equity (PE)
peer counselors, 198–199
Penny, Daniel, xix
person-centered therapy, 75
Pfizer, 96, 162
pharmaceutical industry
  "astroturf" organizations and, 43–44
  doctors' alliance with, 104–115, 162–163
  expert consensus guidelines, 116–117
  lobbying by, 65, 148, 170
  marketing by, 11, 170
  patents, 108
  price gouging by, 7, 65, 148
Pharmaceutical Research and Manufacturers of America (PhRMA), 65
pharmacies, 65–66, 110
pharmacy benefits managers (PBMs), 63–66
phenobarbital, 15
PHI. *See* Protected Health Information (PHI)
Philip Morris, 167
physicians. *See* doctors
Physicians for a National Health Program, 163, 181, 186–187
Physicians Foundation, 126
placebo effect, 120–121
PLOS Digital Health, 98
police encounters, 31–32, 49, 187
Porter, Roy, 12, 13
Portland Fire and Rescue, 187
post-traumatic stress disorder (PTSD), 121, 129–130, 144
Potter, Wendell, 176
Powers, Roy, 29–30
Practice Fusion, 71–72